GLORY GLORY!

For my mum, Ann. Old Trafford born and red – though she still says 'yoo-nigh-ted' like a yonner. George Best once turned up at her house in his E-Type Jag to take my auntie out. Grandad wasn't impressed and told him to shift his car.

GLORY GLORY!

MAN UTD IN THE '90S
THE PLAYERS' STORIES

BY ANDY MITTEN

VSP

Published by Vision Sports Publishing in 2009

Vision Sports Publishing
19–23 High Street
London
KT1 1LL

www.visionsp.co.uk

ISBN 13: 978-1905326-69-3

Typeset by Palimpsest Book Production Limited,
Grangemouth, Stirlingshire

A CIP record for this book is available from the British Library

Printed and bound in the UK by CPI Mackays, Chatham, ME5 8TD

CONTENTS

INTRODUCTION

On 1st January 1990, Manchester United drew 0–0 against Queens Park Rangers in front of a sparse 34,824 Old Trafford crowd. The stadium still had terracing on all four sides and was in need of serious investment. United's line up was: Jim Leighton, Viv Anderson, Lee Martin, Steve Bruce, Gary Pallister, Mike Phelan, Lee Sharpe, Clayton Blackmore, Brian McClair, Mark Hughes and Mark Robins. Two days earlier, just 9,622 watched United in the last game of the 1980s, a 2–2 draw on the banks of the River Wandle at Plough Lane, Wimbledon. Even the nearby dog track looked more glamorous.

United were then in the middle of a ten-game winless league run. Wimbledon and QPR would both finish the season ahead of 13th place United, who limped home just five points clear of the relegation places with a goal difference of -1. So would Southampton and the Citys of Norwich and Coventry. The crowds for United's final two league games were 29,281 and 35,389, but even those low figures were inflated by the inclusion of absent season-ticket holders. Bryan Robson, United's best-paid player, earned less than £3,000 a week and Liverpool were champions again.

By the final days of the same decade, Manchester United were reigning English, European and World Champions. They became the first English team to win the treble in circumstances

1

so dramatic that those fortunate enough to be in Barcelona still shake their heads in disbelief. Old Trafford was virtually rebuilt and had been expanded several times. Full to its 55,000 capacity every week, that total would soon rise to 60,000, then 68,000 and 76,000. United did not even play domestic football for the first three weeks of the new millennium because, as reigning European Champions, they were set to participate in an inaugural tournament in Brazil, where, despite Real Madrid being among the opponents, United were the side more fêted by the Brazilian media. Players like David Beckham, Ryan Giggs, Paul Scholes and Roy Keane were global superstars. Off the field, United had capitalised on the success and the value of the club had increased one hundredfold from £10 million to almost £1 billion.

The club could lay serious claim to being the biggest in the world, with the pulling power to draw 80,000 to friendly matches in Australia and China. Roy Keane, the best paid player, was about to conclude contract negotiations for a new deal worth £55,000 a week. With Keane signed and content, United would go on to retain the enormously successful Premier League by an 18-point margin over Arsenal. Liverpool? They haven't been champions since.

It's easy to look back to the start of the 1990s and cast them as dark days in Manchester United's rich history, but they didn't feel oppressive as I worked on the first few issues of the *United We Stand* fanzine I'd started with schoolmates at the end of 1989. We'd photocopy issues and staple them together after school before selling them outside Old Trafford. We visited away grounds for the first time, wide eyed as we wandered into Anfield, Stamford Bridge or Villa Park. Football special trains – the detritus of the British Rail stock – were still running, match tickets were cheap (my junior season ticket worked out at £1.35 a game in 1990) and plentiful, and players' shorts were still tight. United were our local team and we followed them wherever they played. We still do.

When we wrote to Alex Ferguson asking for an interview, he wrote back stating that, while he was not a fan of fanzines, he liked *United We Stand* and he'd be happy for us to talk to him. And when I met him in a Trondheim hotel on a pre-season tour of Scandinavia, I recorded the interview on a giant red ghetto blaster which had played the Stone Roses, Electronic, Happy Mondays and Inspiral Carpets on a loop as we travelled northern Europe on tickets which were not always fully valid, slept under United flags in railways stations and ate cheese and ham sandwiches every day for two weeks.

Back home, Manchester was an exciting place to be and the shoots of recovery after decades of post-industrial decline were sprouting in the city. And nowhere was that better illustrated than by Manchester United's resurgence.

Editing *UWS* was great fun and I enjoyed the ride. When we interviewed the United secretary Ken Merrett, I took a mate along, simply because he was bored and it was the school holidays. Merrett looked confused, but went ahead anyway.

As our addiction to United took hold, we'd travel to every single game home and away, where we'd meet like-minded Reds from all over Britain and beyond. By 1991 we were organising coaches to away games, sometimes four or five, to hostile places like Leeds. I was 18, but looked 15. When I told the police I was in charge of the coaches, they'd laugh. Football fans were considered scum and that made me really angry because I knew different. After one game was cancelled at Leeds, I rang around everyone who had booked on the coaches from a box room in Gorse Hill to see if they would be travelling to the rearranged game. Most of the numbers bore the 061 telephone code of Manchester, a few prefixes for Bolton, Wigan, or one of the old industrial satellite towns that fringe Manchester. There was one code I didn't recognise: 0892. I called it. A cheery female answered.

"Hello. I'm not sure if I've got the right number, but someone called Grant booked on a coach."

"Oh, he's my boy. He's just called. He's still in Manchester and there's no buses back tonight."

She was southern and sympathetic, conjuring up the image of the perfect mum found in advertisements for washing powder. I replied, "Well, can you ask him to call the coach company to let us know if he'll be travelling with us on Wednesday for the rescheduled game?"

"Of course I can, darling," she replied. "When he gets back from his wretched trip I shall tell him. I'm sure he'll be going back up. He's incredibly dedicated you know."

It transpired that her son Grant had undertaken the following journey to watch a 90-minute football game on the Sabbath: walk to train station, train to London (no ticket), coach to Birmingham and the 'midnight express' coach to Manchester. He'd arrived in Manchester at 3am and spent the night sleeping rough in the city's Chorlton Street bus station, a haven for addicts and prostitutes. He'd walked the grey, rain-lashed January streets of the city in the morning, killing time until the buses were ready to leave for Leeds. Except they never left for Leeds, and Grant's long journey back to Sussex was about to start again. A journey that started Saturday morning and ended on Monday afternoon. And would start again on Tuesday for the game on Wednesday. And he did that every week.

I was intrigued. Grant did book on for the return leg and I met him at Chorlton Street. He looked like a hero in a Hollywood movie, more Take That than football anorak. His girlfriends were sensational, and could have modelled for Victoria's Secrets or Myla.

We became mates, travelled together and he soon moved to Manchester, one of those enduring friendships created through the love of a football team. We picked up more lads along the way.

On my first day at university, we had to stand up and introduce ourselves and give a short biography. One stood up, said his name, listing his interests as liking Manchester United and despising Leeds United. He then sat down to the aghast faces of the other students. A year later and without funds to buy a proper train ticket, the same lad hid underneath seats on a night train from Ostend to Budapest, just to watch United play in Budapest.

Another character, Ted, collared me outside the Glastonbury Festival in 1993. It was midnight and I was preparing to sleep in a car. He recognised me from *UWS*, told me that his family lived locally and offered a bed. Hallelujah. We became mates and Ted entered the United world. Fifteen years later, I met two England fans who, when I mentioned that I supported United, asked me if I knew Ted, a person they spoke about in reverential tones.

By the time of Barcelona away in 1994 there was a gang of 30 of us, watching Manchester United home and away, week in, week out. One of the old hooligans pulled me to one side and said, "You're our future firm – it's brilliant to see so many of you coming through." Some went that way; it was never my scene.

We'd spend all our spare time sourcing cheap travel in the days before budget airlines, helping each other out with away match tickets and obsessing about the latest casual fashion trends. At one point there were that many of the lads meeting on Warwick Road by where we sold *UWS* that the police told us we were causing an obstruction.

Our addiction to United worsened. One was labelled a part-timer because he didn't go to Galatasaray – away. Four of us lived in a big house in Urmston which became a headquarters for *UWS* and away-game operations. I briefly dated Brian Kidd's daughter Claire – a fantastic girl from a wonderful family. When she came to my house for the first time, my housemates put pictures of her dad around the walls. From the 1970s. That took some explaining, but she saw the funny side and three weeks later invited us all to her 21st birthday party. I had serious words with the lads not to act up and get starstruck. It started to go awry when one pointed at a pair of Wellington boots and cried, "Look, Kiddo's wellies!' I told him to calm down and sent him into the kitchen for a beer . . . where he was followed by Sir Alex Ferguson. I'll never forget the look on his face when he turned around to be confronted by Ferguson saying, "How you doing son?"

Pre-season tours to Asia became the norm in our house. One afternoon, I caught a housemate on the phone to an addiction counsellor. He'd taken time off work to go to a December mid-season friendly in Belfast because someone had told him that it was an official United game. Unable to locate a ferry from Stranraer at the right time, he'd gone into meltdown. He confessed to the counsellor that he was petrified in case someone close to him arranged their wedding on a day when United played or if he came down with flu and was unable to attend a match. He'd spoiled relationships with beautiful girls since being a teen. The diagnosis? He loved Manchester United more than anything else. We'd justify attending the smallest friendly game on the strength that it was the debut of a certain player – as if the players cared.

The huge-selling French magazine *L'Equipe* sent a journalist and photographer round to see what life was like in a typical Manchester house during a time when much of the city had been seduced by Eric Cantona. With four young lads, ours was anything but typical, but *L'Equipe* wanted it to be as English as possible, so they photographed us in front of a fireplace holding cups of tea under the gaze of a Cantona poster. Short of having slices of roast beef draped across our face, we'd reluctantly fallen into fulfilling their fantasy of Little England.

We were largely ambivalent about the players themselves. We recognised their talents and sang their names, but despite their clichés about "great fans", we reckoned they had a low opinion of supporters – which was no surprise when you saw the type of fan which approached them. As Gary Pallister explains so graphically later in this book, United fans had ready access to players at the start of the 1990s. By the end of the decade, these fans had become a hindrance for players, the interaction usually limited to one-off, in-your-face auto-graph requests at airports or outside grounds. That was when the fans weren't shouting abuse. The only real fans the players seemed to get to know properly were wealthy club sponsors, but even this was more of a one-way relationship, where people wanted the glamour and status of association with the club, rather than a genuine friendship.

But paths did cross. The whole first-team squad walked into a bar where we were drinking in Copenhagen in 1993. Roy Keane had just joined and I wished him well, until a drunken Mark Hughes interrupted and asked who the fuck I was. Angered, I asked him the same question. Hughes then asked where I was from.

"Urmston, Manchester," I said, causing him to sneer, which well you might if you're from the global metropolis of Wrexham. I was fuming. I'd spent hours as a 13-year-old colouring in a 'Sparky Come Home' banner which I held up on the Stretford End. Other players looked up, realised that we weren't interested in any autographs or their company and that they'd walked into the bar we were in. Hughes too saw sense and quietened down.

A year later, I was offered a job editing the official Manchester United magazine, where one of the first tasks was to interview Hughes. He didn't recognise me. I didn't take the job full time, because I had to think about what I was going to do after my journalism degree finished.

I'd already had a lucky break when, by chance, I had my dictaphone in my pocket during the violence the night before United's game in Istanbul in 1993. It recorded the gunshots and my own worried screams after I was hit by what I thought was a brick thrown from an Istanbul tower block. It was actu-ally a melon. The BBC and my tutors were delighted, but I wasn't keen on walking away from *UWS* and agreed to free-lance for United's magazine. That meant interviewing virtually all of the players, an experience I found hugely pleasurable and I still enjoy interviewing footballers to this day.

Current footballers are restricted in what they can and can't say. They are under contract and in a working situation where the thoughts of their colleagues and especially their manager matter. While Samuel Eto'o or Roy Keane may have made for great copy by speaking out, they created problems for themselves by their frankness. After hundreds of interviews with some of the biggest names in football, I found that speaking to just retired players was usually far more interesting. They had more time on their hands and were happy to reminisce, glad they could finally speak their mind.

So that's why I didn't go for the likes of Ryan Giggs, Paul Scholes, the Neville brothers or David Beckham in this book. They are outstanding talents, United legends and perfectly pleasant individuals whose lives have been great successes, but that doesn't always make the best story, the most engaging interview. And what could David Beckham say? One on one in a pub, I think he'd be charming, but he's surrounded by a team of public relations advisors and I'd never want the type of 'to be fair to the lads' type of interview which would ensue – though it's doubtful they would even agree to it in the first place.

So I approached characters, each of whom has their own merits. I knew some of the players well and hoped that they would trust me. Others intrigued me because I'd heard so little about them since they left United. From the feedback to *We're the Famous Man United*, the book I wrote about the 1980s side, I found out that fans were more interested in reading about the less high-profile men – Billy Garton or John Gidman, rather than Bryan Robson.

I wanted to know what really happened with Jesper Blomqvist. Was David May really as crackers as his teammates suggested? Why had Martin Edwards never told his side of the story? Why did Jordi Cruyff hate his time at United so much? What was Andrew Cole really like? How did Nicky Butt view his time at Old Trafford now that he was away from it? And what about Lee Sharpe, a huge star in his day? I hooked up with Gary Pallister, the British record transfer signing who was so tall that he looked like a freak in his first United team photo. It didn't help that the photographer put him at the end of the row, mind. His opposite in size was Paul Parker, whose company I've always enjoyed. And what of Lee Martin who scored the winning goal in an FA Cup final at 22, and the brooding King Cantona himself?

I was fortunate enough to spend quality time with all of them. Geographically, the diaspora of former Manchester United players from the 1990s spread far greater than in previous decades, meaning that I had to travel far and wide while writing this book.

It's always better to do interviews face-to-face, to get to know your subject, to look them in the eye. And for them to get to know you and to do likewise. These men played during a time when football's profile rose exponentially, switching from the back pages to the front. Some of them had had negative experiences at the hands of the media, so they initially were naturally cautious and even mistrusting.

I spent three days in Stockholm with Blomqvist, staggering the interview in different places and was rewarded with a comprehensive picture of his life. The meticulously organised Edwards initially allotted me three hours at his home in Cheshire and then told me I could have as much time as I liked. Cantona was interviewed in a seedy Marseille hotel, Cruyff in an uptown Barcelona café. The always honest Parker invited me into the kitchen of his Essex home and rattled on while he searched for his mobile phone. Pallister stuck to his beloved sofa in his beautiful Yarm home. I met Butt at Newcastle United's training ground, where he made me a cup of tea, switched his phone off and said, "Let's talk properly."

There was no danger that May would be anything other than funny and frank during an afternoon in Manchester, nor that he'd be late to pick up the children he adores from school. A serious accident on the M62 near Salford meant I was an hour late to interview Sharpe in Leeds, but he was fine about it and didn't cut short our time. Cole was in brilliant form at Mottram Hall and texted after to say how much he'd enjoyed talking, while Martin was typically friendly and down to earth at his new home on the Wirral.

I enjoyed every interview immensely and hope that the players did too. I've kept in touch with several and tried to help them as they helped me. I've given them a lot of space to offer their opinions and only tightened up their words for the purpose of clarity, but hope that I've retained their own voices in an authentic manner. You won't be hearing the players saying 'the Old Trafford faithful' in these pages, as some ghost writers would have it, because players don't speak like that. They frequently do say 'minging', 'cabbaged' and 'trolleyed', and they swear constantly.

In terms of interview technique, I'd like to think that it's more Radio 5 than Radio 4. The subjects have been gracious enough to give me their time for a small fee (and several donated that to charity), so I believe I should be decent enough to let them have their say, while not ignoring any negatives which have cropped up in their career.

While nobody criticises Professor Stephen Hawking for being a bad footballer, footballers are often derided for being inarticulate and semi-educated, working-class boys unfairly compared to middle-class rugby union and cricket players. That doesn't mean they are thick. The people I interviewed as part of this book were incredibly bright, insightful and honest.

I must thank lots of people. First, my publishers Jim Drewett and Toby Trotman, two match-going AFC Wimbledon fans enjoying their team on the rise. They were happy for me to write this book while travelling the world and I'll never forget writing about David May's exploits on a revolving dance floor in Swindon while looking at penguins in Antarctica.

Joyce Woolridge was unstinting at wading through huge amounts of copy, often at short notice. There should be a statue of her outside Lostock Public Library in Stretford. And thanks also to Martin Cloake at Vision Sports Publishing, who read the manuscript.

Jim White, Jonathan Northcroft, Hugh Sleight, Graham Hunter, Stuart Trueman, Mark Pearson, Andrew Dickman, Stuart Mathieson, Paddy Barclay and Paul Davies all helped. As did the *UWS* and *MLF* boys. And an obvious thanks to my fiancée Ba, a Brazilian who can't get over how the one true religion is football in England's north. I must also thank my family for their continued love and support.

And thanks to you, the reader for again supporting my books. It costs money to fly to Stockholm to meet a footballer and you pay for that. I only hope you enjoy this book as much as I have writing it.

Glory, Glory, Man United.

Andy Mitten
September 2009

1
ANDREW COLE
'He gets the ball he scores a goal'

ANDREW COLE
MANCHESTER UNITED

"I was living by myself, doing the laundry in Clifton, the poshest Bristol suburb, playing for Bristol City, when I came outside to see a note on the window of my car," remembers Andrew Cole. "I didn't have a mobile phone then. The note was from my teammate Russell Osman and it said, 'Coley, give me a call.' I called Russell and he told me Kevin Keegan wanted to phone me and he'd given him my home number. So I went home and waited for the call.

"He said, 'Hello, Adrian.'

"I said, 'I think you have got the wrong person, because I'm Andrew.'

"He said, 'Ah, sorry, sorry. Anyway, we'd like you to come up as we're interested in signing you. Is there any possibility that you can get up to Newcastle tomorrow?'

"Me being me, I said, 'I can't come tomorrow because I have to finish my laundry. I can come the day after though.' He was a bit taken aback, but I did my laundry. And went the day after."

Throughout his career, Andrew Cole has had a reputation for being a difficult customer. His offhand response to Keegan when offered his break into the football big time, when most other players would have been obsequiously grateful is, he admits, typical of his tendency to do something awkward, something individual, often not in his own best interests. "Me being me." He was one of the last people I approached to be in this book. Perhaps it was because of what I'd heard from others. A former editor of *FourFourTwo* magazine resigned from his position, citing the restrictions put on his magazine by Cole's agents when they interviewed him and his strike partner Dwight Yorke in 1998. So many questions were off limits that the editor felt it was more like a public relations exercise than an interview. And there is still contempt in some commentators' voices when they refer to his request to be known as 'Andrew', not 'Andy' as he was dubbed for most of his career, as if it springs from affectation and pomposity, rather than the fact that it is his preferred name.

Andrew Cole, as I quickly discover, is polite, frank, funny and friendly. We speak for over three hours and later, as he drives his son to play at Manchester City's youth academy, he sends a text to say how much he's enjoyed talking about his life. Cole also insists that his fee goes to the Alder Hey Children's hospital in Liverpool, a hospital which months later would provide care for Sir Alex Ferguson's grandchildren after a car accident.

We meet at Mottram Hall, a four-star hotel 20 miles south of Manchester. The interview begins with us both laughing over the story of how Sir Alex Ferguson discovered United had won the league for the first time in 26 years in 1993 while playing golf on the leafy links of this exclusive golf club with his son Mark. By the 17th hole, Ferguson heard a car screech to a halt and a stranger with a huge grin on his face poked his head out of the window.

"Mr Ferguson," he shouted, "Manchester United have just

won the league." The 18th hole was abandoned as the Fergusons strode up the fairway past a group of Japanese golfers. One had the logo of Sharp, United's sponsors throughout the 1990s, on his bag.

"United have won the league," shouted Ferguson senior, assuming he was a United fan.

"Ah . . . what you mean?" replied the bemused Japanese golfer, leaving Ferguson feeling a little stupid.

Nestling in the shadow of the Peak District, there's snow on the ground now, 14 years to the day since Andrew Cole moved from Newcastle to Manchester United for a then record £6 million fee in January 1995. There are no golfers, no Sir Alex enjoying his favourite view over Cheshire from the 14th hole, none of the United stars who live among the local opulence of Prestbury, Mottram, Alderley Edge and Wilmslow. Instead, local kids delight in using their sledges down the undulating fairways.

"I was born in Nottingham in 1971," begins Cole, as he sits down, casually dressed in jeans and a leather jacket. "My parents came to England from Jamaica in the 1950s. My grandfather was already here and he sent for his daughter to find work.

"Dad went to London first, then Birmingham and finally Nottingham. He became a miner, but in Jamaica he cut the cane fields in Kingston. I've been over there and it's a lovely country, which could be a lot better. Perhaps Jamaica took its independence far too early.

"Dad was working at the time of the miners' strike in the early 1980s. It was a difficult time in Nottingham. If he crossed the picket line he would be called a Judas. He didn't. My dad shielded his family. My brother became a miner too. He wanted to go into the British Army but dad wouldn't let him. He went mad and told him that he'd get him a job as a miner instead. I remember my brother coming home and saying, 'I ain't crossing no picket line.' A very quiet man, dad never said a word about the strike, and still has hasn't. He takes a lot on board and keeps it in. Mum is sprightly and speaks her mind. They are like chalk and cheese and are still together in Nottingham."

Cole was the second youngest of eight, six of whom were girls. Mum was a school cleaning lady and money was tight.

"I know what a working-class background is, I really do," says Cole. "My parents took a lot of flak to get in the position they were in. When they arrived, people said, 'You've come to take our jobs.' Dad shielded us from a lot of abuse, but it wasn't easy. I would see adverts on television for toys we could never have. If I wanted new football boots I couldn't have them. I had one pair of boots with rubber studs which I wore down so much that I started to wear them as trainers. And if I had a hole in my trainers, I'd put something in like a piece of card to keep the water out.

"I was a bit naughty when I was young, which didn't do me any good. I knocked around with kids who were a bit older and grew up fast. What did I do? What didn't I do? A bit of this and a bit of that. It was the environment I was in. Lenton was about ten minutes from the city centre and it was tough, yet it gave me a good grounding."

From the mid-20th century onwards, Lenton absorbed a large number of immigrants from Britain's former empire, especially the West Indies, India and Pakistan. Its Kimbolton Avenue was dubbed Britain's most burgled street by the *News of the World* in 2006, with one article stating, "rows of rundown red-brick Victorian houses in a road strewn with rubbish and burnt-out cars are a stark and embarrassing image of Blair's Britain today."

"I saw too much when I was younger so when I saw bad things happen as I got older they didn't phase me," continues Cole. "There was a small element of gang culture. If we went to a certain area then it would cheese someone off and go off. It's a lot worse now."

When he wasn't involved in mischief, Cole loved football, an activity which didn't win approval from his family

"For some reason, I got a white Man United away top which I wore all the time, even though I knew very little about United. My old man used to tell me to play cricket instead of football. He'd say: 'You're from the Caribbean and you're black: you should play cricket.'

"I'd reply, 'I'm English, born in England and I play football.'"

"'That's rubbish,' he'd say. 'How are you ever going to make money out of football?' He could never understand football and he still can't. He watched me play, but he couldn't understand it. Cricket, cricket, cricket, that's all that mattered to my dad."

Cole's father had words of wisdom in other areas. "He'd say, 'I know how you are and you have to listen. For you to succeed as a black kid, you have to be better than the white kids before you can get anywhere.'"

Despite Nottingham Forest, the reigning European champions, playing on his doorstep, Cole never visited the City Ground.

"My mates loved football, but we never watched it. Never. In those days it was going off all the time. Being black, nah. Not a chance I would go and watch a game in case someone called me a black this or black that. We played football on the park, jumpers for goalposts and all that, but we never watched it."

But he has vivid memories of Forest's back-to-back European Cups, recalling, "The players came past where we lived on a bus with the trophy. I followed the bus and ended up lost in an area I didn't know. When I watched them on the bus, I never ever thought that I'd win that trophy which players like Trevor Francis, Tony Woodcock and Peter Shilton held up."

Rather than these Forest stars, Cole's idol was the black West Bromwich Albion striker Cyrille Regis. "He was a pioneer," says Cole. "He took so much abuse, so that people like me could play without problems. He was a tank, strong as an ox with a powerful strike. I loved watching him on television scoring great

17

goals, loved the way the commentator said, 'Regis!' He brushed off so much abuse and held himself well. He always had respect for himself, Cyrille. I've told him that too. It was an honour to meet him, a major honour and I took my hat off to him."

Samuel Eto'o said that you have to run like a black man to live like a white man. Cole nods when he hears this, before returning to the subject of a misspent youth.

"School was a write-off because I let it be. I regret it now because I had the capabilities to do a lot better. I tossed it off, when I should have got my head down. I've got a boy at 13 now and I encourage him to work hard. He wants to be a footballer, but I tell him that school is important.

"Football was important to me and my mates maybe knew that I had a future because if there was going to be trouble they would keep me away from it. They never put me in a difficult situation."

Already a striker, Cole was excelling in a Nottingham Forest feeder team each Sunday, playing for a different Saturday side, plus turning out for Nottinghamshire schools.

"I was doing pretty well at 13," he recalls. "I got offered trials at Sheffield Wednesday, Forest and Arsenal. Me being me, I didn't go to most of them. My brother would get the letters and open them excitedly, but I wasn't bothered."

One of those envelopes contained an offer of an England trial, but still Cole wasn't interested.

"I didn't want to go," he says. "The geezer came to my house and drove me there, probably because he knew I wouldn't show. I got through every trial to the finals. I got where I was in spite of myself. There was always divine intervention, I kept getting another chance."

At club level, he was on the verge of signing for Arsenal or Nottingham Forest, but didn't like the way he was treated at Forest.

"I couldn't take to some of the people there, didn't like the environment. Brian Clough was there with his green sweater, dominating. I've got a huge respect for what he achieved as a manager with Forest. When I was later an apprentice at Arsenal, I would clean the away dressing rooms. When Arsenal played Forest, Clough would see me, plant a big kiss on my cheek and say, 'Ah, young man, this is the one from Nottingham who got away.'"

Cole signed schoolboy forms with Arsenal on his 14th birthday in the front room at home. Weeks later, he left to go to the National Football School for outstanding talent at Lilleshall, where he continued his misspent schooling while playing every day.

"A lot of the England Schoolboys don't end up making it. They think they have made it before they have. We had a Vietnamese boat boy in our year and he was at Tottenham. They were saying he was going to be unbelievable. What happened? Nothing."

At 16, Cole moved to Arsenal as an apprentice. "I really enjoyed it," he explains, "but again there were several examples of divine intervention. My youth team coach Pat Rice was a right prick, but a prick in the right way. He was right on top of us all the time and giving us jobs: cleaning the floor, sweeping the stands and cleaning the bogs. I hated it. I was the foreman, with responsibility for the other first-year apprentices. If something went wrong – if boots weren't cleaned properly – then it came back to me. We always rowed until he took the foreman's job off me. I found the jobs a chore, didn't get the argument that cleaning a floor was character-building. Looking back now, that's exactly what it was. And Pat Rice was exactly what I needed. He knew that I was a feisty so and so who always spoke my mind, knew that I was always getting into altercations and wouldn't back down."

Cole's reputation soon spread. "George Graham pulled me into his office one day and said: 'You think you're the bee's knees, don't you?' I was 15, but I wasn't having him taking the piss and came back with, 'No. And I'm not having you tell me what I am.' Gorgeous George just shouted, 'Out!' and pointed to the door. Their problem was that they knew I had something and could play. I knew that too. I had to have that self-belief, but it came from scoring goals wherever I played, including England Schoolboys."

Cole excelled with Arsenal's youth team and was occasionally invited to train with the first team. Life was good.

"I was living with my sister and her boyfriend who was a bit of a boy, a bit of a legend. He always looked after me."

The young striker was with Arsenal when they won the league at Anfield in 1989.

"I am very good friends with Michael Thomas and he still talks about that frightening night. Michael and David Rocastle would take me out clubbing when I was 16 or 17."

Cole shakes his head sadly when he mentions Rocastle's name. His parents had also emigrated to England from the Caribbean and he was an Arsenal star. He died in 2001, aged just 33, from an aggressive form of non-Hodgkin's lymphoma, a cancer which attacks the immune system.

"Rocky was brilliant with me," says Cole. "My eyes were opened by him and Michael and I treasure those memories. We'd go to Shoreditch where they played R'n'B and reggae. Soul II Soul were big at that time. They'd bring a lady over and say, 'Have a dance with her.' I used to think, 'But I'm only a boy!' Still, I'd get up dancing. I grew up fast, you have to in London. The acid scene was big and we'd go to raves in old aircraft hangers. We never knew where we were going. Thousands of people were there dancing all night. I knew that people were doing drugs, but I never did. I was protected from that, the music and the company was good enough for me."

Paul Gascoigne was also on the scene. "Gazza was big mates with Rocky and Michael and we'd go and watch Tottenham. Arsenal players watching Tottenham! There were no problems though, it was all boxed off."

Cole appeared in a few reserve team games for Arsenal,

but wanted to play more frequently. He appeared in a pre-season tournament for Arsenal's first team at Highbury and was sub twice for competitive matches.

"I travelled with the first team a few times but I never started," he says. "My relationship with George Graham wasn't the best: I didn't like him and he didn't like me. I'd detected that from an early age."

Cole's desire to play saw him loaned to Fulham in 1991 for three months, where he played 13 games.

"I had to take my own kit and wash it: that was a culture shock," he says. "I drove across London every day in my XR2. I put myself in a murderous debt for that car after paying five bags [£5,000] for it. Rocky and the lads would kill me for that car. 'Coley,' Rocky would say, 'Have you shagged in your car yet? You must have.' I loved all that talk."

Jimmy Hill was at Fulham and told Cole that he wanted to speak to him.

"You think you're a bit of a player don't you?" Hill said. Cole didn't reply. "Whereas I don't think you're ever going to be a player," continued Hill.

"That's your opinion," replied Cole. "You're entitled to it." Then he walked out.

"I never spoke to him for years until he came up to me when I was at Manchester United and said 'Remember that chat we had? I was wrong, wasn't I?'"

"You definitely were wrong," Cole replied, and walked away.

"What I didn't tell Hill," says Cole, "was that I used people like him and George Graham to spur me on."

Cole went on a further loan to Bristol City, a league below the newly-created Premiership.

"I did well," he says. "I was scoring goals in front of 15,000; that's all I wanted. People started talking about me. Pat Rice called me from Arsenal, telling me that Derby County wanted to buy me. 'So Arsenal want to sell me then?' I asked. There was a pause, then he said he'd get back to me. He never did."

Bristol City made Cole their record signing when they paid £500,000 for him in 1992.

"I didn't have an agent, but went with my brother to negotiate," recalls Cole. "He told me not to sign anything. I was impatient and signed a three-year contract straight away, worth £450 a week. I got a signing on fee of about £20,000. I thought I was minted.

Cole loved Bristol, initially living in the Avon Gorge Hotel and then a waterside apartment, though it meant moving away from his girlfriend, Shirley, a Brixton girl whom he'd met at Kevin Campbell's brother's wedding. Of that encounter, he reminisces, "She looked decent and we had the banter. I didn't know whether it would be one night and then I'd crack on with someone else. We're married and still together 18 years later!

"The senior players at Bristol started talking about me in a good way, people like Leroy Rosenior, Mark Aizlewood, Russell Osman and the Polish magician, Jacki Dziekanowski."

With 20 goals in 41 appearances other clubs began to show interest. "The Bristol City manager Denis Smith called me in and told me that Nottingham Forest, of all clubs, had come in for me," recalls Cole. Smith said, 'I'd let you go tomorrow, but they have only offered £600,000. We paid £500,000 for you. If they come back and they offer over a million, I'll let you go.'"

Forest never came back and were relegated that season. Newcastle United were the next club to approach Bristol City. Riding high at the top of football's second tier, the Geordies wanted a striker, hence Keegan's phone call to 'Adrian'.

Cole's line was suddenly busy. Out of the blue, he received a call from Paul Elliott, who was working as an agent.

"'Hi Coley,' he said, all friendly. 'How you doing, brother?' I'd never spoken to him before, but I listened to what he said because I knew that he'd been a top-level player. I also felt that this transfer was going to be out of my own brother's depth to deal with. I genuinely thought Elliott was trying to help me out when he said, 'I've got someone who can help you out with the deal.'

"Michael Thomas had also put me onto the solicitor Michael Kennedy, but I didn't end up using him. Instead, I ended up using an agent, whom Paul Elliott had recommended. I went up to Newcastle in his car.

"I didn't know about the numbers, but a deal was done to sell me for £1.75 million (a club record fee). When it was concluded, the agent said, 'That'll be £30,000 for my services.' I asked if I could pay in instalments, but he said, 'No, I want the money now.' I had to pay him out of my signing on fee.

"I've never heard from Paul Elliott or the agent since. The same geezer got involved when Ruel Fox signed for Newcastle, but Foxy didn't pay him."

The incident angered Cole. "I don't think that top players actually need an agent," he says. "They need a financial advisor and solicitor, but not an agent. Because if you play well the offers are going to come."

Cole was paid £1,200 a week and his good form continued, 12 goals in 12 games as Newcastle were promoted as champions in 1992/93. As club owner Sir John Hall set about realising the vast potential, St James' Park was rebuilt and Newcastle returned to the top flight. The Geordies played at Old Trafford at the start of the 1993/94 season, when Cole scored in a 1–1 draw. He would score 41 goals that season, yet all wasn't well.

"It was difficult being a Newcastle player," he says. "No disrespect to their fans, but if you are scoring goals up there then they absolutely adore you. I found that very difficult. I was a young man and struggled to deal with it. I just wanted to play football, do my best, go home and go out with my mates."

Going out was a big problem.

"Some punters would say, 'Well done.' That was fine. Others wanted to hold court with you. I could be having a meal with my missus and people would come up and want to get involved in the conversation. I found it very awkward and still do. It did my fruit in. I loved my football at Newcastle, but I felt trapped. And the more goals I scored, the worse it got. From the milkman to the bloke in the paper shop, everyone wanted to talk about football, football, football. There was no escape from it."

The Geordies went on to regard Cole, who linked up effectively with Peter Beardsley, as their greatest goalscorer since the Gallowgate's 1970s hero Malcolm Macdonald. He preceded Ryan Giggs as PFA Player of the Year and while he struggled with the adulation, he was receptive to other aspects of the hero worship.

"I loved it when they made that song up, the one about me getting the ball and scoring a goal. I was buzzing my tits off, I've got to be honest. My initial reaction was, 'I must be doing something right.' I was happy that I was entertaining the punters and the Geordies love their football, but I needed a break from it. Manchester was different because it's much bigger and there's a lot more going on."

After 68 goals in 84 games, Cole left Newcastle for Manchester United in January 1995 because his relationship with manager Kevin Keegan had soured.

"Kevin was absolutely brilliant when I first went there," he says. "I was the centre forward and he built a team around me to score goals for his football team. Then we had a disagreement and after that he was a changed man towards me. If you cross or upset Kevin then he falls out of love with you.

"The fall-out was trivial. We were about to play Wimbledon in the League Cup. I was messing about in training. It was cold and I was knackered from the game on Saturday. 'What's wrong, do you not fancy training?' Kevin asked. 'To be honest, no,' I replied. 'If you don't want to train, you might as well fuck off in then,' he said.

"So, me being me, I went inside and didn't come out. He

probably thought that I would go back out, but he didn't know my character. Kevin saw that I was leaving and asked me what I was doing. I argued that I was only following his instructions.

"I went south to my missus in Brixton and told her about what had happened. She asked me if I was for real and had a go. I ended up having a ding dong with her until she dropped down a couple of gears and saw it more my way."

Newcastle lost against Wimbledon that night, with supporters and the media wondering why Cole was absent. Keegan responded to questions by saying that Cole had walked out of the club. The story went big as Cole decided not to go into training the following day. Then Cole's new agent, Paul Stretford, called.

"What you doing?" asked Stretford.

"What do you mean, what am I doing?" Cole replied.

"You can't just walk out."

"I did what I was told to do."

"Well you're going to have to get yourself back up the road tomorrow."

Cole went back two days later.

"I was treated like a criminal. Photographers were coming up to me at the airport and getting in my face. I had to have a meeting with Freddie Shepherd, the Newcastle chairman. He said, 'Coley, what's the problem?'

"I told him that it had been blown out of proportion. He asked if there was a problem with my contract, which had been increased to £4,000 a week and I said that there wasn't. Then we began to talk and it all came out. I told him that I wasn't happy living where I was and Shepherd sorted everything out. He was really good, paid up my rent and moved me into an apartment he owned in Gosforth. I was happy there, but it was never right with Kevin after that. I was determined to do my best for Newcastle United, but it didn't work out that way. We played a game against Blackburn in January 1995 and Kevin didn't say a word to me."

Cole went home and watched Sheffield United against Manchester United. The phone rang. It was Stretford.

"Andrew, you know you said that you'd leave Newcastle to go to one other club?"

"Yes."

"The deal's on. Man United. I'm not messing about. Get yourself and your essentials together and I'll be up in three or four hours."

Cole was told that Joe Royle had tipped Alex Ferguson off that all wasn't well between him and Keegan and that Newcastle would let him go if the price was right. The news would have delighted Ferguson, who had been looking for a new striker since the start of the season. Mark Hughes was 31 and Ferguson had spoken with Everton manager Royle about taking Hughes. Ferguson felt that teams were changing their tactics to play United, becoming more trenchant and defensive. His solution was to find a striker who was so quick that he could create spaces in tighter areas of the box. Two were identified: Cole and Stan Collymore at Nottingham Forest.

"Andy had the speed and movement that could exploit the short passes from Cantona," said Ferguson. "And Collymore had the ability to turn and run at opponents. After initial enquiries about Cole were discouraged by Kevin Keegan, I made quite strenuous efforts to do business with Frank Clark, the Forest manager, over Collymore.

"It so happened that on the day I phoned with the intention of making a big offer for Collymore, Frank did not return my call, having apparently gone home with flu. I went back to probing Kevin about Cole and this time, after a little sparring on the phone, he said he would part with Andy for £6 million plus Keith Gillespie."

Collymore, another player represented by Paul Stretford, was gutted. He had performed exceptionally well in games for Forest against United and, with speculation reaching fever pitch, was expecting to join United.

"I couldn't believe it when I heard," said Collymore. "It was made worse by the fact that Andy Cole was Stretford's client too. Stretford had assured me that the move to Old Trafford would happen if he kept plugging away at Fergie, and now it had collapsed. I tried four or five times to call Stretford on his mobile and he was very curt with me. He kept telling me he couldn't talk. At one stage I was in denial about it. I didn't want to believe the Andy Cole move was happening. Stretford never rang me back and I was livid with him. I didn't blame Fergie. That's just business. But the fact was that Stretford had shoehorned his other client into Manchester United at my expense."

Stretford eventually returned Collymore's calls and blamed Frank Clark, saying – correctly – that it had been taken out of his hands. Collymore was asked if he would be interested in a move to Liverpool, who were interested and, so Collymore was assured, on the dawn of great things.

Cole's £6 million fee was a new British transfer record and almost twice what Ferguson had paid for Roy Keane only 18 months earlier, but the United manager knew that he wanted to do the deal straight away, which was no surprise: Cole was the most prolific goalscorer in England and had scored 41 goals in the previous season.

Stretford picked up Cole and drove to Manchester, passing the United coach on the M62 as it was returning from Sheffield.

"I thought, 'These will be my teammates tomorrow and they haven't got a clue that I'm coming,'" smiles Cole.

"I stayed at Paul's and I met the manager the next day. He was saying how he saw me fitting in the team. All I could think about was signing. I wanted it to happen so much. I had a really long medical – they even checked my toenails. It was a great day for me when I signed, a really great day.

"My parents were pleased and shocked at the fee. Rio Ferdinand said to me recently, 'Look what Darren Bent went for, what would you be worth now Coley?'"

Most United players were earning £5,000 a week in 1995 and Cole was no different. Eric Cantona was on £5,400 basic.

By coincidence, United met Newcastle that weekend, but Keegan and Ferguson agreed that neither Cole nor the Northern Irish winger Gillespie, who had been a makeweight in the transfer and had made nine United starts between 1993/95, should play.

"I'm not being disrespectful to Newcastle, but standards were higher at United," says Cole. "The dressing room was a Who's Who of world-class players and I struggled to get my head around it at first. I felt that I was still a boy who was still learning my trade. Kiddo came up to me and welcomed me to his United. Then he said, 'If you think that 40 goals a season at this club is good enough then you are wrong.' Then he walked off. I couldn't believe it, but over the years I realised where he was coming from. Goals weren't enough at United: you had to become a team player, the complete footballer. That's what killed Ruud van Nistelrooy's United career. He scored, that's all. That started to annoy the players. United need more than a goalscorer."

Cole maintains that he always played his heart out for United. "Always," he says strongly. "Some of those players were gifted for fun – far more gifted than me. I knew that I'd have to knock my pipe out all day long if I was going to win over the supporters."

Historically, big money strikers from Nottingham like Peter Davenport and Garry Birtles had struggled.

"I can understand why," says Cole. "It's not easy being a striker at Old Trafford; it's daunting. Expectations are so high. You need confidence and peace of mind to come through. I did well, but I was always looking over my shoulder because United are always bringing in centre forwards – just as the club have throughout history."

Two weeks after joining, Cole watched his strike partner Eric Cantona jump into the crowd at Selhurst Park.

"I thought, 'What the fuck is going on here?' I caught it out the corner of my eye."

Perhaps because of Cantona's absence, Cole's first season at Old Trafford could have had a better ending. He did score five goals in a record 9–0 victory over Ipswich Town, but claims that game doesn't really stand out in his memory. What does is United losing out on the league to Blackburn on the final day of the season at Upton Park.

"I got a lot of criticism that day," says Cole. "Ludek Miklosko was unbelievable in the net. I hit the post but we couldn't get a winner. Those people in the media who had said I had been brought in to win the championship were now saying that I had cost United the league. I took too much of it to heart. I was devastated by how much flak I took because it implied that I wasn't committed to United. I was – I'd even missed the birth of my first child to play for United a few weeks before."

Sir Alex Ferguson was always on hand to encourage Cole. "One journalist, Matt Lawton, was giving it me more than most. The gaffer told me that he wouldn't know how to play football if he tried and that made me laugh. I just wanted to dig the journalists out, but the gaffer made light of it. He was always convinced that I would come good for Manchester United and I believe I did."

Cole settled in south Manchester, where he still lives. His second season also brought his first league title.

"It was a major season for me," he says. "I was playing up front with Eric for most of it. He was the only player I saw who the manager never had a go at. We all went to a film premiere and were told to wear black ties. Eric turned up in a cream lemon suit with Nike trainers. The manager told him that he looked fantastic. I liked Eric and considered him friendly."

Despite winning the double, United went for another striker in 1996, Alan Shearer. When Shearer chose Newcastle for

£15 million, United signed Ole Gunnar Solskjær from Norwegian club Molde for £1.6 million.

"I didn't think he was old enough to play for Manchester United," says Cole. "I thought he was about 15. But what a finisher. His impact from the bench was phenomenal. He'd get crucial goals – goals which would make him a United legend."

Roy Keane was another player with whom Cole enjoyed a positive relationship.

"Not everyone did," says Cole, "but we didn't have a cross word. He knew my character and I knew his. I called him 'Schiz' and got away with it so he must have liked me.

"We came in at half time at Highfield Road one year. We'd not been playing well and Schiz started raving at Gary Neville. Nev gave it him back and Roy flipped and started chasing him around the dressing room. It was hilarious. The manager came in and settled him down.

"We went to Spain one year to train. Schiz always ended up taking Quinton Fortune out with ferocious tackles. The gaffer saw this one and came over, telling him to calm down. Roy told him to keep his oar out. The manager abandoned training. The lads couldn't believe what they were seeing.

"I had a set-to with Teddy on the pitch. Everybody knew that Teddy wasn't my cup of tea and I wasn't his. We came in at half time and it was going to go off between me and Teddy. Schiz calmed me down, but then he wanted to start fighting Teddy.

"He could be really, really cutting. He used to hammer Yorkie and tell him that he was really, really shit. During a game. He'd hammer him for his touch. Yet he never did it to me."

Injuries restricted Cole's appearances in 1996/97, but he scored a key goal at Anfield as United moved towards another title.

"The manager always had a thing about Liverpool," says

Cole. "He used to say, 'We've got Liverpool at Anfield and I'm going to play Coley because he always scores at Anfield.' I used to love playing at Anfield. Loved the songs which United fans sang."

Cantona left in the summer of 1997 and Cole's bugbear, Teddy Sheringham, arrived.

"Our problems started when I made my England debut," explains Cole. "I replaced Teddy. I was making my debut. Maybe I was naive, but I think he should have wished me all the best. I was nervous, as anyone would be. Instead, he walked straight past me and blanked me. It's not like I told Terry Venables to take Teddy off.

"So I was devastated when Teddy Sheringham signed for United because I couldn't stand him. We played a friendly in Milan in 1997, just after he'd signed. He said something on the pitch. I didn't like it. 'I'm only trying to help you,' he said.

"'I don't need your help, you fucking prick.'"

Ironically, the striking partnership between the two thrived.

"Pally pulled me to one side once and said. 'I know you don't like Teddy, but keep doing it together.'

"I always tried to be professional on the pitch and to be fair I think Teddy did too. You don't have to be best mates with the people you work with. I got on with everyone and had a good life, but me and Teddy – nah."

Cantona's retirement saw Cole emerge as United's main striker. He was the Premiership's joint top scorer with 18 goals, but United finished the season without a trophy, in spite of some great moments. One was Cole's hat-trick against Feyenoord away, a game which saw United and Feyenoord hooligans clash in Rotterdam city centre and inside the De Kuip stadium.

"That was a good night, one of the stand-outs in my career. Those Wednesday night Champions League games were superb, especially at Old Trafford.

"We didn't win the Champions League that year though.

We used to watch videos of our upcoming opponents and I don't think it did us any good because they were invariably the best bits. We'd watch a team like Monaco and think, 'Fuck me, they're absolutely brilliant.' We stopped doing that in 1998/99, stopped worrying about our opponents and look what happened."

Arsenal won the league in 1998. "I always considered Arsenal our main rivals – most of the players did because we had ferocious games against them," says Cole. Roy Keane certainly did. "For me Arsenal are our biggest rivals," said Keane. "They have been our biggest challengers in the last 11 or 12 years. I know games against Liverpool, City and Leeds mean a lot to the fans and I can understand that but Arsenal are our biggest challengers."

United signed another new forward in 1998. "The manager wanted Patrick Kluivert," says Cole. The Dutch striker refused to speak to United and joined Barcelona. "If Kluivert would have arrived then I'm sure I would have been on my way," says Cole.

Kluivert's intransigence meant Ferguson realised his long-standing ambition to sign Dwight Yorke from Aston Villa for £12.6 million in September 1998.

"With Teddy, Ole and Yorkey, I still wasn't sure of my United future," says Cole. "I was the one player United could have got good money for selling."

"My fears were realised as I was on the bench a lot at the start of the season and missed some big games. I was started in a league game at Southampton [in October] and we won 3–0, with me, Dwight and Jordi Cruyff scoring. It was only the second time Dwight and I had paired up and I think the manager saw something."

He did. "I have given all the strikers a go alongside Dwight Yorke now," said Ferguson. "He has looked the part, whoever he has played with. Good players can play with anyone and Dwight has so many different aspects to his game. I must say that I liked the look of Andy Cole with him and I think it's a combination I shall pursue. They seem to have struck up a friendship and are developing an understanding."

The partnership would prosper. "I liked Yorkey. We were totally different. Dwight was, 'Look at me, I play for Manchester United, I've got a nice bird and car.' I'm the opposite. I bought a Porsche one year but was so self-conscious that I couldn't drive it. It took me two months to drive it to training. Yorkey had no such worries."

United met Barcelona in the Champions League group stage in 1998/99. The Catalans were favourites to win the competition and had the added incentive of the final being staged at their Camp Nou home – in their centenary season. Xavi made his European debut at Old Trafford as the two teams played out an epic 3–3 draw.

"I was on the bench wishing that I was playing," says Cole. "Barça were playing sensational passing football. Two of their goals were so slick, but United kept coming back at them and it was end-to-end stuff."

The return was at the Camp Nou at the end of November. In between, United played their other opponents in the tough group from which two would qualify, drawing 2–2 away to Bayern Munich, destroying Brondby 6–2 away and 5–0 at home. By the time of the Camp Nou clash, Barcelona had to win to stay in the competition.

"I recalled our 4–0 defeat in the Camp Nou in 1994, and set against this background it would have been understandable if we had gone to Spain to make sure we didn't lose," said Ferguson. "But I always had this wonderful dream of having a team ready to attack and beat them."

As the players trained beneath the towering stands of the 114,000-capacity stadium, Cole pointed to the corner flag beneath where the travelling support would be and said, "If I score I'm going to run to that corner."

A vengeful United attacked, but were behind after a minute.

Yorke equalised after 25 minutes before combining brilliantly with Cole, who put United ahead in the 52nd minute. Cole ran to the corner, where a group of United fans were sitting in the home end and piled forward to the corner flag in delight. Rivaldo levelled for Barça, before Yorke struck again.

Up in the press box, the hugely respected Scottish journalist Hugh McIlvanney, who was working with Sir Alex Ferguson on his 1999 autobiography *Managing My Life*, was purring, "Brilliant, brilliant, brilliant."

Rivaldo and Luis Figo, arguably two of the best players in the world, roared back at United in a desperate attempt to stay in the competition. The Brazilian equalised to make it 3–3 and hit the bar in the dying minutes. Barca were out. United and Bayern were through.

"We had nine clear chances and Barcelona had 11 or 12," said Ferguson.

Inter were beaten in the quarter-final, Cole and Yorke charging into them in the first leg at Old Trafford which United won 2–0.

Ferguson said, "Now I just have a smell about Europe, I think we have a terrific chance to go all the way. Our concentration was first class."

The Juventus of Zidane, Davids, Deschamps and Inzaghi were United's opponents in the semi-final.

"Juventus are the best team I've ever played against," said Roy Keane when I interviewed him in a Philadelphia hotel in 2003. The interview was scheduled for 30 minutes, lasted 90 and included two major arguments. "They battered us at Old Trafford in the first leg. Giggsy scored in the last minute, but we should have been 2–0 down at half time."

Juventus were favourites, a status they immediately justified by surging into a 2–0 lead inside 11 minutes after two goals from Filippo Inzaghi. First-half goals from Roy Keane and Dwight Yorke put United level in the match and ahead on away goals in the tie.

"The manager was totally calm at half time," recalls Cole. "It was like he was reading it from a book and really inspiring. He said, 'Get another goal and we'll win this game.' He was totally relaxed about it. We went out and battered them, steamrollered them, absolutely battered them. It could have been more than 3–2 because we pulverised them. I got the winner five or six minutes before the end, but that night was about others. Scholes was awesome, Roy too – especially because they knew that he would miss the final. Roy was mind-boggling."

Keane deflected such praise: "I don't necessarily think that it was my best game but people have since jumped on the bandwagon and said that I scored and got booked and all that. But I suppose if you look at the game, the fact that we were 2–0 down and the opposition you might see it differently." Keane was awarded a rare '8' by the notoriously hard-to-please *Gazetta Dello Sport*.

"It was proper rowdy on the plane home," adds Cole. "Everyone was buzzing their tits off and having a drink. Juventus are a proper football club. They had great players like Zidane and we'd just smashed them everywhere, physically and tactically. I'm sure the Juventus players thought we were on something."

The atmosphere was different in Sitges, the seaside base for the United players 20 miles south of Barcelona, for the final.

"The mood was almost like the preparation for some third-round Milk Cup tie at some Division Three club," says Cole. "We didn't do anything special, a rest on the afternoon then listening to the gaffer's pre-match talk which seemed to get longer and longer as the seasons went by."

Bayern Munich, whom United had already faced twice, were the opponents in the final.

"We'd played well against them and were confident," says Cole. "But we never turned up for the final. I was very disappointed with my performance. I had done well in that competition all season; me and Yorkie had scored 53 goals between us. We were the best team in that competition, but not in the Camp Nou."

Cole was substituted for Solskjær in the 81st minute.

"Ole and Teddy did it for us, no question. We should have won the competition a year later, but Redondo did us with an unbelievable bit of skill."

Cole was again United's top scorer in 1999/2000 with 19 goals from 28 Premiership starts. He also enjoyed the trip to Brazil for the inaugural World Club championship.

"Me, Butty, Roy and Giggsy were sat by the pool at our hotel in Rio. We talked about going up in a glider, which flew off from a cliff nearby and over the Atlantic Ocean. I realised it was Friday 13th and ducked out, so did Giggsy. Next thing, we hear these screams. Schiz and Butty were up the sky having the time of their lives. We were pissing ourselves, it was brilliant. The manager had no idea what was going on."

Three weeks in the South American sun did United no harm, as they returned to win another title. Cole scored the only goal in the top-of-the-table clash against Leeds and netted his 100th United goal in the spring, just before injury saw him miss out on Euro 2000.

Injuries continued to affect him in 2000/01.

"I didn't have the best luck with them," he rues. "I came back pre-season with bronchitis, then the next year with pneumonia. The gaffer was spitting bullets, but I got through it."

United signed Ruud van Nistelrooy in 2001. Here, finally, was the new striker who pushed Cole to the sidelines.

"The formation switched to 4-5-1 with Ruud as the 1," explains Cole. "The manager kept saying, 'Don't worry, you'll get your games.' But I didn't.

"One day I knocked on the manager's door. I'd always had a brilliant relationship with him and he was great in that meeting. I was desperate to play in the 2002 World Cup, but needed to be playing every week for that to happen. I was 30 and there was a lot more football in me. I told him that I didn't want to be sat on the bench. I didn't want to steal a wage. I wanted fans to come up to me and say that I had put a good shift in for my wages. There are players who are happy to pick up their wages and see out their contract. I'm not one of them. I wanted to see out my contract at United. The last contract I signed would have brought me up to a testimonial, but it didn't materialise that way. Keaney told me that I shouldn't go, saying that I would regret it for the rest of my life. He was right, but I wouldn't listen at the time.

"The manager told me that he didn't want me to go, but said, 'I know how you are, understand where you are coming from and will let you go.' In hindsight, I should have swallowed my pride."

Cole made the short move to Blackburn Rovers for an £8 million fee in December 2001. Within two months he had won the League Cup, scoring the winner against a Tottenham side managed by Glenn Hoddle, the manager who had refused to pick him so often when in charge of England. He scored 13 in just 20 games that season, before reforming his striker partnership with Dwight Yorke the following year.

"Blackburn is a good family club and I enjoyed it there. I didn't take to Graeme Souness at all times and struggled to work with him. He kept on saying what he'd done at Liverpool as a player, what he'd achieved. I'd played with great players who never talked about what they'd won."

Cole didn't make the World Cup squad and was unable to add to his international record of 15 caps and one goal. Glenn Hoddle, in defence of his decision not to select Cole for the World Cup in 1998, accused him of needing six or seven chances to score one goal.

Cole played 83 times for Blackburn, scoring 27 goals, but his relationship with Souness deteriorated to such an extent that he reported him to the PFA, accusing him of victimisation.

"Every day was a fight with Souness. I could have done

that for ever, but I was bringing my problems home with me."

Thirteen years after leaving, Cole returned to Fulham, where he was their top scorer in the 2004/05 season.

"I needed to play for someone who I liked and respected and that person was Chris Coleman. The only time it was difficult was in the winter, because my family was still in Manchester. I'd just sit alone in my apartment. I was enjoying playing and got another great goal against Liverpool, but I wanted to move back home."

Manchester City approached Cole.

"I'm not going to lie, City was good. I was apprehensive about going there because I would be seen as a red. That's because I am a red. I have a season ticket at Old Trafford and sit in the main stand in a normal seat. I just mingle in, paying my money like everybody else.

"A City fan came up to me on a pre-season tour of Bangkok and said, 'I remember how you celebrated against us for United.'

I got a few goals, played well and before I knew it the City fans were singing my name. There was uproar when I left."

Cole wanted to finish at 35. City offered him a one-year contract, but Portsmouth offered him two years.

"I wanted to stay at City, but Stuart Pearce voiced concerns about my injuries. I told him that I was going to Portsmouth, City budged and offered to pay me appearance money, but I'd made my mind up. City got me on a free and sold me for £500,000."

Cole scored three in 18 at Portsmouth, went on loan to Birmingham and then moved to Sunderland to play under Roy Keane and alongside Dwight Yorke.

"It was very difficult," he says. "Roy as a manager was very different to Roy as a player. They say management changes people. It was hard for me and it was probably hard for him. I didn't call him 'Schiz' . . . I changed it to 'Skip'!"

Was Cole easy to manage?

"I changed a lot from 21 to 31. I mellowed. I can sit down and hold court with people a lot more now, when before I would have said 'Fuck off.' Everything was a row for me when I was younger. Scholesy, of all people, described me as 'miserable' at Butty's wedding in 2008. I laughed at that. We used to always be at the back in pre-season training; we know each other."

After seven Sunderland games, Cole was loaned to Burnley in 2008.

"It was like being 21 again," he says. "I was scoring and manager Owen Coyle was good to work with. He wanted to sign me for another year, but the board wouldn't sanction the money, except on a pay-to-play basis.

"In passing, someone asked if I would be interested in playing for Forest. It was my hometown club and my grandfather was a big Forest fan, so I thought, 'Why not?'"

Cole joined Forest in the summer of 2008.

"I realised straight away that it was a mistake," he says. "Nigel Doughty, the guy who ran the club, interviewed me before I signed. He explained that he'd done due diligence on me, before asking why I was joining Forest. I thought they wanted me, not the other way round. Doughty backed down, put a kid's rucksack on and got off! I was left in the room with the manager.

"Forest were selling season tickets off the back of me signing but by August I wanted to retire. It was so hard to play in that team because they were all kids. Kids who play 20 games think they've made it. I told the manager in October that I wanted to retire. I wasn't playing and felt like I was stealing money. I had to give them three months' notice. Two weeks later they said I could go – implying that I hadn't done it for them. They then put the story out that I walked out of Nottingham Forest. I nailed all of them."

After scoring 229 goals in 499 games of professional club football, Andrew Cole retired in November 2008. Only Alan

Shearer has scored more than his 187 Premier League goals. Shearer didn't win a European Cup, however. Or five titles.

"I intend to do my coaching badges and see where we go from there. My son is at the Man City academy and I want to do some more media work, which I have enjoyed, though I'm not into tucking the lads in and criticising them because I've played the game. All that should keep me ticking over. I was talking to Incey the other day about my future. I like the idea of management. As for United, those good old days, they seem like only yesterday."

2
LEE SHARPE
'Dance, dance, wherever you may be . . .'

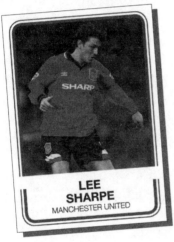

LEE SHARPE
MANCHESTER UNITED

1st December 1991. The cold and mist of Merseyside mean that there are few takers among the 4,500 travelling Reds for the 'Highbury massacre' T-shirts being sold outside the away end at Goodison Park. The shirts, which have been knocked up in no time by Manchester grafters, celebrate United's 6–2 demolition of Arsenal less than three days earlier, a result which stunned United fans at a time when away victories were not taken for granted. Star of the shirt is Lee Sharpe, 20 years old and wheeling away from the North Bank, arms open in celebration, looking like the coolest man in the world in United's acid-blue away shirt.

Winger Sharpe was the Highbury hat-trick hero. The Black Country boy was on the fast track to stardom and celebrity, the first pop-star footballer of the Premiership age, the man who set a precedent which future United stars Ryan Giggs and David Beckham would follow. Good-looking, fashionable and personable, Sharpe was as popular with hardcore Reds as with the thousands of teenage girls who would join his fan club.

His popularity was enhanced yet further when he scored the game's only goal in the Goodison cold. As he celebrated, Sharpe did a little shimmy, dancing back and forward in what became known as the 'Sharpey Shuffle'. The United end, half of which was unable to see much more from the atrocious view offered by the Park End terrace, loved it, but not everyone shared their appreciation.

"We were all well pleased when we got back on the bus," recalls Sharpe. "Three good away points and we were looking forward to getting back to Manchester for a night out. We waited as the manager had a drink with the Everton manager. While there, he saw my celebration on television. He came back on the coach, stormed up to where I was sitting and roared, 'Who the fucking hell do you think you are?' I was shocked. I'd just scored the winner at Everton, my fourth goal in two games, but the manager went on, 'What's all that carry on after you've scored? Fucking stupid dancing, what the fuck do you think you are doing? If I see you doing that again you'll be out of this club.' There was no point saying anything so I just looked down at the table like a naughty schoolboy."

The others players wondered what was going on. "I'm not saying that the manager didn't have a point," adds Sharpe when we meet at the trendy Malmaison hotel in Leeds, the city where he has lived for over a decade. "He's a great football manager and nobody can argue with his track record, but I've thought about it since and I wouldn't have changed my celebration. I'd scored a goal: why shouldn't I have gone mental with the people who paid my wages? Lads my own age who'd paid good money to travel away with United. I felt like them and wanted to be with them for 30 seconds of madness.

"I wouldn't have done it if we were losing and I still can't understand why the manager had a problem with it. It's like he didn't want me to have a personality. Something was lost between me and the manager that day."

Sharpe was tuned into and part of the prevailing vibe in

Manchester. *United We Stand*'s front cover reflected the mood, with the headline 'Rave On Sharpey'. To the soundtrack of the so-called 'Madchester' music of the Stone Roses and the Happy Mondays, Sharpe was another example of Manchester moving into ascendancy after too many championship-free years and rampant industrial decay. There was a long-overdue, palpable feel-good factor in the streets of Manchester and its environs.

On the pitch, Merseyside's dominance waned as United served notice that they were back: first with the FA Cup, then Rotterdam, then the league title. The double followed. Sharpe was the face of these times, the boy about town in the casual clobber who attracted more female attention than Brad Pitt at a divorcees' disco. Basically, Sharpe could pick up virtually any girl he wanted in Manchester.

"That was always nice," he says, smiling. "I had a few quid in my pocket, was a young lad playing well for Manchester United. There was a bar at the back in Discotheque Royale where all the United players went. You could not move for girls trying to get close. The City players had a bar on the other side of the club, and there would be one or two girls there. I just thought it was part of being a footballer and was determined to enjoy it while it lasted."

Critics of Sharpe say his star didn't burn brightly for long enough. Sharpe disagrees, more than happy with his career which took in 263 United matches between 1988 and 1996 – more games than Jack Crompton, Paul McGrath, Gordon McQueen, Ray Wilkins, Eric Cantona and Ruud van Nistelrooy.

"I'm a Black Country lad," says Sharpe. He still has a discernible Midlands accent, though the edges have been smoothed down by his years in the media. "Dad [Leo] was a massive Birmingham City fan and he was swinging me towards a football before I could walk. He played semi-professional for Causeway United and tried to get a trial at a couple of professional clubs, but never got anywhere. He was a quick and aggressive little winger.

He was a decent player but mouthy and the opposite in temperament to me and my brother John."

The two Sharpe brothers would watch their dad play each Saturday.

"Mum would send us off with a bag of sweets and we'd watch the first ten minutes of the game before wandering off and playing somewhere. I had a happy childhood. My parents were not rich but we wanted for nothing. We lived in Blackheath, a working-class estate between Birmingham and Wolverhampton and played outside all of the time.

"Dad worked in a factory but was made redundant so he set up a small industrial company. Mum supervised a team of cleaners. Then we moved to Halesowen, which was a bit posher."

Sharpe's hero was his granddad. "I spent loads of time with him," he recalls. "He was a truck driver and I loved going in his truck with him. I thought I was a proper trucker when I was seven, thinking I had responsibility for unloading, but it was really my granddad doing it. I travelled around the country with him and it was a big adventure. From him I learned that you had to work in life."

But Sharpe didn't want to drive a truck, setting his sights on becoming a professional footballer. It wasn't always easy, despite his obvious talent.

"I was a good player and played for my year and the year above, but I couldn't get into the district side," he says. "That was more about politics because the manager was picking players from another Sunday League team, Worsley Wasps, and ignoring players from our side, Stourbridge Falcons. I actually played for the district side for the year above me."

Like many footballers, Sharpe didn't thrive academically. "Every school report was the same," he recalls. "'Lee has ability and brains, but he does not apply himself.' I was too busy looking out of the window or practising my autograph in the back of textbooks for when I became a famous footballer. I was a daydreamer. I wish I would have worked harder at school and I'm thinking of studying again. Other parents would put their kids under pressure to succeed and the kids would get stressed, but my parents never did that. They wanted us to be happy and we were."

Sharpe was a popular pupil. "I had a girlfriend called Debbie from the age of 13 right through school. We were on and off for years and she moved in with me in Manchester until Fergie kicked her out and told her to move back home. I've not spoken to her for years. She lives in Brighton now, but my sister keeps in touch. I'm the eldest, then my sister and our younger brother John. John was at Man City for a few years, but Alan Ball let him go."

Sharpe supported Aston Villa as a boy, and again this was his grandfather's doing.

"Granddad said, 'You're not supporting who that duck egg [Sharpe's dad] supports.' So I supported the Villa of John Gidman and my dad was fuming. I went a few times with my mates, but not often. We had to get three buses to get to Villa Park. It wasn't the safest place to go and my mum was very protective."

At 15, Sharpe took his GCSEs and reaped the dubious benefits of all those years perfecting his signature. "My results were pants, but I wasn't too worried as I'd signed on with Birmingham City to play there all summer. I didn't really like it, though, as they had a lot of players from a team called North Star, who had been there for ages and they were rivals with us."

Former Manchester City and England striker Kevin Reeves was in charge of Youth Development at Birmingham. "He called me and my dad in at the end of the summer and announced, 'We think that Lee has got more ability than all of the six lads that we are going to take on, but we're not going to sign him because we think he lacks the aggression to be a top flight pro.' I wanted to smash him in the face. Surely that was his job to make me more aggressive? On reflection, I wasn't that bothered because there was a clique there and I hadn't been there that long. Of the lads who got signed up, one or two played for Birmingham a few times but that was it."

Sharpe then went on trial at distant Torquay United.

"I was a left winger and the lad who played left back in our junior team was a bit of a tough nut. Because I wasn't, he helped me out and we had a good understanding. One of his granddad's mates knew someone who had moved to Torquay and did scouting there. Torquay took a few lads from our team and my mate asked if it was all right if I went along, explaining that I had just been released from Birmingham City. I travelled down and played three games in three days. I did really well and the manager offered me a place on their YTS [Youth Training Scheme]. I returned to the Midlands and had a trial for West Brom, where I played as a centre forward. I was knackered and West Brom said to my dad, 'If he has been offered something by Torquay then he should snatch it with both hands.' My dad explained that I had just played three games in three days, but they were not interested and were quite dismissive."

Torquay's pre-season started on 1st July, but Sharpe's mother didn't want him to go.

"She wasn't happy about the situation. I had an option for a trial at Wolves – again as a centre forward, but we eventually decided that it was right to go to Torquay, where I played as a centre forward in the reserves. It was very difficult moving away from home, but Torquay was a brilliant little place. The weather was better than anywhere in the country; I was in good digs with a very friendly family. It was a big house in the centre of a terrace with three bedrooms on the first floor and a big kitchen downstairs. If the digs were not good then I doubt I would have stayed. The husband worked away and the wife was a real motherly figure. Torquay was also full of Swedish students learning English, so there was plenty of eye candy."

Sharpe enjoyed his time on the English Riviera and Torquay's exacting regime gave him the wake-up call he needed.

"It was a great introduction to professional football. It was really hard physically, but I pushed myself like never before. Two or three lads jacked it in because it was so hard. The hard training made it easier for me when I trained with United."

As a first-year player, Sharpe's main job was to clean the referee's room, sweep the terraces after a first team game and replace the divots in the pitch. "The manager called me in and said that I was looking a bit tired and jaded. They felt that I was homesick and sent me back home for a week. I had been at home for two days and had gone to see the PE teacher at my old school when a message came through from Torquay. One left-sided player was injured and the only other one at the club was away for a family bereavement, so they sent for me."

Sharpe was only 16 so his dad drove him to Exeter, where he came on for the last 20 minutes in the Devon derby at Exeter City.

"I did all right and stayed in the first team for a while. We played Tottenham a few weeks later. I nutmegged someone and Ossie Ardiles came over and pushed me in the back. I knew I had made an impact.

"There were some characters in the Plainmoor dressing room. On our end of season do, the club's leading striker, who was staying in our digs, came back drunk and got into bed with my dad. We had another lad who was renowned for getting sent off, chinning people and knocking them out."

Torquay manager Cyril Knowles protected Sharpe by starting him in home games and bringing him off the bench away. Sharpe thrived, and didn't hesitate when charged with taking a penalty at home to Cardiff City.

"That made me a bit of a local hero," he recalls, "and life was good. I was getting £30 first-team money to add to my £27.50 a week apprentice wage. I felt rich. Even though I was 16, I could get in the local nightclub Monroe's by borrowing the pass off another player. There were lots of girls around, plus a school right opposite the ground with lots of good-looking fifth and sixth formers. They were the same age as us and we'd chat them up."

Sharpe played against Colchester United one Friday night in 1988. He remembers being clouted a few times and receiving a few elbows in a 0–0 draw. "My parents had come down from Birmingham to watch and they took me back to my digs before driving home. I was in bed at one in the morning when the landlady's mate Jackie shouted up the stairs, 'I don't know what the fuck you have been doing, but the manager is downstairs with the club secretary.'"

Torquay's manager Cyril Knowles and the club secretary were waiting below in the kitchen. "I got changed and went downstairs wondering what it could be about. I was shitting myself. They sat me down and said, 'We have just left the ground and a Jaguar was parked there with no lights on. As we walked past, a door opened and a voice said, 'Get in we'd like a word with you.' We crapped ourselves at first, but went over. Alex Ferguson was in the car with Archie Knox. They took us for a drive around Torquay. They want you at Man United. They're staying overnight and want to see you at ten in the morning. They're not leaving Torquay until you have signed.'"

Sharpe was stunned as Knowles gave his honest opinion about the offer, saying that he would be better off moving, getting better coaching and fewer kicks, playing some games in the reserves and going on from there. Then they went.

"I was 16," recalls Sharpe. "I didn't know what to say. I went into the front room and told my landlady Irene. She yelped. Dave Caldwell, an experienced Torquay player who was seeing Irene's mate Jackie, gave me some advice and told me what to ask for. I wanted to tell my parents, but couldn't because they were on the motorway and there were no mobiles then. I kept trying them at home and mum answered after the fourth time at 2.30am. She was worried that something was wrong and I asked her to put Dad on. Dad was silent when I told him. But he wasn't starstruck.

"'Man U's a big place,' he finally said. 'I don't know whether you'd be better staying another year where you are before going somewhere as big as that.'

"'I know what you mean, Dad, but I have to go. The chance might not come up again. The manager thinks I should go up there and learn to play properly.'

"'Yeah, yeah, of course,' Dad conceded. 'It's a great club. You should go.'"

Sharpe was up early the next morning and put his only shirt and tie on.

"I was dressed like Rick Astley with a paisley shirt on," he says.

Cyril Knowles was already in the boardroom with Ferguson and Knox, where they did a deal – £180,000, plus a friendly and other payments if Sharpe played a certain number of games for United.

"I was taken into the boardroom and Alex Ferguson was there. I was shitting myself. It was weird, I'd only seen him on the television and there he was asking me how I thought I'd played. I said, 'Not great.' Fergie said that I'd done OK and that I kept getting up after being knocked over, which showed determination. He said that I was brave, a hard worker, a good athlete with pace who looked like I'd fill out. He explained that I'd receive excellent coaching at United and start off in the reserves."

Ferguson had been alerted to Sharpe by an unofficial United scout, Les Noad, a former journalist from Manchester who had retired to Torquay.

"What I saw that night left me in no doubt that I wanted his signature on a contract without delay," said Ferguson later. "He was quick enough to catch pigeons and had good physical lines. An excellent crosser of the ball, he was brave enough to take advantage of that and his other assets."

In the Plainmoor boardroom, Ferguson started to talk about money. "He offered me a four-year contract worth £170 a week, with a £5,000 signing-on fee," says Sharpe. "If I made the first team, my wages would go up to £320 and I'd get £150 per appearance. I just sat there saying nothing, mumbling and nodding. I would have signed anything."

Business concluded, Ferguson and Knox returned to Manchester and Sharpe went to change out of his shirt and tie. At midday he had to be sweeping the detritus of the crisps and pies and Bovrils of the match the night before from the terraces.

"I had a big grin on my face and Cyril Knowles gathered all the apprentices after we'd done our chores and said, 'Sharpey's off to Man U.' They couldn't believe it."

Sharpe gathered his scant belongings and caught a train to Manchester a few days later. Alex Ferguson was waiting to greet him at Piccadilly Station.

"I wasn't expecting that, but he took me to his Jag and then to Old Trafford where he gave me a guided tour of the ground. He introduced me as 'the new player' to everyone as if I was a million-pound signing. He made me feel so special and gave the impression that he cared for me. He then drove me to some digs and told me that I'd train with the first team the next day."

Sharpe was also given a lift to the Cliff the following morning. "It was so different to Torquay. The cars in the car park were really posh, the pitch was like a lawn and all the kit was laid out perfectly. The towels were clean and everyone had their own space. At Torquay you had to buy your own top and trackie bottoms and you washed your training kit your- self. Outside, players were hitting perfect passes and killing the ball dead with one touch. At Torquay we played Murder Ball behind the social club."

His induction into this dream world continued when the first team started to emerge from the dressing room.

"Players like Bryan Robson and Gordon Strachan were there in real life," he says, "I felt like I'd won a competition to spend a few days training with United. Steve Bruce told Fergie off for not introducing me to the rest of the first team."

After a few days, Sharpe returned to spend the rest of the season with Torquay, before moving to Manchester in the close season of 1988. He spent that summer having driving lessons and passed his test.

"I bought an Escort with my signing-on fee, which I later found out was two cars which had been welded together. The bonnet used to fly up if I went above 80mph."

Sharpe lived in digs in Salford with Shaun Goater and Mark Bosnich and several other players. "I would go to Makro in Irlam and buy big boxes of jelly fangs and Maltesers, which the other lads would rob," he remembers. "I'd get back from night matches and Shaun (who was from Bermuda) would be sat there in front of a full fire wearing as many clothes as possible, plus gloves and a hat. It was like a sauna and he would moan, 'It's freezing isn't it?'

"There was another lad who we called The Dong, a bit of an oddball who carried his kit around in a bin liner. He was an Irish lad who said he wanted to quit football, busk and be a tramp. He had a photo of Spiderman and a broom in his room and would talk about being mates with this broom. He'd get a bus and stay on it until the end, then come back. He was a right winger, lightning quick with a funny run. He played like he was in the 50s – he'd stop the ball and sprint with it. I heard he committed suicide and that his parents blamed United."

On the field, Sharpe's progress was swift. "I played in the reserves a few times as a left winger, but was tried at left back in a practice game against Newcastle due to injury and I did well. A few days later the manager asked me if I was ready to play in the first team. I said, 'Er, yeah.' I'd been at United six weeks."

Sharpe made his debut in a 2–0 home win against West Ham in September 1988. "I was very nervous and couldn't believe it when the team was read out. I watched the other players go through their pre-match routines. Steve Bruce always put his shorts on last. Paul Ince and Gary Pallister, when they joined United, used to have miniature bottles of brandy and take a little swig before we went out.

"I marked the winger Mark Ward. The roar of the crowd soon becomes background noise because you are concentrating and trying not to make a mistake. I was quicker than Ward so he couldn't push the ball past me and I did OK."

Sharpe kept his place and enjoyed some early highlights, like the 3–1 win over Liverpool on New Year's Day, 1989. A week later, United played QPR in the FA Cup, a tie which stretched to three matches. For the second game at Loftus Road, an injury-hit United side contained several young players nicknamed 'Fergie's Fledglings' by a media who sensed a new beginning for a struggling United side.

Of those much-heralded young players, only Lee Sharpe and Lee Martin would go on to make over 100 United appearances, though Mark Robins and Russell Beardsmore both played over 50 times. Robins and Martin would play crucial match-winning roles in future FA Cup ties, Robins famously scoring the only goal against Nottingham Forest in a key third-round tie in 1990 (always remembered as the match which saved Fergie's job) and Martin scoring the only goal of the 1990 FA Cup final replay.

Injuries and loss of form meant David Wilson, Tony Gill, Deniol Graham and Giuliano Maiorana, a winger from Cambridge, all faded from view, but Alex Ferguson's willingness to blood youngsters had been demonstrated, a philosophy which was repeated with great success throughout the 1990s.

"There was a buzz around us," says Sharpe. "Most of us were reserve players in digs together. We looked like kids compared to the older players. It was still my first season at Old Trafford and I didn't expect to feature at all in the first team. I'd been told that I would be in the reserves for two years, so it was really exciting just to be involved in the first team. United had so many injuries that the manager had no option to start with so many youngsters against QPR."

Sharpe moved out and in with his girlfriend. "But the manager said it was affecting my performances and told me to get back into digs after nine months. She wasn't pleased about it, but what could I do? I was soon back in the spartan digs, with shit food."

Sharpe's popularity with the fans was also rising. He even had a terrace song, to the tune of *Lord of the Dance*: "Dance, dance, wherever you may be, we signed the young kid from Torquay. He soon settled in and he soon made his mark. He is the boy that we call Lee Sharpe."

"I was getting recognised. I would go to functions with the team and started to get known more and more, but all my mates were lads from the reserve team and I'd knock about with them. We'd go in the Priory pub opposite the Cliff and play on the pinball machine or visit a snooker club. We'd go to Saturday's, a cheesy nightclub beneath the Britannia Hotel, but I was too young to get in. I showed my players' pass and the doormen were good with us. I've got happy memories of that time."

Flush with his first-team bonuses, Sharpe would squander much of his money on clothes.

"I got some lairy stuff which I rarely wore, but I was really into clothes. I bought a few Stone Island coats which sparkled at night like a cat's eye. Flannels and Life were the best shops, then Comme des Garçons and Richard Creme."

A hernia injury kept Sharpe out for much of 1989/90, though he suffered his first Fergie hair dryer in the dark month of December 1989, when the manager shouted, "Sharpe! I don't know what the fuck you're doing out there; you might as well be sat next to me, you're fucking rubbish! I don't know what's going on in your head."

It wasn't until the following season that Sharpe really found form.

"I was flying that year," he says. "I scored a hat-trick against Arsenal in a League Cup game at Highbury. It was like I'd achieved my life's ambition . . . and then I went back to my cold digs in Salford to reflect on it. I did a few interviews with papers, which the manager bollocked me for."

In one game against Sunderland, Sharpe destroyed the opposing right back to such a degree that he was withdrawn at half time. His pace was peerless; his crosses hit so true that he was voted PFA Young Player of the Year in 1991, superseding Matt Le Tissier and preceding Ryan Giggs. Sharpe was also awarded his first of eight England caps and began to make his mark in European competition as United reached the final of the Cup Winners' Cup against Barcelona.

"I shit myself in Rotterdam," he says. "I was just so, so nervous before the game and I don't think I played particularly well. Brian McClair came up to me after the game and said, 'You were shitting yourself weren't you?' It was the most nervous I've ever been for a game in my life. I saw interviews on television beforehand where Ronald Koeman was being asked what he thought of Lee Sharpe and I was a bit blown away by it all; I had just turned 20."

The United players had walked out into the rain and onto the pitch at Feyenoord's De Kuip stadium before the match.

"The place was chocka," says Sharpe. "Two-thirds of the ground was United and there were hundreds of flags. It was an unbelievable atmosphere with fans singing *Sit Down* by James and *Always Look on the Bright Side of Life*. Phenomenal."

Sharpe was rewarded with a new contract worth £1,000 a week and finally allowed to move out of digs into a new house in Timperley, a suburb near Altrincham.

"My mates would come up from Birmingham and we'd go around Manchester. I was pretty much famous by then, and we'd get in all the bars and clubs for free. The girls were lining up. My mates used to say that there should be a red light outside my house because it was like a brothel. Every Sunday there would be girls draped everywhere, asleep in our beds, on the floor, the settee . . ."

Keith Fane, the public address announcer at Old Trafford, helped him start a fan club. "I was getting a lot of post, people asking for signed autographs and pictures. I couldn't cope with it all. Nobody ever made any money from the fan club, but the money from memberships helped pay for photos and administration."

Sharpe's fan club was ahead of its time, and became briefly notorious for organising membership functions at Sharpe's favourite Manchester club, Royale's, for which 2,000 screaming females would turn up. "It was fun for a while, but Keith got a bit carried away with it and I had to pull back from it."

But he was brought abruptly down from the highs of Rotterdam by the lows of a debilitating bout of meningitis before the start of the 1991/92 season.

"I bought this huge, stupid, St. Bernard dog," explains Sharpe. "I couldn't control it so had to pass it onto someone who could after nine months. I don't know what I was thinking. I couldn't even get the dog into my car so I borrowed a Rascal van off a mate to get the dog about. I'd just brought the dog back to the house one day when I started getting pins and needles in my right foot. I started tapping my foot to get rid of it, but they started working their way up my shin and calf to my knee. I tried to pick the TV control up put there were pins and needles there. Then they came into the side of my face and my tongue. I started to slur my speech – all this happened in the space of half an hour before going away."

Sharpe called the club doctor, who came immediately to his house.

"He gave me some paracetamol, told me that I'd be OK and that I should go to training in the morning. He thought that it was food poisoning which would soon leave my system. But within an hour I started vomiting and didn't stop for 24 hours. I had to be taken to hospital and put on a drip because I was dehydrated. I was then diagnosed with viral meningitis. What happened to me was classed as an attack and I would have another three of them. Nobody knew how long it would last."

Ferguson sent him back to his parents, where he had his final attack in bed at 5am one morning.

"My mum thought I'd had a stroke. My local doctor came, shit himself and told me to get to Manchester to see the specialists. Mum and Dad whisked me straight up the motorway to BUPA, the private hospital in Whalley Range which I always went to. To make things worse, reporters started coming to the hospital and saying, 'We're investigating reports that Lee's illness is drug-related.' I told them to print and see what happened."

Manchester is the hub of Britain's second biggest conurbation with a population of 2.5 million. But it displays a village mentality when it comes to gossip, with the exploits of Manchester United footballers top of the 'he said/she said' gossip agenda.

"There were rumours that I was taking drugs," says Sharpe. "I wasn't. I wasn't even into the Hacienda rave scene. People would come up to me and say, 'I saw you in the Hacienda last Saturday' when I'd not even been there. I'd go to the cheesier clubs like Royale's, have a couple of drinks to get Dutch courage and chat a few girls up and get them back to my house. I was done by two in the morning.

"The former United player Ralph Milne didn't help when he did a story with a tabloid saying that when United played in Rotterdam, some of the younger lads had been smoking weed in Amsterdam the night before the game. I was in Rotterdam preparing for the match, but because he didn't name anyone, people put two and two together and got five."

No newspaper would dare to print a rumour they couldn't substantiate, yet Sharpe's image was damaged.

"The rumours upset me because shit sticks," he says. "I once went to watch United at Villa and went in the United end with my dad. As we tried to find our seats, some lads asked me if I wanted a line of coke or an E. They'd formed an image of me which simply wasn't true. I'd never taken class A drugs, nor had I ever felt the need to. I had enough things to buzz off in life without them. I'd had a few spliffs and that was it, but I stopped having those after Chris Armstrong tested positive for dope at Spurs."

Sharpe's lifestyle didn't meet his manager's approval. "Alex Ferguson had his spies out and didn't like what he heard. He started to tell me that I should be married, gave me the hair dryer treatment a few times and lots of tickings off. He told me that my clothes were too fashionable, my car too flash, that my hairstyle wasn't sober enough. Giggsy played the game better than me. He had a flash car, but drove a boring club car to training. The manager once called my mum and said, 'Lee seems to have developed a taste for young ladies.' The reality was that I went out on a Saturday night. I didn't drink heavily and never once broke the rule of going out 48 hours before a game. The rest of the time I'd be at home, wrestling with confidence, dwelling on things."

Sharpe overcame his illness and returned to form in the 1992/93 season. With Sharpe on the right and Ryan Giggs on the left, United won their first championship since 1967. Sharpe was frequently sublime and remembers the day that it was won, after his childhood heroes and United's title rivals Aston Villa were beaten by Oldham.

"We'd lost the league to Leeds in 1992 – a crucial lesson for us all. There was a nervousness towards the end of that season because we didn't believe we could win the league. Outwardly, people were saying, 'We're going to win it'; subconsciously there was too much pressure. The disappointment made the players more determined."

When the team demonstrated its resolve by finally clinching the title, Sharpe didn't waste time in celebrating what he calls "my most memorable trophy" and his response to the news became the stuff of legend.

"I was sat in the house with my mum, dad and brother. We jumped around when the reality sunk in that the league had been won for the first time in 26 years. I called a few of the lads but their phones were engaged. I thought, 'What do I do now?' It wasn't like I'd been in the situation before. My dad said, 'Let's drive down to Old Trafford, there will be a few people down there.' I got out of the car at Old Trafford and there were perhaps a thousand fans around. After ten minutes there were ten times that. I was picked up and thrown up in the air by supporters on the forecourt and security had to rescue me. They took me into the stadium because the situation was becoming dangerous. I had to sneak out the other end of the ground and get away. One of the best days in my life nearly ended being one of the worst.

"I didn't get hold of the other lads until late and I was one of the last to arrive at Brucey's house. Most of the players were half-cut but I was driving so I didn't drink much and left about midnight.

"There were a couple of sore heads in the changing room the next night before the Blackburn game. The manager kept his team talk brief. He said, 'You've just won the league. The fans have been great so let's go out on a high. We don't want to lose this game. And I don't even want to know what went on last night.' Then he smiled. It was probably the only time that he didn't mind us having a drink the night before a match.

"We only started to knock the ball about a bit once we'd gone a goal down. The atmosphere was special and we really soaked it up on the lap of honour. We all went out after the match together for a second night of celebrations."

Sharpe was now an experienced member of the United team, yet he still listened to his superiors.

"Robbo pulled me to one side after one game and said, 'You didn't play well today, did you?' I hadn't done. He went on, 'You are young, you will have bad games, but do you know why that was? Are you eating well, getting enough sleep?' It was nice to know that he was looking out for me. He would kick a player in a match if he was kicking me. Robbo was immense – he controlled everything from the pace of the game to the referee and the crowd. He calmed people down in times of trouble. He was like a father on the pitch, pure class."

Sharpe only began to appreciate what Robson gave to the team when he joined United.

"I'd preferred brilliant passers like Glenn Hoddle, or Gordon Cowans at Villa," he explains. "Then I arrived at United and saw Robson first hand. I was in awe of the man, how much ground he covered and how much he bossed the game."

Robson was also the team's social convenor. "He would tell the manager that the lads were going out for a drink when there was no training. The manager wouldn't like it, but could see that sometimes the players needed to sort problems out between themselves. Male bravado and egos needed checking. Keano, Incey, Bruce and Robbo were the strongest personalities. Work colleagues became mates in those sessions and you're more likely to run your nuts off for your mates."

Robson was a great help in other ways. "Robbo negotiated contracts for me and Giggsy in 1993," Sharpe says. "We just sat in negotiations with Martin Edwards, but let Robbo do the talking. He got us deals worth nearly £6,000 a week – up from £1,000. Giggsy and I danced out of the room. We bought Robbo a nice Gucci watch as a thank you. Then I bought a big house in Hale Barnes, proper footballer land, half a mile down a country lane backing onto a golf course."

Giggs and Sharpe were mates, the good-looking young stars of a resurgent Manchester United side riding the new wave created by the Premiership and Sky television.

"I knocked about with Giggsy at the start, then Keaney and Pally," explains Sharpe. "Keaney is one of the funniest men ever – he's bonkers. He was very aggressive and competitive and I'd like to think that I calmed him down a little. He'd scream at me sometimes if I didn't give him the ball, so I'd just smile at him. My job wasn't to pass the ball to Keaney every time I got it! He was very quick witted and would take the piss out of everyone, like Pally for his clothes. Pally actually wears nice clothes; he's just a bit of an odd shape.

"Keaney hated hangers on, but sometimes he was a little too aggressive and quick to judge. People would have the best intentions and maybe they'd have a drink, but you are in a job where the people are making you who you are, you have to be a bit patient."

Sharpe and Keane became good friends. Paul Parker called them 'Piss' and 'Shit' and would leave the dressing room when they walked in to escape abuse, usually about his clothes.

When champions United started the 1993/94 season away to Norwich, Sharpe warmed up with a big black eye.

"I'd been kicked in the face by some little idiot," he says. "He was a lad who I'd say hello to when I saw him out and about. I was in Coco's [another cheesy nightclub] in Stockport and he was coked up and thought we were talking about him. He started pushing and shoving. The doormen came over and kicked him out. The lad was waiting for me outside. I didn't want any trouble so I arranged for a mate to get his car, which I planned to jump into. I got into the car, but couldn't close the door and the lad yanked it open. He offered me out.

"There was no way I wanted trouble and I told him that I didn't want to scratch my knuckles on his face. He wouldn't let go of the door so we tried to drive away. As we did, the lad volleyed me across my nose and face with his foot. There was blood everywhere. The lad ran off and got into a car. We chased after him. Me and my mate were trying to drag him out of the car when the police turned up. They put him in the back of one van and me and my friend in another, while we explained what had happened. None of the papers got it until I started warming up at Norwich. The headline was 'Take That'.

"As for the lad, we went looking for him and he put an

injunction on me. The police came to the training ground and told me that I had to stay away from him."

Two weeks after the incident, Sharpe was recalled to the starting eleven. He scored twice in United's 2–1 win at Villa Park and celebrated by doing what he described as 'The Three Amigos' in front of some United fans holding a giant 'Manchester 2000' flag for the city's optimistic Olympic bid. He scored against Southampton in the next game and West Ham in the one after.

Yet despite these performances and United winning the league and FA Cup in 1993/94, Sharpe doesn't have particularly good memories of that season.

"I felt like I was sidelined," he says. "If you watch the video highlights of that season then they show me flying and playing some of the best football of my career, but I had a hernia problem which kept me out for a while."

With Andrei Kanchelskis on one wing and Ryan Giggs on the other, Sharpe was no longer a shoe-in for the starting eleven either, but he remained an important member of the squad.

"I came on as a sub for the last six minutes of the 1994 FA Cup final, but that wasn't ideal. As the players celebrated after, the manager poked me in the back and said, 'What the fuck do you call that?' He was pointing to a tattoo I'd had done. It was nothing to do with him."

Things seemed to be improving when Sharpe began the following season, 1994/95, as a starter and later scored probably his finest United goal, backheeling a Brian McClair cross against Barcelona.

"I celebrated by pretending to shag the post!" grins Sharpe. "It was the best goal I ever scored, professional football at the highest level. I also set up United's other goal for Mark Hughes in a 2–2 draw."

In a pattern that was all too familiar, a high point was followed by a setback. Just a week later, he fractured his ankle in a League Cup game against Newcastle. So bad was the swelling, he wasn't allowed to fly to Barcelona for the return leg, but that wasn't his only worry.

"The manager thought that I had too many interests outside of football, which wasn't true. I lived for football, was always on time for training and at the front of the running. The manager kept telling me that he wanted me to play in a defensive position but I didn't fancy that."

The emergence of the class of 1992 further limited Sharpe's appearances in the following season, 1995/96. "My confidence was erratic. In my final two years I played in different positions and didn't enjoy it. I was a bit-part player and just wanted to play wide on the left or just inside. That didn't happen. The manager picked his best team and had it been any other club I wouldn't have been competing with Ryan Giggs for the same spot. He's one of the best wingers in the world so I can't really complain."

Sharpe roomed with the emerging David Beckham. "Becks was my gimp," he smiles. "He'd clean my shoes and make me cups of tea. He was a good lad, Becks. Never lairy and loud and a great player technically. He's had a very similar upbringing to me with a very supportive family. He's well-mannered and mad into football.

"He probably looked up to me and even came to one of my fan club afternoons. My dad told him that if he trained hard, he could have all this, pointing at the 14-year-old girls queuing up for my autograph. Becks shook his head, looked at the ground and said, 'Nah, I never will. Sharpey's a legend.'

"You have to say Beckham was right. He may be a global superstar, but has he ever sold out Discotheque Royale on a Sunday afternoon?"

Sharpe chips in with a story about one of Beckham's peers.

"All the first-team players were watching the young players in a game one day at the Cliff and these lads were being told by the manager who was going to be kept on and who would leave. There was a story that they were going to let Scholesy go because they couldn't work out his best position. At the precise moment they were talking about Scholes, he got the ball on the edge of the D, dragged it past two defenders, shuffled between a couple more and slotted it in the bottom corner. He never left United."

While Scholes was United's future, all Sharpe hoped for was an easy way out of United. "Because I'd not played that much in the past two seasons, I thought that the manager would have given me a free transfer. It wasn't like United had not got their money out of me was it?"

Instead, Sharpe became Leeds' £4.6 million record signing in 1996 (a significant mark up on the £185,000 he cost United from Torquay in 1988). Ferguson has always rued his failure to get the most out of Sharpe.

"I look back on my dealings with Lee Sharpe as a disappointing episode," said Ferguson. "Here was a boy who had a chance of making it big. He had everything a wide player needs to be successful in top-flight football other than the ability to beat a man by dribbling."

Ferguson put his "failure to make the best of his immense potential" down to Sharpe's lifestyle, claiming that he had warned him that fast living would slow him down. He has warm words for Sharpe's personal charm and his "wonderful smile", the same which worked its magic on many young women at Royale's, but also concluded that he should have been a far more significant figure at Old Trafford.

Sharpe moved to Elland Road in the summer of 1996. "I felt that Leeds were a big club on the up and had decent players. I got a 25 per cent pay rise, but more importantly, Howard Wilkinson promised me regular football which is what I wanted. After a few weeks he said, 'You're doing far better than I expected, the left-hand side of the pitch is yours. Get at players and take them on and get crosses in. Score a few goals, play with a smile on your face and enjoy yourself.' That was exactly what I wanted to hear and why I moved."

A month later, Wilkinson was sacked.

"George Graham arrived and said that he wanted to avoid relegation," recalls Sharpe. "We were ninth in the league – the players were stunned. It was the worst thing that happened to me. As an attacking midfielder, it was a nightmare season because we were so defensive and only scored 28 goals in 38 games. He didn't like big-name players."

Sharpe's trip across the Pennines from Manchester United wasn't much of a problem for Leeds fans surprisingly.

"Leeds fans were and still are pretty good with me considering what went on and the rivalry with United," says Sharpe. "Only two had a dig because of where I had come from. I went to a bar with a mate not long after I had signed and a lad said, 'Once a scum, always a scum.' A few years later, the same man came up to me and apologised. That was a turn-up for the books."

On the field, more ill fortune followed when Sharpe snapped his cruciate ligament the following pre-season. "I came back a year later but Graham wouldn't play me. People suggested it was because I'd dyed my hair blond!"

He liked Leeds as a place to live and was in a relationship with Joanne, who he's been with on and off for over a decade.

"That's one reason I've stayed living in Leeds. The other is that it's a decent city, not unlike Manchester with a decent nightlife."

Always sociable, he enjoyed the characters at the club. "There was a lady who worked at Leeds's training ground. She had big tits and one of the players really liked big tits. She was a lot older than him and I told him not to, but he shagged her one night. In the throes of passion she was saying, 'Talk to me, talk to me.' He didn't know what to say, but she kept saying, 'Talk to me, talk to me.' Finally, he said, 'Why's there no Vimto in the drinks machine?'

"There also was a blind masseur who used to work at Leeds. His wife would put his clothes into different bags, so he knew what to wear when we were away on trips. We used to change the order round."

In 1998, George Graham's assistant David O'Leary took over at Leeds and told Sharpe to get a new club. He went to Sampdoria where David Platt briefly managed, and describes his one-month time in Genoa as "nice, but lonely; nobody spoke any English. Platty was pushed out, the old manager Spalletti returned and he wanted to bring in his own players."

Sharpe moved again, to First Division Bradford, where his luck finally turned. "We got promotion to the Premiership, a real achievement – as was staying up." Bradford then gambled on expensive recruits like Benito Carboni but were relegated and another managerial change saw Sharpe loaned out again.

"I enjoyed Portsmouth under Graham Rix," he claims. "I played centre midfield, played well and had responsibility. Rix was a good listener – even though he rarely took on board what we said! I wanted to sign for Portsmouth, but the Bradford chairman Geoffrey Richmond wouldn't let me go."

Back at Bradford, there was more unrest at t'mill. "I was convinced the chairman was picking the team – a problem for me as he wasn't my biggest fan. I've always loved training but I didn't want to go in some days because I knew that I wouldn't be picked. I'd wake up and think, 'What excuse can I give today?' I wanted to jack football in."

In 2001, Sharpe's best friend Mark Russell committed suicide. "He was a golfer and we spent a lot of time together, he was like a big brother to me. He had a mental illness, attacks of schizophrenia, and thought that the world would be a better place without him so he committed suicide after taking an overdose. That was a massive loss."

Sharpe, meanwhile, found himself on the move again.

"I needed another Graham Rix who would give me responsibility but I didn't find that at Exeter City, the club where I had made my debut for Torquay, and I only played a few games. It was hard dropping down, it's not the same game as at the top level. An offer came from Iceland. I fancied a change and it was a spectacular country with very friendly people, but it wasn't what I was looking for and I returned after six weeks. Although they were amateurs, their rules were very strict. I wasn't expecting to take the piss and I was fit. I did a full pre-season and never left my house, then a mate came over after five weeks. We went out on Saturday night after a game and the manager pulled me in and told me that I'd been spotted out in Reykjavik. He then said that players were not allowed out for seven nights before the game. I walked away then."

Sharpe consulted his ever-supportive parents. "Mum had been to Exeter and heard the abuse I was getting, partly because I'd been at bigger clubs. You get used to that as a player, but it's not nice for your parents. Dad knew that I wasn't enjoying my football. I told them that I wanted to retire. My mum said, 'I don't blame you. You've done nothing wrong and you don't deserve the abuse that you are taking, it's getting a bit personal. It's time to get out.'"

Sharpe walked away from the game, aged 32.

"I spent the next year depressed and not knowing what I would do," he recalls. "I was lucky in that I've always had good family and friends. My friends have been constant over the years, I've never really knocked around with footballers. I played a few times for my mate's pub team and took over a pub. I got ripped off in that deal though because the takings were nothing like the previous landlord. He told us that it was doing £8,000 a week. We closed the doors at the end of the first week having taken £900. I then did an autobiography, which was quite therapeutic. It made me realise who were ships in the night and who were proper friends."

In 2005, Sharpe found an alternative career when he appeared on the first of several reality television programmes.

"I did *Celebrity Wrestling*. I got offered £10,000 for a week's work, but broke my rib and only wrestled for a day. Because I had a laugh with all the crew, some of the bookers told me that they would let me know about a new programme called *Celebrity Love Island*."

Sharpe was selected to go on the island, where most of the other females, especially Abi Titmuss and Jayne Middlemiss, were attracted to him.

"It was a test for me because I actually like my own privacy. Once I got into it, I really enjoyed it. That made me famous again with a whole new group of people," Sharpe says. "Kids and housewives would come up and say, 'You're that lad off *Love Island*.' They had no idea that I'd once been a footballer.' I started seeing Abi Titmuss for a while, she's cool, bright and funny."

In 2007, Sharpe got to use his other skills when he appeared on *Dancing on Ice*. "Ice skating is really hard," he says. "It was good fun."

"I've had an up-and-down couple of years," he concludes. "It's hard when you step out of football but I'm fortunate to have good family and friends. The hardest bit is working out what to do after football. The PFA don't really help. You finish paying your subs and that's it for them.

"I felt out of love with football. Fifteen years being told where to go and what to do can take its toll and having been at United and Leeds it was hard going to smaller places and not playing. I hadn't planned on retiring, I thought I'd play until 35 or 36, but I became despondent. When I quit, I didn't want to play, watch or even talk about it. It's only now that I'm starting to enjoy watching, talking about it and playing it again."

Sharpe played 'it' for Garforth Town, a semi-pro side in the Northern Counties East League. Gatherings of 200 (double their average) contrasted acutely with his time at Old Trafford.

"I wasn't trying to make a comeback," he offers, smiling, "I struggle to motivate myself in the gym and see playing as a good excuse to keep fit and have a laugh."

It was a long way from a decade ago when Sharpe was in his prime.

"I look back at my time at United almost like being another life. I have little contact with United although I look out for their results and play golf with Gary Pallister. I play off one; Pally's a proper bandit off 16. I occasionally see Brucey and Robbo, but I'm not one for looking back. My medals are actually in my parents' loft."

That's not to say that Sharpe wants to blank out the memory of his time at United. "Not at all," he affirms, "I had five happy years – from 17 to 22 – when I played regularly in an ever-improving team with players like Bryan Robson, Mark Hughes and Eric Cantona.

"Hughes made playing easy. I'd hit the ball to him and he'd control it with his head or chest, even with two big centre halves marking him. Then he'd knock the ball back to me and make me look good.

"Cantona was magic. He turned games, even if we had ten men. He was charismatic, we got on well."

As for himself, Sharpe reckons that he can pick out "a dozen to 20 games which stand out", the Highbury hat-trick being the main one. But the bad times he endured have also left a lasting impression.

In 2008, he started returning to Old Trafford to help out on the corporate hospitality side. "I'd watch the matches. Berbatov is quite casual and great to watch. And I like to see Carrick play too. He never gives the ball away."

And now he looks to the future, even to settling down. "I'd like children myself, like to take them to football, golf and tennis. I've grown up a little bit over the last year or two. I'm not after a WAG, but someone with ambition who is inspiring, someone with a bit of spunk about her. I'm very choosy when it comes to long term relationships, so we'll see."

3
ERIC CANTONA
The King

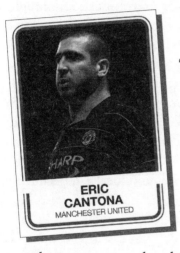

**ERIC
CANTONA**
MANCHESTER UNITED

"**M**y best moment? I have a lot of good moments but the one I prefer is when I kicked the hooligan."

Eric Daniel Pierre Cantona gives his verdict thus on his time at Manchester United. Curiously, in one sense, many of those United fans who were besotted by Cantona during his five tumultuous years at the club might agree with him. His leap into the crowd and into the chest of a spectator berating him at Selhurst Park in 1995 was the defining event for United's supporters in the 1990s. It polarised football not just in England but around the world. You were either against Cantona or with him. And for some the adoration which they had felt the minute he first strutted onto the Old Trafford turf – collar turned up, chest puffed out, holding himself ramrod straight – ratcheted up several notches to the point of blasphemy. Cantona was now United's ultimate Red Devil, rebel supreme, the new Demon King of Old Trafford, or simply 'Dieu'. When he returned from his ban, fans paid for a billboard on the fore-court at Old Trafford saying: 'We'll never forget that night at

Selhurst . . . when you buried that 30-yard screamer against Palace.'

"I remember it," Eric says. "And I remember the goal. It was against Wimbledon. They played at Selhurst Park too. I liked the words on the poster. And I liked it when I was in court and the fans supported me. They travelled from Manchester in the middle of the week to Croydon. I could feel that support and it helped me a lot. The club also supported me. So I stayed."

The FA-imposed ban was harsh, with Sir Alex Ferguson saying, "I don't think any player in the history of football will get the sentence he got – unless they had killed Bert Millichip's dog." (Millichip was then FA chairman.)

Cantona is speaking in Marseille on Bastille Day while thousands fill the streets in celebration, the air a pungent mix of the sulphur from spent fireworks and the salty spray from the sea. Marseille's brilliant white urban sprawl is in vivid contrast to the azure sky. We meet near the Old Port – where England fans had running battles with feral local youths during the 1998 World Cup finals.

When Eric Cantona appears, he is wearing a French national shirt and sporting a beard flecked with grey. He is taller, wider and more imposing than you might imagine. Formidable bushy eyebrows frame his dark, impenetrable eyes. His gaze is direct, but also guarded and wary as he weighs up the strangers around him. He dismisses the notion of a fee for talking, saying, "For me, it is not about the money."

In current football parlance, everyone is a legend and the words 'charisma' and 'aura' have been debased by too frequent and unwarranted use. But not in this case. Cantona is a magnetic, commanding personality to the point of being, frankly, a little frightening.

What has become forever known as the 'kung fu kick' is almost a Kennedy assassination moment for United fans. I can recall exactly what I was doing at the time: I was in the crowd, midway up the Arthur Wait Stand which was full of Reds. As the game went on, I couldn't take my eyes off him. He seemed to be seething inside, full of resentment. When he was sent off, Andrew Cole rushed up to the referee and told him exactly what he thought. Eric walked off, turning down the collar of the black United away strip. The next minute it was bedlam, and most of us didn't know why. When the story of what had happened next filtered around the ground there was palpable disbelief among United fans.

Cantona was, and remains, unrepentant. "I did not punch him strong enough," he says, with regret. "I should have punched him harder. I didn't watch it after on television. Because I knew. All I had was journalists around my house. That's all I could see. My house was small. They blocked the light." Initially, Alex Ferguson thought Cantona was finished in English football.

At a press conference afterwards, Cantona would utter only a single sentence, which has also entered football folklore. "When the seagulls follow the trawler," he took here a short pause while he sipped some water, "it is because they think sardines will be thrown into the sea."

After miles of newsprint had been expended explaining the significance of this cryptic utterance, Eric commented, "My lawyer wanted me to talk. I could have said, 'The curtains are pink, but I love them.'"

"I played that moment at Selhurst Park," he admits. "It was a drama and I was an actor. I do things seriously without taking myself seriously. Even when I kicked the fan it is because I don't take myself seriously. I didn't think because of who I was I had a responsibility not to do it. No, I was just a footballer and a man.'"

Cantona was shepherded off the pitch that night at Selhurst Park by the much loved kit man, Norman Davies, and sadly I have to tell him that he has since died. Norman's funeral was attended by many United players and staff past and present.

Eric is visibly moved, "No, no, no, no," is all he can say for a while.

By the time Cantona joined Manchester United in 1992, he had served notice that the normal rules did not apply to him. His signing came as a shock. Martin Edwards claims the credit for it elsewhere in these pages, and many predicted that the mercurial Frenchman's stay would be short and that he and Ferguson would soon clash. But they didn't. Lee Sharpe and others among Cantona's new teammates point out that it was because Ferguson, the disciplinarian, simply cut Eric much more slack. In 1995, Cantona had turned up to Norman Davies's leaving function at Manchester's august Midland Hotel wearing an open-necked shirt, single-breasted Thierry Mugler suit and a pair of Nike trainers. Which would have been fine, if the dress code wasn't black tie. Ferguson didn't bat an eyelid. His teammates laughed about it. Eric was popular, even if some were envious about the freedom he was afforded.

"With Eric, the manager had to watch his feelings, mollycoddle him, because he was supposedly an off-the-wall genius who needed to be treated differently to get the best out of him," says Lee Sharpe. "I really liked him, but it was one set of rules for him and another for the likes of me. Yet in the press the manager was praised for treating Eric differently. You still hear people saying that he tailored his management to individual needs. But I don't think he adapted his style for me."

Alex Ferguson put it another way, demonstrating that the Frenchman is not the only one with poetic leanings. "If ever there was one player, anywhere in the world, that was made for Manchester United, it was Cantona. I think because he had travelled to so many different countries. There's a bit of a gypsy in some people. He'd been searching all his life for somewhere he could look at and feel, 'This is my home.' And when he came here he knew, 'This is my place.' You could just tell."

Cantona is happy to tell the story of his 'gypsy life' and

how he ended up in his 'true' home in the North of England. "I was a happy child," he begins, perched incongruously on a chair in front of a flip chart. "We had a strong, close family, which gives you the best education you can get. We were working class and satisfied with the small things in life. We were polite and always said please and thank you. We were respectful to others and enjoyed life. We sang, smiled and loved. We were immigrants, Mediterranean people.

"My father came from Italy, my mother from Spain, from Barcelona. I was there when I was a child to see my grandfather. I was ten and liked it very much. He came to France after the civil war in Spain. He was not allowed to return for 15 years under the Franco regime."

Driving to Marseille for the interview from Barcelona where I live I retraced the route of Cantona's grandfather into exile in France, all 500 kilometres, coincidentally through the towns of some of Eric's former French clubs – Montpellier, Nimes and Martigues. He did it on a donkey and it took two weeks. It was more than long enough by car.

"When I finished in Manchester I went to live in Barcelona for three years," Cantona continues, "to relive those childhood memories. To read and live. I liked Barcelona."

The Cantonas (Eric was still with his former wife Isabel when they moved in 1997) lived in Espluges, a wealthy neighbourhood close to the Camp Nou, where their son went to an international school. One day, his pencil case went missing. A trivial matter you might think, but Eric didn't like what he heard and he turned up at the school to confront a startled British teacher, who offered apologies and promised that the school would buy a new one. Cantona listened and then replied, "It is not about a replacement, it is about respect." While in Barcelona, Cantona watched many of the players he'd played with lift the treble in 1999.

"When you see teams win things you want to be involved. But I had been away from football for two years. I was proud and happy. I knew ten of the players and Ferguson. I was very happy for him. I would have loved to have been on the pitch in Barcelona. Of course."

Eric goes back to his life story. He emphasises that he was just a child when he left his family in Marseille to work with one of French football's greatest creators, Auxerre manager Guy Roux.

"It was 600 kilometres away. I was 15. For us young players, Guy Roux was like a father. In some clubs it is not so close. I liked and respected him. Some coaches are not so close to their players, but Guy Roux made sure that Auxerre was like a big family. If I had moved to another club it may have been difficult, but in Auxerre I found another family."

Cantona believes passionately in family values and respect, but this has not been the main theme of his football career. He has been defined instead by rage, an incandescent anger which has periodically burst into life and risked his continuation in the sport he has loved. In France, he burnt every bridge from Martigues to the Seine. In 1988, aged 22, when the French national coach Henri Michel failed to select him, he called him "un sac de merde" [a shitbag] live on television. Eric later described himself as "like a fuse wire", waiting to explode. He earned a ten-month ban, but refused to repent. Such behaviour he claimed as his due. "A young man," he argued, "has a right to rebel." He was further disciplined for the minor infringement of hurling a 'sacred' Marseille shirt to the floor after being substituted in a friendly game.

Following a move to Montpellier, he fought with a team-mate whom he believed had criticised him, flinging his boots into his face. Sent off for throwing a ball at a referee, he was summoned before a disciplinary committee, one of whom commented beforehand, "Behind you is a trail of sulphur." On receiving their verdict, Cantona walked the length of the table behind which his four judges sat, stared each in the eye and addressed them individually with a single word: "Idiot".

In the petty authoritarianism of football, these were heinous crimes which effectively threatened his career.

"If I don't feel the environment is good, I didn't want to be there," offered Cantona at the time. "I need to feel good. Maybe that is why before I had problems. Maybe the atmosphere in a club wasn't how I dreamed it would be. I needed time or I gave up or I tried to find words to explain what I wanted. It is like with a woman. Sometimes you can't find love. Sometimes you can, but it is still not right. It's good to be in love, but you want more: you want to give, you want to receive. Sometimes that doesn't happen. I'm not sure that I would like to be with a woman who is like some of the chairmen I met. They didn't deserve to be loved."

He crossed the Channel, thinking that he was signing for Sheffield Wednesday.

"I was there for one week and I thought I was there to sign," he says. "My lawyer was there and he spoke to try and find a way with the contract. I trained and played in a friendly game. We won 4–3. I scored three goals. After one week, he [Sheffield Wednesday manager Trevor Francis] asked me to spend one more week on trial.

"There were not a lot of foreigners in England then, maybe some from the north of Europe but not many from the South. Maybe they were suspicious, but I was a French international. And Sheffield Wednesday wanted more time to decide about me. That was not a very good way to go about things."

Cantona moved instead to Leeds, where he became a cult hero and won the league. And then he left, only a few months later.

"I had a bad relationship with the manager," he says. "Wilkinson. We didn't have the same views on football. I am more like a Manchester footballer. At Leeds football was played the old way. I think you say kick and then rush. But it was very important to play for Leeds at first because I learned a lot with this kind of football. And we had success."

The first most United fans saw of Cantona was in a league

game at Old Trafford in September 1992, when he pulled Pallister and Bruce around and nearly scored with an overhead kick. Given the vicious rivalry between United and Leeds, it was unheard of for a Leeds player to be applauded, but the whole of K Stand clapped Cantona.

"You dream about things," he says by way of explanation. "You feel like you lived in a situation before."

He finally ended up in Manchester in December 1992, where he promptly turned his collar up.

"That was not a gimmick," he says. "I put my shirt on. It was a cold day. The collar stayed up so I kept it like that. We won so it became a habit to play with my collar up."

Eric's arrival caused a stir in the dressing room that never really settled. David May remembers it vividly. He had not been at Old Trafford long and was just getting to know his new teammates before his first away game.

"I was in awe of Eric and so were all my family," explains May. "I wasn't rooming with anybody. Pally and Brucey were together, Denis and Keaney, Incey and Giggsy. So I was on my own."

Still considering himself an outsider, May went to his room and lay on one of the two double beds. Then he heard a click and saw the door open.

"Eric walked in," recalls May. "I was thinking, 'Oh my God, I don't need this. I'm rooming with Eric.'"

May was polite and tried not to appear starstruck. "I later went for dinner, but didn't know what time to return to my room. It was all about what I thought Eric would want. Should I go back early or late? Be loud or quiet? So I went back early and sat on my bed watching TV."

Cantona lay on the bed across from May. Aged 28, he had become used to the anodyne features of four-star hotel rooms. He was already at his eighth club and knew the life of a professional footballer well, the hours in soulless hotels, the pranks, the expensive phone calls to family.

The conversation in the May-Cantona bedroom was hardly flowing, so May duly called home.

"I rang to say hello and ask my family how many tickets they wanted for the game," he recalls. "Our Pete answered. He was excited about me playing for Manchester United and asked who I was rooming with."

"'I'm with Eric,' I said quietly, trying to sound like it was the most normal thing in the world.

"'Dad!' Pete screamed. 'Dad! He's with Eric! He's with the King!'

"Eric was lying on his bed and heard everything," adds May. "He just smiled and carried on watching television. I looked across and just shrugged my shoulders."

When the Frenchman arrived, United had not won the championship in 26 years. When he left, retiring at his peak, before any hint of physical deterioration could diminish the legend, the Old Trafford trophy room had needed major extension work to accommodate the trophies he had inspired the team to win.

"We had been crowned champions of England by default the day before," Cantona recalls of the title win in 1993. "Now we wanted to play like champions. Our supporters would see us as champions. The lid was ready to jump off, mouths were ready to open. It was a feeling of the greatest delight and madness.

"The songs that came from the depths of the crowd were so beautiful that for an instant I didn't want to have to play, but would have liked to stand still somewhere and just listen.

"At quarter to seven, Steve Bruce led us out onto the pitch and the voice of the people became clearly heard. Kenny Dalglish claimed that Blackburn were going to beat us. The loudspeaker system had started with Queen's *We Are the Champions* and now it was *Simply the Best* by Tina Turner. After a few bars, it looked as if Paul Ince was going to start a dance on the field. Blackburn made a fast start but then three goals for Manchester United!

77

"We brandished the cup before Sir Matt Busby, the man whose most beautiful children had perished in that air catastrophe. We did a lap of honour to cheers from all around the ground. When I compare this spectacle to all the shows in the world, this isn't far from being the most perfect because, just as in certain theatres, the audience is almost part of the play.

"I went back into the dressing rooms. The champagne could flow all night. My shower was long and enjoyable. I didn't go to the celebrations which were given in our honour by a supporter who owned a hotel in the town. I wanted to get home to Leeds to be with my young son."

The following season, Cantona also showed immense personal courage. He faced up to Turkish riot police in the tunnel after a Champions League fixture and received a battering for his pains, an incident which was hushed up by the authorities, but again has passed into Manchester United folklore.

Nowhere was his *sang froid* demonstrated so well than in his skill at penalty-taking. Some players refuse to ever take spot kicks, but Eric enjoyed nothing more than this test of his nerve. As he stepped up to take a penalty against Chelsea in the 1994 FA Cup, opposition captain Dennis Wise attempted to psych him out by offering him a bet on the outcome. "OK, a hundred pounds," smiled Eric, before burying the ball in the net. It all added to the spice.

Not only was Cantona a dedicated trainer who set new standards for the rest of the United dressing room, he was also that rare thing in English football, a man with intellectual pursuits who was not afraid to invite ridicule by publicly discussing philosophy and art. This aspect of his character was not quite as influential with his fellow players.

Cantona has always understood his football as a performance. He has a passionate interest in art, instilled in him by his Spanish grandfather Pedro who was an accomplished abstract painter. Among others, Cantona admires the art of the short-lived Cobra school, which argued that artists should paint like children, expressively and spontaneously, aiming at a form of art without restraint. What few Cantona paintings have been seen are brightly coloured, swirling designs, thrown onto the canvas with freedom. Cantona usually paints for personal enjoyment; he knows he is not a great artist, but he has spoken about how he desires the release of creation, the performance of art.

Lee Sharpe has a comic routine which, amongst other things, touches on what the rest of the team thought about Eric's paintings. Eric was asked to do a painting to be auctioned as part of Bryan Robson's testimonial. He was happy to oblige. When the canvas was unveiled, the players were in agreement that it was 'shit'. Steve Bruce opined that his son could have done better, which shows, at least, that Eric had achieved the effect the Cobra school was aiming for. Brian McClair was once, in all seriousness, asked if Eric read his poems out in the dressing room. Unsurprisingly, the answer was no.

Cantona has, in the past, professed himself often stimulated by interviews. Halfway through, I hope one question I've carefully prepared will intrigue him.

"Camus or Sartre? Who would have won in a verbal joust?"

"What?" he bellows, exasperated.

"A verbal joust."

He looks momentarily perplexed.

"The philosophers." I explained.

"Ah, Camus," he replies, saying it correctly. [I speak Spanish, but not French].

"Or Sartre," rolling the Rs and giving a deep belly laugh at my Mancunian pronunciation. "I didn't understand. I thought you meant a camel or a sauterelle – a grasshopper. I liked this comparison. But the philosophers? There would be no winner. They were open people with their own ideas, but they would listen to the ideas of others. Truth was not everything. You argue to improve your point of view. If you think you know everything then you stay in your own world and go crazy. And then kill yourself. It is important to be open and to have your own point of view, but be open to change."

It became a cliché that he was the final piece in United's jigsaw, the missing part that transformed a nearly team into one which dominated. Cantona's rise to stardom in England confused the French, whom he continued to represent at international level, though his relationship with the national side was always fraught. He played in that infamous France v Bulgaria match in 1993 when David Ginola gave the ball away to Kostadinov, who scored and put France out of qualifying for USA '94.

"It is a very bad memory because we did not lose a game until we had three games to go," he says of France's ill-fated campaign. "We played in Sweden. If we had won, we would have qualified. We drew after leading 1–0. They equalised ten minutes from the end.

"So we had two more games, against Israel and Bulgaria. We beat Israel 4–0 away, but lost 3–2 to Bulgaria at home. If we had drawn, we would have gone through. We were 1–0 up and I scored the goal. They scored and, again, getting the winning goal in the last seconds.

"Bulgaria and Sweden qualified and both of them reached the semi-finals of the World Cup. France could have done at least as well as they did. We had the best team, but we didn't really handle the situation well, despite our players having a lot of experience. Because even with experience, you can make a mistake. But you have to learn from mistakes to improve, both in football and in your life."

In Manchester, his stock continued to soar. George Best, never one to lavish praise where it wasn't earned, gave him the ultimate accolade: "I'd give all the champagne I've ever drunk to be playing alongside Eric in a big European match at Old Trafford."

"Football is art and Best was an artist." Cantona was quick

to return the compliment, but according to his own particular frame of reference. "Not every picture is a good one. All art is about trying to explain yourself. Everyone can do that – the man behind the bar, the man sweeping the streets. It is up to those watching to decide if you are successful at your art. But it is all art. You are an artist if you explain yourself with beauty, with particularity."

In 1995, although he seriously considered walking away from football, he returned to Old Trafford for another two years, inspired, as he said earlier, by the supporters who rallied to his defence. Which was good for United, as his goals were often important, match-winning ones. Roy Keane described him as the best finisher he's seen in one-on-ones. Those who watched him score United's only goal in a key title battle away to Newcastle in March 1996 would not disagree.

"I worked a lot and I was relaxed in those situations," says Cantona. "You have to find the timing when the goalkeeper comes towards you. If he is too close then you don't have the angle to score a goal. If he is too far then you are too far and you will not be strong enough to be precise. When the goal-keeper is three metres away is good. That's when you score the goal.

"When I was young I used to miss. I tried to understand why I scored in training but not in the game. It was about timing. It's the same for the dribble. If a defender is too close you cannot dribble, if he is too far away then he can anticipate."

Alan Hansen's verdict on Cantona's first match back after his ban, against Liverpool on 1st October 1995: "You couldn't have asked much more of a man who was under the most intense pressure, but he appeared about as relaxed as someone wandering down to the shops for a pint of milk."

Practice made Cantona almost perfect, though critics argued that he didn't perform as well or score goals in big European games. Cantona shakes his head.

"I scored goals in the European Cup. Like I scored goals

for France. I played 45 times for France and scored 20 goals. I scored one goal in every two games in Europe. That's not bad." He smiles to himself as he says this.

"When you are a striker you can prove yourself with numbers. You can play ten games, score five goals and assist five goals. You can give an answer very quickly if the press are against you by scoring goals.

"When you are a midfielder or defender you can't do that. If they don't want to see that you are a good player they won't see it. That's why I was a striker."

In 1997, he suddenly retired. His teammates generally weren't as surprised by this as they might have been. They sensed that his attitude had changed markedly, that the spark had gone out of his game. Eric agrees.

"I didn't want to play any more. I'd lost the passion. I think I retired so young because I wanted to improve every time, to be a better player. For myself and the team. To win trophies. To have a feeling of improving. When I retired, I didn't feel that I could improve any more. And I lost the passion at the same time. The passion comes with the motivation of improving. If you lose the passion, you lose the motivation. Money? No."

This prompted me to ask, "If someone asked you to pay £100 to play in an FA Cup final would you pay or not?"

He replied, "It was a dream for me to play because I did not have to pay. We were paid, but I would have played for nothing. There is lots of money involved in football and the players take their share, which is normal. But it is not money which motivates, it is a dream."

Cantona left a city and stadium he loved. He could often be seen around Manchester, watching films at the art cinema the Cornerhouse, or drinking and playing pool in the quieter pubs. United supporters liked it that he lived in a modest house, not in a Cheshire 'palace'. The admiration was mutual.

"The atmosphere is special for the players [inside Old

Trafford] because we can feel that the fans make the sacrifices to be in the stadium. We can feel that football is in the blood of the fans.

"I do miss Manchester a lot. I like the culture, Oasis. And the others. The Stone Roses. I liked The Smiths before I moved to Manchester. Morrissey, I liked the things he did and the way he did them. Very much. A lot of people in France liked him.

"Manchester United is so strong and you can feel that in the city. There is a lot of energy in Manchester in football, music and culture. Maybe it's because of the rain. I only lived there when I was a player. I went back to live there recently for one month to shoot *Looking for Eric* with Ken Loach recently. Some cities you have beautiful things to see and visit; in Manchester they have energy.

"I could feel something in this city, the energy from the history of the city. People try to find things in Manchester, to create things.

"My friend Claude Boli [footballer Basil's brother] lived in Manchester at the same time as me. His girlfriend had moved there as part of her studies on the textiles of Africa, the fabrics and the cloth. That was her passion. I thought that they were all the same, but the different tribes have different cloth, different textiles. And of course all of the cotton originally travelled to Africa from Manchester and then by a boat from Liverpool."

Outside the scruffy hotel situated amid a seedy social housing project and discount stores, gangs of young men of North African descent in Olympique Marseille shirts throw tiny firecrackers to intimidate pedestrians. The explosions punctuate the interview and remind Cantona of the present and his current project. Cantona is extremely busy. His family have helped bring the FIFA Beach Soccer World Cup to Marseille and it will begin in two days. Billboards advertise the tournament around France's third city, while teams of men in Argentina and Japan tracksuits acclimatise by walking the streets, dodging the sleek Le Trams and enjoying the attention their tracksuits bring – even though none of the players are recognisable.

"Now I am in Marseille, a football city where OM [another of Cantona's former teams, Olympique de Marseille] is like a religion," he goes on. "It's a cosmopolitan, passionate city and the people live for football."

Cantona is happy to be back for work reasons, as manager of the French national beach soccer team.

"I am very proud," he explains. "We have been organising the Beach Soccer finals to come to Marseille for six years and this is the culmination of the work that my brothers have put in. Marseille is a passionate city, like Rio de Janeiro, which staged several Beach Soccer finals, so I think it will be a success." Cantona played in the French team which won the Beach Soccer World Cup in Brazil in 2005.

"I played only one game in the finals. I started playing Beach Soccer in 1997 and played for three years before becoming player-manager. In the World Cup finals of 2005 I played just one game. I played for a few minutes and I scored one goal. To win that World Cup was as important as anything I achieved as a player on the grass."

The statement surprises me. "Really?" I ask. "As important as scoring the winning goal in an FA Cup final for Manchester United against Liverpool?" That strike became King Eric's signature goal. When he received the ball he appeared to be cramped for space. There appeared to be no way he could get a shot on target without changing his position. But Eric leaned backwards, arching his body while remaining perfectly balanced, impossibly striking the ball into the net. How could such a big man, commentators wondered, move with such delicacy?

"Really," insists Cantona. "We had helped develop a sport which was almost nothing in Europe. And we were World

Champions. It was a big moment. I did not have any interest in beach soccer as a child. The beach in Marseille had no sand, just small stones. The game was born in 1992. My youngest brother Joel played one tournament in Brazil in 1996 and he really liked the game. He spoke about it a lot. I retired from football in May 1997 and played my first beach soccer tournament in September 1997 in Monte Carlo. I really liked it. It is a beautiful game. I wanted to help the organisation. It gave me satisfaction to help create something."

As it turns out, France underperformed in this tournament, losing to Italy in the quarter-finals. Brazil won the competition for a 12th time. The only other winners, with one title each, have been France and Portugal.

Cantona's other profession is acting and, since this interview took place, he has been touring Britain for the launch of the Ken Loach film he had just been shooting. *Looking For Eric* has garnered excellent reviews and it is easy to see why. For United fans of a certain age it is a powerful exercise in nostalgia. The Manchester postman, Eric, who is the protagonist of the film, attempts to console himself as his life falls apart by smoking weed and watching footage of Cantona's greatest performances in the 1990s. Cantona materialises in his bedroom and acts as a guide through the postman's difficulties, spouting philosophy as well as reflecting on his own career. It captures brilliantly how Cantona became an obsession and a muse particularly to hardened northern males who are notoriously difficult to impress. It was apparently Cantona's idea that a film could be made with this type of storyline. Throughout the film, Cantona gives ample evidence that he is not afraid to send himself up. Although his acting hero is Mickey Rourke he has a very different screen persona and a surprising gift for comedy.

Acting has gone some way to replacing the buzz of football. Eric observes, "You can lose your mind, like when you score a goal. You can share it with 60,000 people and you can feel the energy. Football and acting is very similar for me because they are passionate. You get a similar feeling when you are on the pitch and on a set. But the feeling is stronger on a pitch. When I lost that feeling I stopped to play. I felt like I could not improve.

"In acting, I work hard to try and improve. I don't like it when a football coach tells you which way to play. I like to improve myself as a person. Often there are players who have only football as a way of expressing themselves and never develop other interests. And when they no longer play football, they no longer do anything; they no longer exist, or rather they have the sensation of no longer existing."

Elsewhere he has claimed that he has mellowed with age. "There was a time," mused Cantona, "When I would lose my temper regularly, when I felt that I had to stand up and say something about the things that made me angry. I used to take a stand and rage against injustice all the time. Now I know how things will turn out and that has taken the fun out of losing my temper. There was a time when I could derive a certain pleasure from trying to work out what to say and do next. But not any more."

And he has continued to watch United from afar, voicing his concerns for the club publicly.

"I can understand why the supporters were concerned after the Glazer takeover," he says. "The philosophy of the club will never change while Ferguson is at the club. After he leaves . . . that is what makes me worry. Ferguson is so strong, so popular. He can control everything. For the moment nothing has changed at Manchester – apart from in an economic way."

Asked "Who was the greatest French footballer ever – Platini or Zidane, or someone else?" it is really no surprise when Cantona replies, "Somebody else. Me."

Cantona's talent has never faded in his own mind, nor in the minds of those who loved him. He still retains the ability to make generous gestures which endear him to people. Brian

McClair tells the story of how Eric was more than happy to help him out with an appearance at a function in Ireland in support of his testimonial year. One of Eric's shirts was to be auctioned and an Irish fan, with a tattoo of Eric on his back, was bidding for it. Eric promptly bought the shirt, then gave it to the man.

At the end of the interview I tell Eric about Gary and Wendy Knight. Gary is a friend in Manchester whose wife Wendy had given birth to a stillborn child. The couple are on a mission to raise money for charity and phoned that morning asking if I could get any footballers to sign any memorabilia to be raffled. They have chosen their moment well. I ask him to sign something which could be auctioned in a Manchester pub.

"I would like to do this," declares Cantona, except there was nothing like a shirt or poster to sign. We are, however, standing by that large flip chart of A2 paper.

"Just write something on there," I said, eyeing the big felt markers.

"What?" he asked.

"You've just told me that you're an artist. Show it," I reply. "Or write a message to the people of Manchester."

With that, Eric does a Miro-esque squiggle and a message. So as not to crease it, I 'borrowed' the hotel's roll of flip chart paper and tucked Eric's work in the middle.

Smartly framed, that squiggle was auctioned for £2,500 in a pub in a working-class area of Manchester. The couple would have been happy with a tenth of that – which is what a signed Ruud van Nistelrooy shirt raised.

4
DAVID MAY
'. . . Superstar, got more medals than Shearer'

DAVID MAY
MANCHESTER UNITED

David May winces and laughs as he tells the story of United's celebrations after overcoming Newcastle's 12-point lead at the top of the Premiership to win the league at Middlesbrough in 1996.

"I had a bottle of champagne in each suit pocket and two in each hand as we celebrated all the way back to Manchester," he recalls. "I was thinking, 'This is the life.' I probably played my best football at United that season. I had a consistency that comes with playing every week which I didn't have in my later years at Old Trafford. I was trolleyed by the time we went out in Alderley Edge later to continue the celebrations.

"We'd won the league and I'd heard the song about me that day for the first time, 'David May, superstar, he's got more medals than Shearer'. That stunned me. There had been better United players than me who had never had a song about them. People still come up to me and sing it in Manchester.

"I was annihilated and, somehow, pissed all over the taxi and the driver on the way home. Despite this, the driver still took me to my house in Rochdale where I gave him £50."

But the smile was wiped off his face when events took a darker twist the following morning. Regional news reported the story of a taxi driver who had been beaten up in Rochdale the night before.

"I was out of it," recalls May of the morning after, "cabbaged at home in bed and uncontactable. I was still wearing my United suit. I could remember very little. The other players thought it was me who'd attacked the driver."

May was called by Dave Fevre, the United physio.

"Where are you?" asked a concerned Fevre, who would later follow Brian Kidd to May's former club Blackburn Rovers, "The gaffer is going mad."

"Why?" asked May.

"Because you assaulted a taxi driver in Rochdale and it's on the news."

"The fear swept over me," remembers May as Fevre hung up with the ominous words that Ferguson wanted to see him in the morning. "I was dead."

As requested, May made his way to the Cliff.

"I was bricking it when I went to see the gaffer," he recalls. "I knocked on his office door and waited for the 'Come in.' Then I walked in sheepishly."

The United manager got straight to the point.

"What the fuck have you been up to?" asked an angry Ferguson.

"Gaffer, I'm really sorry and I'll pay for whatever I've done."

"Fucking right you'll pay for it, son. What were you thinking of?"

"I'd just won the league for the first time, Gaffer," explained May.

"But you've got Liverpool in the FA Cup final on Saturday. I'm fining you two weeks' wages. We've had to pay the taxi driver to keep it out of the press."

"Then he got a message that another taxi company had contacted Old Trafford to complain about my lagging in the cab," May explains. And he just started laughing and said, "What were you thinking of? Go and train."

David May was born in Oldham in 1970, close to Boundary Park where the family lived in a two-bedroomed house. His father was a policeman, mother worked part time at home, painting numbers on microchips while looking after May and his two older brothers, Pete and Steve.

"My dad was a decent copper," explains May over lunch in Manchester's striking glass-walled Urbis museum.

"He goes on about how the police have gone too PC these days and how they should be able to give criminals a good hiding in the back of a Black Maria. And you should. Then again, Dad would drive home after drinking and get away with it because he was a copper. Another copper would say, 'Follow me home and you'll be right.' So Dad would go over round-abouts and skirt hedges. That's how it was then. He'd come home after a few drinks and me and my brothers would be upstairs, hear our parents arguing. One Christmas, Mum bought us a dartboard. Dad came in bladdered one night and she put it over his head!

"Mum and Dad are still together and they're great. I had a happy childhood and I was fortunate because Dad's wages were probably higher than average so we had a foreign holiday in Spain every other year. Other than that it was St Ives in Cornwall, which we loved."

May's interest in football began when he was ten. "We had a gang on our street, lads and girls, and we played football all day. There was a mill at the bottom of the road with a big yard. There was barbed wire to stop us getting in, but we'd bend open the fence, sneak inside and play matches against kids from the next street."

His older brothers played Sunday football and May would watch. "It wasn't like I was academic and into homework; in fact I was thick as pig shit and hated school. My mum told me that when I was four I walked home from school, crossing over three busy roads to escape. She said she was cleaning the windows and she thought, 'I'm sure that's our David.'"

May went to primary school in Middleton and secondary in Oldham. "The teachers were on strike so often that we didn't really have a regular football team. If we did, I played left back, then midfield and then centre half. I was put there because I wasn't good enough to play in midfield."

His choice of which professional football club to support was dictated by someone else. "I went to Oldham a few times and stood on the Chaddy End, but Gail, a girl on our street, was a mad City fan. She still goes. I went with her to City from the age of eight until I was 14. We'd sit in the North Stand and my favourite player was Nicky Reid. I later played with him at Blackburn and thought, 'How the fuck were you my favourite player?'

"Denis Tueart, Trevor Francis and Tommy Caton – God bless him – City had a good team. Gail's dad would take us sometimes. He was a keen golfer and had his golf clubs robbed during one match in Moss Side. I told him, 'At least they left you some tees,' to which he probably thought, 'Fuck off you little twat.'"

May had other teenage interests. "I wasn't into clothes, but I liked music. My first record, embarrassingly, was *I'm in the Mood for Dancing* by the Nolan sisters. I bought it twice from John Menzies in Middleton when I was 11. The first time, I was walking home with it when a lad from school booted me up the arse, he'd smashed it. I got into my bedroom to play it, only to discover it was snapped in half. I was devastated. I was on 50p a week spends and it cost 79p. I walked back to Menzies and bought it again."

May stopped watching City when he was spotted playing Sunday football by a scout from Blackburn and offered a trial.

"My dad had no objection so I played for Blackburn's A

team against Formby away in Merseyside," explains May. "I'd never played against Scousers before and was struck by their strange accents. I scored the winner against a team of grown men and the manager asked my dad when I was 16."

"You mean 15?" replied May senior.

"No, 16."

"He's only 14? Then he shouldn't be playing."

West Brom and City were both interested in signing him on schoolboy forms and Tony Book got in touch from the Blues, inviting him for a three-day trial at their Platt Lane training ground in Moss Side.

"I hated it," recalls May. "There were so many kids there, it was like a cattle market with three games going on and very little individual attention. At Blackburn there was one. I was happy at Blackburn so I went back and signed for them."

Blackburn offered May an apprenticeship in April 1986, just before he left school. He moved into digs in a terraced house at 435 Bolton Road, opposite the Fernhurst pub which away fans frequent before games at Ewood Park.

"There were four of us in one room in two bunk beds. Apart from the lads I played with, I didn't know anybody."

May would stay in Blackburn all week and another lad's dad would give him a lift back to Middleton each Friday. In return, May's dad would drive them back to Blackburn on Saturday to play.

Wages were £27 a week, though he gave his landlady Ann £5, which she put away for a lads' holiday, but the spartan life at the digs started to grate.

"I came to hate them after a few months. The landlady was getting £35 per player a week and all we got was potatoes four times a week. I asked Ann if we could have some steaks now and then or some home cooking and she said, 'We can't afford that!' Yet they had just bought a new Mini and a pool table, for which the bastards charged us 50p a week to play on!"

May told Blackburn that he wanted to change and they

agreed to move him close by to live with a couple, Jenny and Dave.

"My old landlady Ann wasn't happy and came steaming into the Fernhurst where I was playing pool," recalls May. "'Who do you think you are commenting on my cooking?' she asked, angrily. She gave me my £35 back which I had saved up for my holiday and told me to get out so I did. The food was better at the new place and I was eating lamb chops and vegetables every night. Jenny was a lovely woman and I loved it there. One of the first-teamers came to stay because I told him about the food.

"'Does she make fish?' he'd asked.

"'I don't know. I've never had fish. You'll have to ask her.'"

The first-teamer asked for fish, Jenny didn't know how to make fish so she rang May's mum, who told her how to cook it. "We had poached fish for the next three weeks," smiles May.

That summer he took his first holiday to Palma Nova, Majorca with his brother Steve.

"We would walk into Magaluf every night," he recalls. "We'd go to a pub, where George Michael was playing *I Want Your Sex*. It was where I lost my virginity, aged 17. I pulled a Danish bird when I was pissed up walking back to the hotel. She was about 20 yards in front of me and I snuck up behind and put my arm around her, saying, 'How are ya, are you all right?' We started kissing and the next thing we were bang at it. I had to go to the hotel to get a johnny, but I had no idea how to get it on. I swear I was trying to put it on backwards. I don't think it was the most pleasurable night for her."

The repercussions of the night's brief romance were not over.

"She came to my hotel the next day and said that she was worried I had given her AIDS," smiles May. "I told her that was impossible as I'd just lost my cherry to her."

Back from the Balearics, May's progress at Blackburn continued and he made his first team debut at Swindon on April Fools' Day in 1988 in the old Second Division.

"I was asked to travel down with the first team and the

manager Don Mackay pulled me aside in the team hotel the night before and said, 'You're starting tomorrow.' I thought 'Happy days' and rang my dad, who drove down to watch me. He's watched every single game that I've ever played."

The game was 1–1 and May thinks he did "all right".

"I've still got a video of the game," he says. "You never forget your debut."

Blackburn played Watford a few days later and the team stayed in the south.

"The lads had told me to take some clothes as we were going out on the lash after the Swindon game. I very rarely drank and hated lager and cider, but we went out in Swindon. Another player, Steve Foley, said, 'You've made your debut as a player. Now make your debut as one of the lads.' He asked what I wanted to drink and the first thing I saw was an advert for Southern Comfort and lemonade so I ordered that. He got me a double and I was soon cabbaged."

The Blackburn players progressed to a nightclub. "I was loving it, but then I turned round and all the lads had disappeared," says May. "I couldn't believe it. Two minutes later they were all back and I was relieved, but then they went again. I was that gone that I didn't realise I was stood on a revolving dance floor and they were all laughing at me. I then decided to order a pint of Pils and danced in front of a girl in a white blouse . . . until I vomited all over her. Howard Gayle, the captain, got me out of there and gave a taxi driver £20 to get me back to the hotel. The price included him cleaning his taxi as I was sick all the way back to the hotel. I was in bed all day the next day. A couple of other players came in my room to smoke joints. I felt awful and the smell made it worse. The manager told me that I wasn't going to play at Watford as I was still pissed. I never told my dad the reason why I didn't play because he would have gone mad."

May loved Blackburn and the various characters in the dressing room. "Simon Garner was a goalscorer who smoked cigarettes like there was no tomorrow. Howard Gayle was a Scouser who always had problems with his hamstrings. It wouldn't happen at any other club, but the manager used to massage them to get him on. When it was the manager's birthday, we threw him in the bath with his suit on! He was a great manager. Imagine throwing Fergie in the bath – he would have killed you."

This was Blackburn before Jack Walker's major financial input and money was tight. "I was on £120 a week," explains May. "Jack joined as a director and started to inject funds, with Kevin Moran arriving from Sporting Gijon."

Needing a win at Barnsley to stay up, Walker entered the dressing room at Oakwell and said, 'If you win, I'll pay for you all to go away to wherever you want.' Blackburn won 1–0. The players had a choice of anywhere in the world: New York, Barbados or Bali. They chose Tenerife for five days and asked Mackay how much spending money they would need. He told them to bring enough for their first night, adding, 'Jack's taking care of it.'

"On the first night we all received a brown envelope with £450 spenders," explains May. "We were made up because it was a fortune. There was a note saying, 'You'll get the other half of your money in two days.' We couldn't spend the money and for the first time I thought, 'Jack Walker is serious here.' My wages increased to £250 a week."

Kenny Dalglish was then made manager and better players started to arrive like Gordon Cowans, David Speedie, Mike Newell, Tim Sherwood, Lee Richardson, Alan Wright, Colin Hendry and Bobby Mimms.

"Kenny didn't play me at first and so I wondered what was going on," remembers May. "We reached the play-offs and I wanted us to lose so that I could go on holiday earlier. I wasn't playing so I wasn't arsed."

To his surprise, May was asked to play at right back in the play-off games, where Blackburn beat Derby and then Leicester at Wembley. They were up.

"It was a reward for all those lovely people at Blackburn and my wages were increased to £500 a week," recalls May. "Then Alan Shearer joined us on £9,000 a week."

May was a near ever-present in Blackburn's inaugural Premiership season.

"We did well, finished fourth and our final game was against United at Old Trafford, when United won the league for the first time in 26 years. I had a car crash on Oldham Road two days before – a woman hit me up the arse so I couldn't play. I still went to the game and sat in the Blackburn end. It was the first time I'd been to Old Trafford as a fan and I thought, 'This is amazing.'"

May was very happy at Blackburn where he usually roomed with winger Jason Wilcox.

"We trashed every hotel we stayed in," he says. "Televisions would end up in baths, we'd put water in the locks so you could never lock your room. Whenever we stayed at a hotel, we'd race from the coach to the reception so that we could get a room straight away. If you didn't your room would be trashed.

"We saw some stepladders in one hotel so we climbed onto the roof to investigate, oblivious to the risks. We'd also push eye holes in hotel room doors through. I once managed to poke the hose from a fire extinguisher through an eye hole into a room containing Graeme Le Saux and Colin Hendry. I switched the extinguisher on and they couldn't escape from getting covered in foam.

"Another time, we stayed in Birmingham and ended up in an Italian, where two really fit strippers were ordered. A couple of the lads who weren't married started nailing them and then one of the coach drivers had a go, but his knob was like a walnut whip. He couldn't get a hard-on – probably because we were pelting him with bread rolls."

May was a popular member of a happy dressing room. "Alan Shearer was a good lad," he says. "He comes across as a bit dour on the television, but that's not the real him. Him and Mike Newell would drive from Formby every day while me and David Batty used to race each other in our cars over the moors between Bolton and Blackburn. At night. With our lights off. I know, I know. Batts was a lovely lad who was into motorbikes."

It was through the Leeds-supporting Batty that May first found out about interest from Manchester United. "We were at Tottenham away and the phone went at six in the morning. It was Batts shouting, 'Scum, scum, scum.' I didn't know what he was on about. Then the same thing happened again half an hour later. I went down for breakfast, where Batts was smiling. He had a paper in his hand which said that United were coming in for me. He didn't like that."

May also had another inkling of United's interest.

"We played Norwich away and Mark Robins, who I'd played Sunday League with and was at Norwich, told me that United had been watching me. I thought, 'Fucking hell.' He was going out with [United chief scout] Les Kershaw's daughter Alison."

May and Robins went back a long way. "I was jealous of Mark when I was younger because he was at United scoring loads of goals and I was at Blackburn," he explains. "I remember seeing him in a new Audi 80 on Oldham Road and thinking, 'He's doing well.' I was in my Ford Fiesta 950 Popular Plus. I would have liked to play with Mark at United. It's probably the wrong thing to say, but Mark's most famous for saving the manager's job with a goal at Forest in 1990. That came very early in his career, but football has been good to Mark and he's still doing well."

When Blackburn heard that United were interested, they started talking about improving May's contract. May appointed Paul Stretford as his agent.

"Paul told me not to say anything and that he would do the rest," he explains. "My family were delighted at the prospect of me joining United. You only get one chance and I didn't want to miss it."

His departure would not go down well in East Lancashire. "Blackburn fans still ask, 'Why did you join United?' Blackburn had pushed United all the way in the league in 1994 and fancied their chances in 1995. Truth is, if Blackburn had signed me on a contract during the Christmas of 1993 I would have stayed. But they didn't start talking to me until my contract was about to expire. I was on £500 a week, £750 for a win. My appearance money was more than my wages. Blackburn offered me £1,750 a week. I thought it was derisory in comparison with my teammates. Some of the lads were on £9,000 a week. Ray Harford, God bless him, offered me £2,750 in a nightclub in Jersey after we'd been over there playing Jack Walker's Sunday league team. Ray mentioned United and questioned whether I would play every week like I would if I stayed at Blackburn. I said, "It's not about that, I've got a chance to improve myself as a player. And it's the biggest club in the world."

Jack Walker called May. "I regret the way I dealt with his call, but I was on a golf course and the reception was bad so I switched the phone off. Jack then called my dad and broke down on the phone to him. He said, 'Tell David that I'll give him a personal cheque for £250,000 to stay.' My dad told him that I had given my word to Fergie to join United."

Robert Coar, the Blackburn chairman, saw the situation differently and described May as "greedy" after he signed for United.

"Tosser," says May. "He'd just signed Chris Sutton for £5 million and paid him £8,000 a week. I didn't speak about money with United. I went to Old Trafford with my mum, dad, girlfriend and Paul Stretford to sign. We spoke to Martin Edwards and saw the gaffer. He showed me around the ground and the museum so that I could appreciate the history of the club. In truth, I wasn't that arsed about seeing it because I just wanted to be part of it."

Sir Alex Ferguson told May, "You'll do well here. Brucey is getting older and I see you as the perfect partner for Pally. Fingers crossed that you'll sign for us."

"Don't worry about it, gaffer, I'll sign," May replied. And he did.

From Old Trafford, Stretford, May and family went to the Trafford Hall Hotel, a popular pre-match pub for Reds. Stretford told him that United were offering a four-year contract at £5,000 a week for the first two years and £6,000 a week for the years three and four.

"We worked out that would be £1.1 million," recalls May, "Before bonuses. I was gobsmacked. So was my dad. And my brothers when I told them. They said, 'How will you spend it all?' Both my brothers could have been footballers. Our Pete could have made it but he was a lazy arse and once women and booze came into it he went that way. Our Steve broke every bone in his body playing football and was really unlucky with injuries. And then there was me, the last chance saloon for my dad – who'd had trials himself for Sheffield United. He's always given me the option. He never stopped me going out, but he'd always tell me the consequences. He'd say, 'You can be a good player or a great player and if you want to be a great player you have to make sacrifices.' So I think he was very proud when I signed for Manchester United."

May joined double winners United in the summer of 1994 for £1.2 million. He celebrated with a party at his house and by buying a Mercedes.

"Two days later, I drove the car to my local pub to show it off to my mates," he recalls. "The landlord asked me to move it because he had a delivery coming from Costco. I got in the car and reversed. The only problem was that I'd forgotten to close the door, which wrapped itself around a lamppost. All my mates were howling at my misfortune. I had to call Mercedes and they sent a big truck to pick my car up in front of everyone."

May then set his mind on United. "Kiddo rang me the

night before my first training session and said, 'Get down there for 9:30 and we'll train at 10:30.' I was in awe of the players when I first went into the dressing room at The Cliff and was shitting myself when I arrived. Schmeichel, Giggs, Pallister, Cantona, Bruce and Keane were all there, the best players in the league. I walked around and shook hands with all of them. Bruce and Pallister could have been awkward, but they both came over and welcomed me. That made me feel good.

"On my second day in training, I was supposed to be warming up the Mad Mullah, Peter Schmeichel. I was clipping balls into him, but then chipped in. He booted it back and started shouting, 'What do you think you are doing? You're supposed to be warming me up you cunt.'

"I booted it back and told him to fuck off. He booted another ball at me as I walked behind the goal. Paul Parker calmed it down."

That was about as loud as May got in his first year, when he was nothing like the joker whom the Blackburn players knew.

"I barely spoke," he recalls. "[Blackburn's] Jason Wilcox used to live in Worsley and would bump into Giggsy and ask how I was doing. Then he said, 'He's mad as fuck, isn't he?'

"'He doesn't say a word,' replied Giggsy. Wilcox was stunned. It wasn't until we had a Christmas do when I went off my head. I was throwing ice cubes and pissing in pint pots. That was the real me."

May's first season at Old Trafford was mixed. His first competitive game was against Blackburn in the Charity Shield.

"When I played at centre half I was fine, but I played at right back for much of the first season because Parks was injured. I didn't have the best of times and I found it hard. Andrei was in front of me, I didn't really know him and found communication difficult."

May was also in awe of the players around him. "I didn't want to have a go at them," he says. "I went on one of the pre-season games and Giggsy was in front of me. He'd come back and help me out, Andrei never did. But in that pre-season game in Ireland, Giggsy came back and I went for a short ball. 'Hit it over the top you knob,' he shouted. I was like, 'Wow'."

Life didn't get any easier. In November 1994, a young IFK Göteburg winger called Jesper Blomqvist consistently got the better of May as the Swedish champions beat United at home.

"He ripped the back out of me," says May. "Then I got torn to bits by the papers. It was a bad month. I'd never had negative publicity before and fans were reading this. Fans were shouting, 'Fuck off back to Blackburn.' It didn't help that I'd been a City fan either. You get a good feeling of how popular you are with the fans when the team is read out before a match. There were a few jeers at times for me and I didn't like that."

All the time, May was adjusting to being a Manchester United player.

"It's strange when you join United," he says. "I'd been famous in Blackburn, but 70 per cent of us lived away from there. At United it's full on. I found that people wanted to latch on and befriend me. Keaney got it right, as he usually did when he spoke, when he said, 'You lose faith in humanity because you think that someone is being friendly but they only want the association. Or tickets.'

"I'd walk into a pub as a Blackburn player and nobody would recognise me. Two weeks later, as a United player, everyone wanted to come over and buy me a drink. You need good friends and family to look after you. Gazza didn't have that and look what happened. He needed help and his friends were not there for him; rather they used him for their own needs."

Solace was found when he met Maxine, the girl he would marry and have children with, in a pub in Rochdale in 1995.

"She came over to talk to me because her mate thought she recognised me and wanted to know who I was," May recalls.

"Maxine said, 'What's your name?'

"'John,' I replied. She went back and told her mate, who lost interest.

"'What do you do?' continued Maxine, when we spoke later.

"'I'm a printer.'

"'Where do you work?'

"'Armin & Butler in Gorton. I do a four-colour machine.' That's what my brother did so I knew what to say. And that's how I met my wife.

"You can't get away with anything at United because you are under the microscope all the time," adds May. "At Blackburn, I did a shit in a box of tissues in the physio's room and put the tissues back in the box and left it on the side. You couldn't get away with something like that at United, but I had my moments. I filled a bucket of water and balanced it on top of Paul Parker's hotel door. The water went all over his room when he opened the door. We went down for dinner later. Parks said he knew it was me and said, seriously, 'You can't get away with this at United, Maysie.'"

May did get away with other blags though, including urinating down the leg of a teammate in the shower, cutting the laces out of Nicky Butt's new trainers and putting Deep Heat in the kitman's shirt.

He scored his first United goal on 25th January 1995 away to Crystal Palace, an event which was completely overshadowed by what happened shortly afterwards.

"My first thought when Eric got sent off was, 'You cunt, I've just scored my first goal for United.' I legged over to see what was going on, but Eric was on his way. Southgate equalised and at full time the gaffer had a go at me for the equaliser. I thought, 'Eric's just jumped into the crowd and leathered someone and you're having a go at me for a goal that was nothing to do with me.'

"I could understand why Eric hit that lad," adds May. "There have been many times when I've wanted to chin a fan for giving personal abuse about my family. When Cantona did it I thought, 'Fair play, Eric.' The lad became famous for that, but then his life was apparently ruined. Good. It's a great pub quiz question though, isn't it? Who scored United's goal on the night of Cantona's kung fu kick?"

May's improvement continued. On 7th May, he once again scored United's only goal in a crucial victory over Sheffield Wednesday at Old Trafford.

"It was my best game for United up to that point and I felt I was getting there," he says. "It kept us up with Blackburn at the top. It was also the first time I felt a spasm in my back."

Blackburn held onto first place and May was "gutted" when they won the league. "I was injured so wasn't playing, but I can remember leaning against the wall outside the Gardeners Arms in Middleton and crying. I was devastated. A lady came up to me and asked if I was OK. I wanted that medal and I'd lost it to the team I had just left. The Blackburn players were right onto me, saying that I should have stayed."

The summer of 1995 proved to be turbulent for United. "Incey, Andrei and Sparky all left in the summer. They were all class players, but Sparky was the best and I was surprised that they all went. Incey was 'big time', but I think part of it was the London Cockney persona. That said, it was him, Pally and Brucey who really supported me when the press were most on my back."

Season 1995/96 was to be much better for May. "Steve Bruce also left United that summer and I had the chance to prove myself to the fans in my favourite position. We won the league and the FA Cup. The '96 FA Cup final was like a dream come true for me. Like anyone of my generation, I'd watched the build up to past cup finals. I'm disappointed that they don't do that any more. I loved the cup final songs, Wembley Way, going there a few days early, rosettes, the lot. It's every professional's dream. My family loved it. Dad never said anything, but I knew he was so proud to see one of his sons in an FA Cup final. I just knew."

Before the final, Liverpool's players took to the field in white suits. "We thought they looked like fucking knobs, absolutely ridiculous," May laughs, confirming the opinions of the majority of the watching world. "They were there in their white Armani suits and ours were from Burtons."

It wasn't a classic cup final.

"We didn't have a chance and neither did they," remembers May. "I half-volleyed my first touch to Denis Irwin. It was a sweet ball, but I didn't remember it until Tony Coton said, 'I knew you'd have a good game after that first touch.' I also knew we wouldn't lose. When we got a late corner, I piled into David James and got a bad dead leg. The ball fell to Eric, who scored. I got up and ran after him. Brilliant."

May celebrated with his teammates after the game, but not to the excess of the previous week. Rochdale's taxi drivers could sleep easily.

The following season saw him play in the Champions League for the first time.

"We played away to Fenerbahçe, who had Jay-Jay Okocha, and the atmosphere was mad. We heard that a Fenerbahçe fan had been shot in the crowd."

The atmosphere that night was indeed feverish. The home fans lit newspapers and the floodlights were turned off as the players warmed up to increase the intimidation. Even with the game underway, the public address system was spewing pro-Fenerbahçe rhetoric. Sir Bobby Charlton went directly to the UEFA official and complained. The announcements stopped.

"I got noticed by Glenn Hoddle for England in that game," says May. "I was sub once against Mexico. Robbie Fowler mentioned me in his book and said, 'I think David May didn't get many caps because he enjoyed a laugh too much in training.' I liked a laugh, but I still knuckled down in training. I just don't think Hoddle liked players who liked a laugh. Robbo got

Hoddle right when he said, 'If he was made of chocolate he'd eat himself.'"

United made solid progress in Europe, with a goal from May helping the side destroy Porto 4–0 at Old Trafford and set up a semi-final tie against Borussia Dortmund.

"I got injured in the warm up and so did Big Pete," rues May. United lost 1–0 and Sir Alex Ferguson said, "Although both Raimond van der Gouw in goal and Ronny Johnsen in central defence performed admirably, the late changes to the team spread an uneasiness throughout our ranks in the first half that prevented us from exploiting our clear superiority. However, any explanation of our failure must begin and end with a simple reality. In the supreme contests of football, you must take a respectable percentage of your chances. In that semi-final, we both missed too many."

"We were unlucky away and we battered them back at Old Trafford but couldn't score," adds May. "It was heartbreaking to go out, especially when they beat Juventus in the final. That should have been ours, but as we saw in '99 you need that little bit of luck."

United still won the league, an event which was overshadowed by Eric Cantona announcing his retirement the day after the final league game of the season.

"I sensed by Eric's body language at the final league game against West Ham that something wasn't right," says May. "A year before at Middlesbrough he was so happy, kissing the trophy and the FA Cup. But despite winning the league he didn't seem happy. I think it hit him losing to Dortmund more than anyone. We'd won the league and yet we still felt that something was missing.

"Could you imagine saying that five years earlier?" adds May. "United fans had become so accustomed to winning things that 'only' winning the league was not considered a success by some. I could see that United were starting to attract glory hunters who thought that success was a divine right. I felt sorry for the long-serving fans who'd watched the team when they didn't win very much and then found themselves being priced out by high ticket charges when the club became successful."

May was firmly established as a United player, though he had already made the majority of his 118 appearances for the club, which yielded eight goals.

He started to pick up injuries in the pre-season of 1997/98 when United played in Bangkok, Hong Kong and Tokyo. That trip was the first time I spoke to May, in the searing heat of the Bangkok sun. A United training session had attracted 25,000 fans and May was sitting on a mat behind the goal when the news went round that Versace had been shot at his Miami home.

"Serves him right for designing those minging clothes," joked May. "Pally will be devastated."

"Pally used to be the worst dresser," adds May, his opinion unchanged 11 years later. "Giggsy and Becks were both tricky dressers and Pally was the opposite. He came into training one day wearing Mary's [Pallister's partner] coat. It was a long black leather jacket which was too tight for him. His defence was that it was Versace. It was minging and I hammered him for it."

May roomed with Pallister after Cantona left. "He was a right dirty bastard," he says. "He used to buy a family bag of cheese and onion crisps and a family bag of Minstrels. He'd lie on the bed, speak to Mary on the phone while scratching his dick and eating crisps. Then he'd offer me some of the crisps. Pally was really lazy. He always got the bed furthest from the door so that he didn't have to answer it if anyone knocked. If they did, he'd say, 'You're closest.' The lads who fitted my kitchen also did Pally's. They told me that they had to go back and move his fridge closer to his living room so that he wouldn't have to walk as far to get his beers from the fridge. He's deadly, Pally."

The smiles among teammates masked May's difficult time with injuries.

"The injuries got me down," he says, "I was just getting into being an established player. I ruptured my thigh but I always thought that I'd get back in. My thigh was 98 per cent right when I played a League Cup game at Ipswich [in October 1997]. The thigh went again and I was out for another two months until Christmas. It snowballed from there. Because my thigh wasn't right, I started getting a sore knee. It got me down. I seriously thought about hanging my boots up. I went to see the manager a few times and he always said the same thing, 'Keep your head down and keep working. You're not the first person to be injured.'"

There was further support from Maxine. "Max kept my head above water," says May. "I would have gone under without her. She told me that there were more important things than football and that if my career ended I would have other options. She said that she would stand by me and the main thing was that we were together. That was comforting, but if you are a footballer you just want to play football."

May was fit enough to play towards the end of the treble season but missed out on a league medal by one game. "We played Leeds away and Jaap was struggling with his Achilles in the warm-up. I think the gaffer wanted to keep Jaap fit for the final so I played."

"David and Wes [Brown] looked as though they were playing their first ever game together, which at this level they probably were!" said Ferguson.

Leeds went ahead, but Keane, just four days after his Herculean effort in Turin, took control of midfield and Andrew Cole equalised. May would feature prominently towards the end of the treble-winning season and performed well, including against Tottenham as United won the league.

"The manager had always said that he wanted to win the title at Old Trafford on the final day of the season," says May.

"We did that by beating Tottenham and did it in style after coming from behind. At times you know you are not going to get beat and I felt like that then. I don't want to sound big-headed, but there was a spirit that wouldn't be beaten. I also felt that, unlike in 1997, it was our destiny and the events what happened reinforced that view. Giggsy's goal against Arsenal in the FA Cup after his mazy dribble, Big Pete saving the penalty in the same match to keep us in the game after Keaney had been sent off . . ."

May admired Keane's commitment and passion.

"I saw Keaney fly off the handle loads of times," he says. "At Deportivo away one year he nearly ripped Ruud's head off, but that's how passionate Keaney was. I would disagree with him sometimes, but deep down I knew that he wanted the best for the team. He had a saying, '99 per cent preparation equals 100 per cent failure' and it's true. Fail to prepare, prepare to fail. That was spot on."

Keane, like May, didn't play in the European Cup final against Bayern Munich. But that didn't stop May celebrating with the best of them as United lifted the trophy.

"My dad always said, 'Make sure you are near the trophy'," he explains. "So I did! I saw the trophy on a chair and thought, 'I'm having that.' So I picked it up and the rest is history, I ended up in half the pictures. Although I didn't play in the final, I was proud of my contribution to the treble. I've been criticised for getting in the trophy photos and part of me regrets doing it now. But then another part of me thinks, 'Fuck 'em.' What would people do in the same circumstances? The lads joked about it with me. I didn't play in the European Cup but I played in the FA Cup final and in some of the league games at an important part of the season. Without winning the league and the FA Cup we wouldn't have won the treble."

May was awarded a European Cup winners' medal. "I didn't kick a ball in Europe all that season so it doesn't mean anything to me. It's in the bank and I don't even look at it."

United celebrated in Barcelona's five-star Arts Hotel. "Simon Le Bon couldn't get in and Ryan Giggs had a fight with Martin Edwards's son and sparked him. It was a brilliant night. I could relive that night every other night for the rest of my life. Everyone was singing away, everyone was with their families. It was brilliant."

That summer, he went to the wedding of David Beckham and Victoria Adams in Ireland. "Becks was a good lad," says May. "He was a sprightly Cockney kid, but his dedication was as good as Eric's. He would train and train and train. He loved hitting dead balls – free kicks, crosses and corners. He's probably the best crosser of the ball in history. He was a good lad with it too, even after he'd met Victoria. I can remember when she first came to Old Trafford to draw the raffle on the pitch and United fans sang *Who Let the Dogs Out?*

"The Beckhams' wedding was an eye opener. I went over to Dublin a few days before with Kevin Moran and Maxine. We were in a bar on the lash with Patrick Kielty and Amanda Byron, who was Miss Ireland. A girl came into bar with lovely long red hair. Kevin got her over and put her hair over my head. 'Mick Hucknall!' he shouted. It was all a laugh.

"The next day, under the headline 'The Darling Buds of May' was a picture of me with her red hair. And another one of me and Miss Ireland in a taxi – but Max was also in the taxi. The girl had spoke to the press, saying that I was a lovely bloke and all that.

"The next day, we were in the hotel and Maxine wanted to borrow Shirley Cole's hair straighteners. I was sent to get them. Shirley told me that I had a cheek to ask for them.

"'What do you mean?' I asked.

"'You got off with a girl and Maxine's here.'

"'What you on about?' I said.

"'Read that,' said Shirley and passed me the *News of the World*. There was a picture of me in a taxi with Miss Ireland. There's worse birds to be pictured with, but imagine if Maxine had not been with me? When I got to the wedding, Victoria told me that I should sue the papers, but I never did."

It was in the summer of 1999 that May realised his time with United was up.

"That was confirmed when the gaffer kept me behind for the Brazil trip which confused me because a few really young players went. Glasgow Rangers had come in for me, Southampton too. I was going to sign a four-year deal for Southampton and the wages were all sorted, but then the manager got sacked. I snapped my Achilles that year and nothing was going right for me."

Life wasn't all bad in 2000. "I became a dad for the first time in 2000 and I've got two great boys who have lovely manners," he says. And he still had a contract at United until 2003.

"I wasn't playing because of all the injuries and it continued to be a struggle for me. Maybe I should have given it up. You end up going out on the lash all the time and that takes you away from your family. I'd get smashed out of my head and I just wanted to drink more and more. I was probably a difficult person to live with. Eventually, the gaffer pulled me and said, 'You've had your fair share of injuries and we're going to have to let you go.'"

"Gaffer," May replied sincerely. "I'm surprised that you've kept me for so long."

"You've been a fantastic servant," said Ferguson. "And you've been unlucky with injuries. There are players who haven't done half of what you have. Don't be down about it."

"I admire him for saying that," says May, "because at times I must have drove him up the wall."

May went to Rangers for two weeks and did the pre-season with them in Germany, but felt like he was always playing catch-up. Alex McLeish was the manager and said, "The season starts next week and we need you fit." May wasn't anywhere near that. Then Burnley, managed by Stan Ternent, came in for him.

"It was like going back to my Blackburn days and it was a bit of a culture shock going from United," says May. "If you want your studs at 9mm then they sort it for you at United; you did that yourself at Burnley. At Burnley we'd have a four-hour coach trip on the day of the game. We spent seven hours on one coach to Ipswich and got battered 6–0. I was seen as a senior player and the manager called me in the next morning to ask my opinion. I told him that the lads had been on the bus for seven hours and so that was bound to affect them.

"I fucking knew you'd say that, you big-time Charlie," Stan said. "What do you want us to do, stay in five-star hotels? We're not Man United."

"Gaffer, the lads will stay in a Travelodge or pay their own way," May replied.

On another occasion, Burnley had two games in the south in close succession.

"We stayed in Watford and were served six pieces of salmon for 18 players," says May. "I told the manager, who was at the bar having a pint. Again, he thought I was big time.

"Soon after we had a game against Sheffield Wednesday on the Saturday and another against Coventry on the Tuesday. Normally, we'd have Wednesday off, but I was told that I'd be in the reserves at Stoke away. We got beat 2–0 on a freezing December night. The gaffer came on the bus after and told me and two other players that we were a 'fucking disgrace'. I wasn't having that and stormed off. The next day he had a go at the other two lads at training and then at me."

"You have two options," Ternent said. "You can go to see the chairman and get paid up. Or you can stay away and we'll pay you until the end of the season."

"Why?" May asked.

"Because I'm not having that yesterday," replied Ternent. "The reserves getting beat 2–0. You're a pro and you should be better than that."

"Gaffer, I was playing with kids," replied May. "I tried to encourage them but the ball kept coming back to me."

Ternent refused to accept his version and a furious May returned to training.

"A ball came to me and I lashed it as far as I could," May says. "The lads told me to calm down but I'd gone, snapped. Stan came over screaming and shouting and calling me a big-time Charlie. I told him to fuck off. He said, 'Fuck off then, you're not ruining my club.'"

"As I walked off, I said, 'I won't ruin it, you've already ruined it, you fat cunt.'

"Stan asked me if I wanted to have a go. I said, 'Go on, then.' He bowled over, head-butted my chest and threw a haymaker. Everyone watching, thinking, 'Fuck me.'"

May got in his car and rang Paul Stretford.

"I told him what had happened and he said, 'Leave it with me.' He rang Burnley and told them that I was going to press charges. The players told me to do the same. I would never have done it, but Paul rang me back and said, 'Stan's going to come to your house tonight to apologise.'"

The rain was falling hard in Rochdale when Ternent arrived at May's house.

"Stan started buzzing on the gates," smiles May. "Me and our Steve were inside and let him stand in the rain for a minute and a half before answering."

"'Maysie, it's the gaffer,' a drenched Ternent said. I let him in. He shook my hand and said, 'These things happen.' I said, 'Gaffer, of all the time I've been in football I've never seen a manager attack a player. Anyway, I can't believe that you missed me.'"

The pair laughed about it and their relationship was fine thereafter.

"I wasn't a big-time Charlie," says May. "I just wanted things done right. He'd always ask for my opinion, which usually was met with, 'We're not Man United.'"

May was released by Burnley at the end of season 2003/04.

"Perhaps I could have played at a higher level, but I just wanted to play football and non-league Bacup Borough was close to where I live so I joined them."

Effectively playing in Division Nine, there were few comparisons between the standard of football at United and a non-league team who played in front of 50 rather than 50,000.

"It was frustrating when you've played with good players constantly throughout your career because you expect the players to be on the same wavelength," cites May. "You'll see an opening which other players don't see, and you think that they must be blind not to see it.

"Rival players just wanted to kick me, possibly because of who I was. Yet they were so slow that you could see any danger coming. There were other differences – the bar was free at United, for example."

Malicious tackles aside, May appreciated the friendliness of the people in the non-league game. "There was one occasion though at Fleetwood when a supporter was shouting 'Munich bastard' at me throughout the game," he states. "After 80 minutes I shouted, 'Fuck off, you fat bastard.' He shut up and at the end of the game he wanted to apologise to me and shake my hand. I told him where to go."

Nor did May cut his United links. He went to the 2004 FA Cup semi-final, where he was in a private box in the Newcastle end. "I was singing on my own in there," he says. "A bloke in front got a bit irate, especially when Scholes scored and I started singing the Paul Scholes song. So I sang it louder. This Geordie was trying to get at me but I wouldn't stop singing."

By that time he set up a company which imported South African wine into the UK. "I didn't know much about wine. In fact all I knew was whether a wine was red, white or rosé. There was a wine-tasting night in Manchester. I didn't know, but it was the Guild of Manchester Sommeliers. I stood up and introduced myself, then they started throwing questions at me about vines and cultivation. I didn't have a clue what to say. If people came up I just read the label to them and asked them if they liked the wine. I ended up walking out shit faced. So I was soon out of that business.

"I went through a divorce from Maxine and now do MUTV and dinners. That is spending money, but it keeps you active and stops you getting bored. I'm lucky to an extent because I was probably from that first generation of footballers who didn't have to go out and work after retiring.

"I look back now at my time at Old Trafford and probably appreciate it more. I still can't believe that five or six lads came through the same youth team. Most of them were United fans from Manchester and most went on to play for England. I doubt that will ever happen again."

Aside from Paul Scholes, whose children go to the same school, he doesn't see too many of his former teammates. "People think that you keep in touch with your ex-teammates, but they are work colleagues, aren't they? I understand why people say it, but it's a job to us. People have asked me if I'm Alan Shearer's mate, but I've not spoken to him since the day I left Blackburn.

"I'm close with my family, my cousins Ian and Lee. We go to the dogs at Belle Vue and the chat between us has barely changed for 30 years. I've my ups and downs but it's not been a dull life."

5
NICKY BUTT
The Gorton lad

NICKY BUTT
MANCHESTER UNITED

Nicky Butt is the only inter-
viewee in this book still
playing professional football, at the time of writing in the
Championship for recently relegated Newcastle. The Magpies' ill
fortune means that Butt will no
longer be one of the few players
– along with Ryan Giggs, Sol
Campbell and David James – to
have played in every Premiership season.

He's also the only Mancunian. Butt hails from Gorton, a
working-class area east of Manchester city centre. It's where
the team that became Manchester City football club was
founded and home to St Francis's monastery. This stunning
example of 19th century High Gothic architecture was designed
by Pugin, but was almost destroyed by vandalism when it closed
in the 1970s. Much of the TV black comedy Shameless is
filmed in Gorton.

Butt is fiercely proud that he has remained a Gorton lad,
unchanged by his success as a footballer. When I remind him
that Pelé named him in his best XI after the 2002 World Cup,
Butt is characteristically self-deprecating. "I think he mixed

me up with Scholesy because we both have ginger hair. Either that or he thought we were one player, so we covered a lot of ground. It was brilliant for Pelé to say that. I'll tell my grand-kids, but it's a load of crap really." He asks for his fee to be donated to Christie's cancer hospital in Manchester.

Gorton is deemed to suffer serious deprivation, the heart ripped out of it by the closure of the locomotive works and the crass, wholesale 1960s slum clearance which flattened much of Manchester's inner boroughs. But Butt has only good things to say about it.

"I was born in Gorton," he begins, speaking in a deep, unmistakeably Mancunian accent, "a nice place, a great place, in January 1975." He's held on to his accent more successfully than he has his thinning, curly hair. "I lived there all my life. My dad still lives there and my mum has a house on the outskirts. Most of my friends live there, so it's very close to my heart. I can't go out for a few pints with my mates on a Friday night [Butt stays in Newcastle for part of the week, away from his family], but it's nice to go out on a Sunday afternoon and have a few beers with friends. Nothing has ever changed. I buy my round like I always have and my mates buy theirs."

Lads from Gorton have a reputation. When he emerged as a first-team player at United, Butt's standing with local fans was enhanced by his association with one of Manchester's rummest areas. Butt is aware of what his life might have been like. "I've lots of friends who've done well for themselves and a lot who've struggled through life as well. I can understand – people fall into the wrong hands. I've got a lot of close mates who have been in and out of prison and it probably could have been me if it wasn't for football. I also had good parents and people I looked up to who kept me on the straight and narrow. I've still got friends who've done wrong – I'm sure everybody has.

"You've just got to be wise enough, and have enough people backing you up, to keep you on the right path. Luckily for me, I was at a club where any messing about at a young age and you would not be going back."

Nicky Butt now has the distinction of being one of four famous people born in Gorton. One is Bouncing Billy Barker, famed for being able to leap over Ashton Canal. Another is Myra Hindley. And the late John Thaw, TV's *Inspector Morse*, was also a Gorton boy. His dad, like Butt's dad Terry, was a long-distance lorry driver, as was Bryan Robson's father. It was Bryan who, in 1993, picked out Nicky as his favourite among the potential young United stars of the so-called 'Class of 92'.

"I used to go away with Dad sometimes for a treat to Scotland, down south and even to France. It was good to go away and be with my dad. We went to see *Raiders of the Lost Ark* in Cardiff once which I thought was really exciting at the time. Mum worked on the fish stall at Gorton market so we always had fish at home. We ate well."

When he wasn't driving, Butt's dad played Sunday league football and Nicky and brother Simon used to watch him.

"I loved football," he says. "I played for the school team in junior school. I was quite small and I thought I was OK, one of the better players but nowhere near the best. What really helped me out was that I usually played with lads two years older than me. When I got to about 13 or 14 I was quite a lot better than most of the lads of my age.

"I was a United fan as a kid but I never went all the time because I was usually playing on a Saturday," he explains. "When I did go, I'd go with my cousin Peter. He was a bit of a lad and his friends were ticket touts."

Butt was soon asked to play for Boundary Park Juniors, who despite their name had no connection with Oldham Athletic.

"The manager Mike Walsh used to approach the best players from all the other teams," he says. "Scholesy and Gary Nev were there and we won almost every week. It was good to get into the habit of winning because we didn't like it when we lost. We probably thought we were the bee's knees because we'd win all the time." Butt's boyhood friend Marvin Hemmings played for Boundary Park too.

"He was really good and played at United with me until he had an accident," he says. "We'd all gone to Spike Island in 1990 to watch the Stone Roses in their famous concert. I still like the Roses now and listen to their albums. A coach ran over Marvin's leg and that was his career finished at 15. Marvin is still my best mate and he was best man at my wedding. He's a bricklayer now."

Butt was lucky that his emerging talent was spotted just when Sir Alex Ferguson was revolutionising United's youth system. The new manager was soon appalled by the short-comings of United's scouting network, where United had just five scouts to cover Greater Manchester, population 2.3 million. At Aberdeen, Ferguson had 17 scouts covering Scotland's five million. Manchester United fan Ryan Giggs was training with Manchester City. By 1988, Ferguson had gone a long way to sorting things out, appointing Brian Kidd as Youth Development Officer, with the task of finding the best boys in the area. Seventeen new scouts were recruited in Manchester and the rewards would be reaped for years to come.

United scout and former player Harry McShane – father of actor Ian McShane – spotted Butt at 13, just as he would later notice Wes Brown, and alerted United, who sent letters offering trials. "I thought I was the only person to get one and went to show off to Marvin," says Butt. "But he had one too."

The trial was at Littleton Road in Salford and Butt remembers it well. "There were hundreds of kids there with packed lunches. It didn't go well for me. United said that I was too small, but that they would keep an eye on me to see how I developed."

He was duly asked back a year later. "I got in second time. Brian Kidd was at United working with the young lads and he had a soft spot for the local lads like me. He's looked after us ever since and I still speak to him all the time. He's a top man, Kiddo."

Butt trained every Thursday night. "Marvin and I would get the 219 from Ashton Old Road into Manchester and then we'd take another bus up to Salford and walk to The Cliff. We'd meet Scholesy in town and he'd join us for the Salford bus. It cost us about a pound to get there and back, but we'd fiddle our expenses and claimed about £5 each week. We thought we were loaded. I've got really happy memories of those times."

Butt left Wright Robinson High School in Abbey Hey at 16, with no qualifications.

"I regret not making the most of school now," he says. "I was never a naughty kid who was always getting told off, but I was always one of the lads who was into having a laugh. Eventually a letter arrived at my house saying that I wasn't going to be able to sit my exams. They said it would be a waste of government funds for me to sit them and for them to be marked. My dad went mad at me, but I think he knew that I was very single-minded on my football, where I was doing well. He was strict in that he'd ground me from going out, but he never hit me. All he had to do was raise his voice and I'd shit myself. I always knew that I could never overstep the mark because he would have killed me. Mum didn't tell me off. I was always a mum's boy and she left discipline to Dad."

As he wasn't sitting exams and any possible apprenticeship at United would be seven months off, Butt had to find employment. "I found a job as a filing-cabinet maker in Belle Vue from November until April," he recalls. "They would come in a flat pack and I would construct them with rivet guns. I would wake up at 5:30am to start. It was hard and it was horrible, but I was getting £120 a week. Believe me, they got their money's worth. It showed me what I would face if I didn't make it at United."

Thankfully, the offer of an apprenticeship duly arrived from United.

"My parents were very proud," says Butt. "They came to

Old Trafford with me and we signed the forms in the reception – there was a queue of us. I was on £29.50 a week plus £40 for my mum for keep. You won't believe this, but part of me thought of not bothering because I could have been earning a lot more in the factory making cabinets."

Younger brother Simon was a talented footballer too. "He did well in trials for Bury," says Butt. "He was a good player, but he was never as focused as he should have been. He never said, 'I'm going to be a footballer.' Then he got into trouble and had to go to prison for a few months. He's my brother, my best mate and a great lad, but he was too easily led. He works in Watford now, road digging in a gang of eight. He likes to earn his money and goes out with his mates Friday, Saturday and Sunday. Good luck to him.

"I try to say to him, 'Simon, you're 30 now. Get a house.' I've offered to buy him a house, but he's stubborn, saying, 'There's no point me having a house because it will get robbed when I'm away.' He's happy where he is."

Butt's preparation could have gone better for his first day at United. "I got the date wrong," he admits. "I went on holiday to Benidorm with my mate Carl Brown who had also signed up for United. My mum and dad only let me go there after I swore to a long list of things I would and wouldn't do on holiday. We landed at 6:30am in the morning and Carl's mum took us straight to training. Nobody at United knew that we'd just come straight from the airport and I don't think they'll know until they read this."

Despite the first day hiccup, Butt settled in quickly. "Eric Harrison was an amazing coach. You knew he was boss. He looked like he hated everybody and had no compassion, but the opposite was true. When I speak to Giggsy about Eric now, we admit that we were shit-scared of him. He gave us almighty bollockings. One, when I was 15, came after I'd played in a Youth Cup game at Blackburn."

That was actually a year before Butt took the apprenticeship.

With injuries and suspensions affecting United's youth team, Butt's school received a call requesting that he took time off to play in the game against Rovers. They gave permission and the young midfielder seized the rare opportunity.

"I thought I was the best," he remembers. "And I wanted to show how good I was, but I had a stinker. Eric gave me a roasting. He told me that I'd never play for United again. He asked me who the fuck I thought I was. He was right. I should have kept my head down and played everything simple. Instead, I tried to show off and it all backfired on me. We won, though.

"I saw Eric in the canteen the next day and wanted to avoid him. He saw me and merely said, 'Morning, Nicky'. I realised then that the bollockings were not personal. If Eric could move on straight away then so could I."

Harrison later described Butt as "without doubt one of the bravest players I have come across in all my time at Old Trafford. He is the one you want by your side when the going gets tough."

Butt has other vivid memories of those days. "Nobby Stiles used to drive us to games in a minibus with benches in the back. If he didn't catch us messing around in the back then Eric Harrison, who would follow the mini bus in his black Sierra, would. We didn't misbehave.

"We knew we had a good team and we wouldn't have been at United if we didn't have ability," adds Butt, "but most of us played for ourselves too much. Eric would keep a close eye on us, but it wasn't until we were 16 and full time that we started to play as a team."

Every player in United's youth team that year received a professional contract. It had never happened before and it hasn't since.

"Some got two years, others one or three," says Butt. "Carl had to go after a year because he had a lot of injuries. He dropped down and down and became disillusioned with football. He used his head though and went into property, buying places and doing them up. We're still mates.

"There was another lad who was built like Mark Hughes. He was brilliant at 16, but when everyone grew he wasn't so special."

There could be no doubting the quality of many of those others surrounding him.

"I never looked around the youth team and thought, 'He's going to make it, he's not,'" he says. "But Gary Nev was always going to make it as a footballer. His determination, focus and professionalism combined with his ability meant that.

"Becks was always a really talented footballer. The thing I really admired about him was that he was single-minded. Eric Harrison would tell him not to try a certain ball – like a 60-yard pass – because it was too risky. Becks would try it in a game and it wouldn't come off. So he practised the next day, time and time again until he perfected that pass. In terms of progress, Becks was always a little bit behind the rest of us. I think the manager described him as a late developer. He was loaned out to Preston at the end of 1994 when none of us were. He came back a much better player and when he filled out a bit he just got better and better."

And Butt is one of the best qualified people to talk about Paul Scholes. "Scholesy was the best player in training. Even when he was 16 and 17, training but not playing with the first team, he was always the best at the small-sided games where you had to keep possession. His awareness, touch and passing were incredible."

But he also wants to put the record straight on Scholes's personality. "One of the biggest myths is that Scholesy is a quiet lad. The press have fallen for it. They think that all he does is spend time with his wife and kids and that he doesn't speak. He's a great family man and he's not one for interviews, but he is one of the driest little bastards you will ever come across. There's a devil side to him, trust me.

"Even the lads who didn't stay at United did well out of football. Robbie Savage, Ben Thornley and Chris Casper, though the latter two saw their careers cut short by injury."

Butt's first professional contract was for £250 a week.

"I thought I was a millionaire," he smiles. "We won the Youth Cup, which was a massive thing for us – like winning the World Cup. The majority of us were first-year professionals apart from Ryan [Giggs] and Colin McKee, who was another excellent player. We'd played Tottenham in the semi-final and they had lads like Nick Barmby, Darren Caskey and Sol Campbell. They were favourites and they all looked like men. Caskey had a full beard and Barmby had played for the first team. We were like boys, but we had discipline. That came from the manager down through people like Eric and Kiddo. I'd see other teams and they'd mess around more than us. We also had Ryan which was awesome for us!"

United beat Tottenham away, largely thanks to their winger, thinks Butt. "Ryan was brilliant, and always so much better than all of us. He had this ability to run with the ball at such speed that I've never seen from anyone else. Here at Newcastle, Obafemi Martins is one of the quickest players I've seen in a sprint, but he couldn't keep up with Ryan with a ball at his feet. Ryan's been one of the best players in the world and I don't think people will fully appreciate him until he's stopped playing. He gets more appreciation now, but he should have had that for a long time."

Tottenham were beaten 5–1 over two games and Crystal Palace 6–3 over the two-legged final, giving United their first FA Youth Cup win since 1964. The United youth team in 1992 can lay claim to being the greatest in the competition's history. The youngsters played like the senior side and of the 14 lads who appeared in the final, only three didn't play for United's first team. Seven would go on to represent their countries.

"We should have won it against Leeds in 1993 the following year, but football can be unpredictable."

Butt made his first-team debut as a substitute, significantly for Paul Ince, against Oldham in November 1992 in a 3–0 win.

"I can't remember much about the game," he says. "Just that I played alongside my hero Bryan Robson. My dad asked me if I wanted a drink after the game in the players' bar. He said that I'd done OK. He's never told me that I've played well in my career. If I played bad then he would tell me straight away. I've played well in big World Cup games and he's just said, 'You did OK.'"

Butt remains close to his father. "My parents split up a long time ago, when I was about 15. It didn't really upset me – I just thought, 'Right, where do we go from here, then?' Dad would still come and watch every single game and come to see me every day. Then mum became ill and was in a wheelchair for a year. She had to go and live with my gran so I would stay more at my dad's. It worked out OK."

With one Manchester United appearance to his name, Butt thought he'd hit the big time. "I thought I'd made it. Though I'd always considered myself to be a footballer. Even when I was 15 I considered that my job. It wasn't about making it or not, because I was a footballer."

Butt went out into Manchester after his debut and waited for the reaction, the glamour and the girls. "We went to Ronnies, Courtneys and onto Discotheque Royale. I'd just played in front of 40,000 and was full of it. What happened? Nobody asked for my autograph, nobody recognised me and no girls came up to me."

In hindsight, Butt sees things more clearly. "I was nowhere near ready for the first team. I think the gaffer just wanted to show the young lads that they could reach the first team, that they could play alongside the big names. It worked for me. I didn't expect to start playing every week straight away, but the debut kept me happy."

Butt would start in the famous League Cup tie away to Port Vale in 1994, in which Gary Neville, Keith Gillespie, Paul

Scholes, David Beckham and Simon Davies started. At the time, there was a deluge of criticism that Ferguson was devaluing the competition by selecting a 'weakened' side. For better or for worse, fielding younger, less established players in the early rounds of both domestic cup competitions is now an established practice, because of Ferguson's stand. Nicky Butt's career also prospered because of it.

"That was a good night for us and even though we won, we were far from first-teamers. I was named in the squad a lot and we'd travel to games hoping to be on the bench. In the end, we'd just end up carrying the skips holding all the kits. We played Blackburn away when they were rebuilding their main stand. I carried the skips to the little temporary huts which Blackburn used for the players to change."

The summer of 1995 was notorious for the departure of Andrei Kanchelskis, Paul Ince and Mark Hughes. Some supporters protested openly about the sale of these stars; most were concerned that the team would be seriously weakened. Butt remembers his own sense of disbelief, tinged, understandably, with other emotions.

"I was surprised as they were three of our best players," recalls Butt. "In fact I couldn't believe it. I read about it while on holiday in Cyprus with mates. I was secretly pleased because it was good for me. Roy had been at the club a year and was doing well, so there was no way he was going. I'd started to feature a bit more towards the end of the 1994/95 season, now with Incey going . . ."

Butt was one of four young players thrust in United's first eleven for the opening game of the 1995/96 season against Aston Villa alongside Paul Scholes and the Neville Brothers. David Beckham and John O'Kane came on as substitutes. The 3–1 loss inspired Alan Hansen's famous, "You can't win anything with kids" remark.

"We all thought the same as all the fans," says Butt. "We were surprised that he'd put so many of us into the first team and thought that the fans would hate us after we lost. The manager had a go at us after the game and that was that. He kept faith with us though and results started to pick up. We won the next five games. As we did, our confidence started to soar. The season went so quickly for us and before we knew it we knew we were going to win the title and were in the FA Cup final."

Like all the other interviewees who played on that day, one thing sticks out in Butt's memories of the day.

"Liverpool wore those white suits," Butt recalls. "I cringed when I saw them. The manager's team talk was written for him: 'Look at them in those suits. If you can't beat that lot then there's no point coming back in the changing room after the match.'"

Dodgy couture or not, United struggled to break down Liverpool for most of the game. "It was possibly the worst ever FA Cup final," says Butt. "Then Eric came up with the goods as usual. I was in awe of Eric. I used to get changed next to him at The Cliff. He wasn't a loner because he would join in with everyone, but he was usually on the outskirts of things. He was a legend, a lovely fella. I saw him at Old Trafford when Newcastle played United a few years ago. I was an England international who had played hundreds of times for United, yet I was excited when he shook my hand and told my teammates that Eric had just shook my hand. I'm not sure what they thought."

Butt established himself as a first-teamer and soon earned a reputation as a prankster.

"I suppose me and Giggsy were the jokers in the dressing room. We used to get a big silver pot of tea at The Cliff after training. One day, Big Pete was standing naked and he went to get a cup of tea. I crept up behind him holding the tea pot. I wanted to put it close to him so that he felt the heat of it and jumped a bit, but he turned towards the pot and made contact with his knob. Everyone looked on as Pete screamed loudly, 'Aaargh!' He knew it was me straight away and started to chase me. I ran out of the dressing room and he pelted after me. Naked. I was hiding from him. I seriously thought he was going to kill me. He ended up getting a big blister on his knob. What must his missus have thought?

"Another time, Gaz Nev got a new black Ford Escort. He was really proud of it, so we got in it and filled it with plastic cups. He came out of training and saw his new car. He was floored. Keaney was a twat for tricks too."

The Butt/Giggs friendship extended beyond United. "We were so alike and he's my best mate in football so we went out a lot. We'd go out to meet the older lads. Robbo or Pally would tell us to meet in the Bull's Head in Hale at midday. It was great for team spirit, but I didn't really want to go because I couldn't keep up with them. I had no choice though; it was enforced. Then we'd go to Mulligans later and Kels."

Both drinking venues were located in the Four Seasons Hotel near Manchester Airport. The United team coach used to leave from there for away games and Mulligans, a pub, was a convenient place to start drinking after hours on a motorway. Kels was the adjacent nightclub which attracted the permatanned Cheshire set, footballers and more than the odd Manchester gangster. Both have now closed.

"The older lads were all good with us. We were part of the team and we went out together. If we didn't then it was frowned upon. After a game on a Wednesday we'd go to Cheerleaders [an American-themed bar close to the Hacienda which was popular with footballers] and then to Charlie Chan's [one of the most famous Chinese restaurants in Manchester's thriving Chinatown]. We'd go upstairs where people would sing karaoke, but not really us."

Butt and Giggs loved Manchester's nightlife.

"Me and Ryan used to go to The Boardwalk and the Hacienda a lot," Butt enthuses. "The Boardwalk was the greatest place in the world, the best club I've ever been to because the music was so good."

Oasis rehearsed daily at The Boardwalk before releasing *Definitely Maybe* and it became renowned as one of the finest clubs in Manchester. Dave Haslam, who wrote the excellent book *Manchester, England* was the DJ at the seminal Yellow Nights which ran for seven years from 1992 and says, "It's easy to get misty-eyed about the past, and I'm happy to admit that in many clubs these days you might get DJs who are better technically than we were at the time, or better toilets, or better security, but you never get a better audience than the one we got at Yellow; very Manchester; a brilliant mix of black and white, students, single mothers from Sale and Droylsden, dental nurses from Chorlton, Cheshire girls, Moss Side boys. You get that kind of club once in a generation." He could have added 'Mancunian professional footballers'. Butt and Giggsy, Manchester boys through and through, wanted, and were allowed to be, part of the vibe.

"We were never into drugs, but we loved the music," adds Butt. "We were young lads who played for United, our local team. We were the champions of England and we'd go out in our own city at night. People would say well done and then leave you alone – unlike the young lads now who get smothered. We were looked after and the bouncers would keep an eye on us. How could life be any better?"

Butt wasn't immune from trouble, however. In 2003 he was arrested after an incident at Brasingamens in Alderley Edge, another Cheshire footballer haunt. One eyewitness said: "We were in the VIP area on a very busy Sunday night when the midfielder pushed into a woman who stumbled and fell. It was accidental, although Nicky had obviously been drinking. The situation soon escalated when the woman's husband remonstrated with Nicky, who lashed out in his direction. There is a Braz [Cheshire-speak for Brasingamens] regular who lives in Marbella, who was standing behind Nicky. He put his arms round him and lifted him off the floor so that Nicky's legs were bicycling in mid-air. He put him down, hoping that this had calmed him, but Nicky went to rush forward again. 'Mr Marbella' repeated the treatment. Still Butt lunged forward. This happened three times in all until his anger subsided. Apparently the woman had been caught by one of Nicky's flailing arms. The police prosecution was later dropped."

Butt was awarded a first England cap against Mexico in 1997 by Glenn Hoddle, though he is vague on the subject.

"I can't remember who it was against and I don't even know how many caps I've got," says Butt. "I've never been one for all that. I'm not as bad as Keaney, but what's in the past is in the past. I don't have anything in my house – no football pictures, no medals. Each to their own. I sometimes go to other people's houses and see what they have done framing pictures and caps and think, 'I must do that.' Nev has got one of my shirts framed at his house alongside one of his, Phil's, Becks, Scholesy and Giggsy. It looks brilliant. Me? My caps are in a bin bag in the attic. I've got United shirts which Albert Morgan the kit man gave me in bin bags. Maybe I'll do something with them when I've finished playing."

While United were dominant domestically, success in Europe eluded the team.

"We were nearly men for much of the 1990s," says Butt. "I played in the 4–0 defeat by Barcelona in November 1994, probably because the three-foreigner rule meant that players like Eric and Peter Schmeichel had to sit it out. I passed the chapel between the dressing room and the pitch. When I walked past it after the game, I thought, 'I should have just prayed in there for two hours instead.' And I'm not even religious.

"We were battered by Stoichkov and Romario, but I actually did quite well playing on the right of a five. The manager [who had charged Butt with squeezing the area in which Pep Guardiola liked to operate in front of the back four] said, 'You were our best player tonight.' What did that mean when we'd just lost 4–0? Ronald Koeman was another great player. I've got a house in Portugal and I see him every summer. He comes up to me on the beach and talks about that game. He must be really into football because he remembers how I played."

United began to improve steadily as they gained more experience in continental competitions.

"By the time I was established in the side, we'd play against the top teams like Juventus and usually dominate them at Old Trafford," says Butt. "I loved those nights because of the atmosphere. We beat Juventus 3–2 [in 1997] at Old Trafford in a brilliant game where Ronnie Johnsen man-marked Zinedine Zidane, but I was taken off with concussion before half time. It was looking good for us that year, but we wouldn't win the European Cup until 1999.

"By the time of the treble season expectations were very high. I've played against some unbelievable players like Stoichkov, Ronaldo and Romario, but the best was Zidane. He was untouchable. In the 1999 game against Juventus, the manager said, 'He's getting to 30 now; get about him; he's not what he was.' Well, I couldn't get the ball off him. He's not even that big, but he was so strong. I swear he had glue on his boot. I would make a tackle and think that I'd won the ball – and he'd keep it, with me looking a tit. I wasn't in awe of Zidane like I was with Eric, but I did think, 'Wow, what a talented player.'

"Keaney's best performance came in the semi-final against Juventus away. After he was booked he knew that he would miss the final, but he played for the team. He got a thing in his head to carry the team. I knew how he felt about that in 2002 when I was booked in the semi-final against Leverkusen. We didn't go through in the end, but I would have missed the final. Scholesy was also booked in Turin. He got another chance to play in a European Cup final. Roy never did."

United confirmed the league title against Tottenham in the final game of the 1998/99 season. "We didn't celebrate it that much. In fact it got to the stage where we didn't really enjoy winning the league because it became the norm. I regret that a bit now. We should have celebrated and appreciated what we had done. But in '99 our attention quickly shifted to the European Cup final, but first there was the FA Cup final against Newcastle."

Butt was in his hotel room near Wembley on the morning of the cup final when there was a knock at the door.

"It was the gaffer and I thought, 'Here we go,'" Butt recalls. "He said, 'Butty, I'm not playing you.' With Keano and Scholesy suspended for the European Cup final four days later, I didn't really expect to play, but I expected to be on the bench and replied, 'OK, gaffer, good luck.'

"'And I'm not putting you on the bench,' the gaffer went on.

"'What?'

"We had a to-do for five minutes. He explained that if I was sub and anyone got injured then I'd be going on. If I was then to get injured we'd be without central midfielders for the European Cup final. I couldn't believe it. I sat in my suit on the bench. Even though we won, I never felt part of it. You never do. We had a small dinner for the families back at the hotel in London and then went on to Barcelona."

The United party stayed in Sitges, a smart seaside town unspoilt by package tourism 20 miles south of Barcelona.

"All of my mates and family went to Barcelona, but the team was a bit out of the excitement. My family told me that that build-up was brilliant. I must have sorted 50 tickets out for the final. I remember having to write out 50 names and addresses of all the people who wanted tickets. To this day I've never watched the game. I'd love to see it and all the build-up."

United fell behind after six minutes through a Mario Basler free kick. Ferguson later recalled, "When Basler prepared to take the free kick and Markus Babbel set about blocking out Nicky Butt on the end of our defensive wall, I was itching to run onto the field to stop Nicky from falling for the ploy. But I was help-less as a gap was created and so was Peter Schmeichel as Basler swept his shot into the net."

"I couldn't do much," Butt agrees. "And after they went ahead they hit the bar and the post. I was knackered. I thought we'd lost the game in Barcelona. We were crap. When Teddy scored the equaliser, I could only think, 'I'm knackered and now we have extra time.' Then Ole scored. We went nuts. It's hard for me to put it into words. We stayed on the pitch for an hour after the game celebrating in front of the fans. I knew that all my mates and family were in there somewhere. In the end, we were told to stop celebrating and leave the pitch so that the fans could start to leave."

Butt remembers his feelings vividly. "I walked back to the dressing room. I'd reached the top. There was no higher that I could go. We'd won the treble and it felt brilliant."

The players eventually made it to the towering Arts Hotel by Barcelona's sea front and Butt finally got to see his family.

"My brother turned up with three or four of his mates. They tried to stop him coming in at first but then they were allowed in. It was amazing. I didn't sleep for two and a half days."

Later that summer, United went on a pre-season tour to Australia and Hong Kong. Sir Alex Ferguson didn't travel on the first stage of the tour and left assistant Steve McClaren in charge, which meant that some of the squad took advantage.

"We had a few good nights out and broke the curfew that had been put on us," grins Butt. "Once, we stayed out until four in the morning in Sydney at a big casino nightclub called Star City. I was with Giggsy and we were ducking and diving up and down fire escapes so that we didn't get caught going back to the rooms late. We got away with it, but Yorkey and Bozzy got caught coming in at five o'clock. They got bollocked."

United had a training session at Sydney's Olympic Stadium the following day. "We were stretching on the floor, then I heard someone snoring. It was Yorkey. He'd fallen asleep. Everyone was giggling, but nobody woke him up. He was fast asleep, but he was still sat up. After four or five minutes of stretching we got up to jog, leaving Yorkey asleep in the middle of the field."

Andrew Cole also remembered this. He tried to help his mate out. "I was shouting, 'Yorkey! Yorkey! Yorkey!' He made a bit of a noise as if he'd heard us, but he was comatose. A few hours later, we were out again. It was the best trip I've ever been on. We went on a big yacht in Australia – what a day."

"Yorkey snoozing in the middle of the Olympic Stadium remains the funniest thing I've ever seen in football," laughs Butt. "The story got back to the manager, who came out to meet us a few days later in Hong Kong. He went nuts."

That tour saw United play in front of 80,000 in Melbourne, 70,000 in Sydney and 80,000 in Shanghai, a level of support which staggered Butt.

"I always knew that United were popular, but it was another thing to see it with your own eyes and it wasn't always a good thing on the pre-season tours. I liked them when I was younger. I was away with my mates and we'd have a free night to enjoy ourselves, but towards the end of my time at United it was crap. We'd be in a hotel for ten days and weren't allowed out. United are so big that you get mobbed even in your hotels."

At one hotel in Thailand, Butt returned from a training session to be met by a flag reading: 'Nicky Butt – you are my God'.

"I still get letters now from people in Thailand," he reveals. "It was mad over there. We couldn't even leave the floor of our hotels and there had to be security on each floor."

Butt always enjoyed a first-class relationship with United fans.

"They were brilliant with me," he says. "Although I played a lot of games, I think I was an average player. Yet, because I was a local lad I was treated like a god."

He had his own song, *Nicky, Nicky Butt* to the tune of KC and the Sunshine Band's *Baby Give it Up*. I have a confession.

It's the only football song I've ever invented. I tell Butt. He smiles. "They sing it for Nicky Hunt at Bolton too," he says. "I liked it and United fans have sung it when I've returned which is nice."

Butt has always tried to do right by his fans. Visitors to Old Trafford can testify that if he was going into the reception he would always stop to sign autographs and say a few words. But he had to learn the nuances of what was happening.

"I always lived in Hale close to Keaney and we used to pick each other up before European away games," he recalls. "We'd walk into the airport and there would be a load of autograph hunters waiting. Keaney would just walk straight through and I thought, 'You can't do that' so I'd sign one or two and keep walking. But it got to the point when I realised that Keaney was being smart. He'd realised that it was the same faces all the time at the airport. Grown men with sheets of photos of players who make money out of autographs who were spoiling it for everyone else. People call you for it, yet what can we do? I've had so many rows at the training ground gates with people who are spoiling it for the kids who genuinely want autographs."

Butt's international career began to take off after a stuttering start. He is not dismissive of his caps. "I usually enjoyed playing for England. I was in and out under Hoddle and Keegan which frustrated me. It pissed me off when I travelled to places like Russia and didn't even get on the bench. I remember being with Pally at one game in Eastern Europe. We were in the stands, quietly fuming. We just left the game to beat the traffic. I couldn't have cared what the papers said, I was that angry."

His international situation improved when Sven-Göran Eriksson was appointed England manager in 2001.

"Sven picked me for his first game against Spain at Villa Park and I did really well as a sitting midfielder. He took to me and played me. That gave me confidence and I got most of my caps under Sven." Eriksson felt that Butt was a seriously underrated player and that commentators failed to notice his particular strengths which lay in doing the simple things well: "He takes up good positions, he is very good at winning the ball, very steady. He goes out there and you will hardly see him play badly." Steven Gerrard was also a fan, citing how Butt did "all the dirty work", in midfield. However, though Butt was getting recognition from his country, at club level he wouldn't find it so easy in the future to gain a regular place. Much of this came from the belief that Ferguson and others shared that to be a commanding team in Europe United needed a midfield creator alongside their undoubted midfield general, Roy Keane. After starting 34 games and making seven substitute appearances in United's title-winning team of 2000/01, Butt signed a new contract.

"A month later United signed Juan Sebastián Verón," recalls Butt. "The gaffer came up to me. He must have known what I was thinking after United signed an unbelievable world-class player for £28 million.

"He said, 'All right, Nick' in his usual manner, which was like a father figure to all of us. 'Don't worry about Verón, you'll always get your 30 games [per season].'

"He'd always said that and had always been good to his word," recalls Butt. "I wasn't a mardarse who would go bleating to an agent or the press, I just did what I always did, I got my head down. I knew how it was at United with competition. I knew that if every single player was fit then I'd usually be on the bench. I was second to Scholesy or Keaney – two world-class players and there's no shame in that. But it often worked out that one would be injured or suspended or the manager would play three midfielders, especially away in big games. It always worked out that I'd play in the big games, but it changed when Verón arrived." Butt still believed in Sir Alex Ferguson.

"I was suspended for Verón's first game at Everton and sat in the stands. He was unbelievable, so good that I never thought that I'd play for United again. But then it didn't go great for Seba. It was a shame for him because he was a lovely fella. In

European games he was brilliant, but I don't think he got to grips with the tempo of the league games. And by the end of the season, I'd played a similar amount of games to usual." Butt had begun to mature as a midfielder of the quintessentially British type, particular during Keane's protracted lay-off from injury. His early tendency to get booked or sent off – inevitable given his combative style – had diminished and his distribution, a previous weak point, improved considerably.

He had started 31 games and been substitute six times that season, a figure which dropped to 22 and 7 in 2002/03 even as Verón's influence diminished. Monaco, under the managership of ex-Chelsea player Didier Deschamps, were reportedly preparing to lure Butt away from Old Trafford with the promise of regular first-team football. But when the Argentine left Old Trafford in the summer of 2003, two other midfielders arrived, the Brazilian World Cup winner Kleberson and the Cameroonian Eric Djemba-Djemba.

"I've never said this before," admits Butt, "but what got to me at United was after the club signed Kleberson and Djemba Djemba. Keaney and Scholesy were still around and Darren Fletcher was coming through. The manager had to give the new signings a chance. Again, the manager told me that I would always play, but I sat down one day and worked things out. I was 28, an England regular and yet I was fifth or even sixth choice midfielder at United. It built up inside me for a while until I went to see the manager. I told him that the situation wasn't for me. Said that I needed to know where I stood. That I wanted to be remembered, not as a good lad and squad player, but as a decent footballer in my own right."

Ferguson sat Butt down and said, "Look, don't do this because you'll regret it for the rest of your life. I don't want to sell you and you don't want to be seen as asking for a transfer." Of all the players he's ever sold, Sir Alex Ferguson still maintains that Nicky Butt was the most difficult to let go.

Butt replied, "I understand all that, but I can't be sat on

the bench watching Djemba-Djemba and Kleberson picked before me, I don't think it's right."

"The gaffer told me to think about it and come back the next day. I went back and told him that I hadn't changed my mind, saying, 'If it's right for the club that I move on then it's right for me.'

"The manager looked at me and said, 'Right. We won't put it in the press that you have asked to leave or that we are selling you. If a club comes in for you then we'll take it from there.'"

That was December 2003. By January it was all over the papers that Butt was leaving.

"It was also when my daughter Jersey was born, a factor which made me want to stay at United," says Butt. "The situation didn't really change though and at the end of that season Newcastle came in for me. I'll be honest, I didn't know what to do at first."

Butt thought long and hard. "Did I stay at United and not be happy, not be myself?" he says. "Come home from training all grumpy, which is not me at all? I didn't want to become vindictive, but part of me was getting that way and I didn't like it. That's not me at all. I've never taken football home and I was starting to."

As Ferguson said at the time, "Nicky Butt has asked to leave, it is a very sad situation. Nicky has given Manchester United great service but he wants to play first-team football. With Phil Neville, and the emergence of Darren Fletcher and Kleberson, it has made it difficult for Nicky to get in the first team so he has asked to leave."

Butt looked at the Newcastle team. "They had quality: Shearer, Kluivert, Dyer and Bellamy. They played in Europe. I looked at other teams. I could never play for City or Liverpool. Arsenal were interested. They weren't happy with Gilberto, but they were rivals to United, so that was a no. Newcastle were a big, big club. They get 50,000 every week. Their fans were really passionate. That was the only club I wanted to leave United for."

Butt left in the summer of 2004, in which he missed the European championship due to injury. That year he received the last of his 39 England caps.

"Nothing happened for ages and at the start of the season I went on a pre-season tour with United to Chicago. I got a call the night of the game from my accountant Paul. I don't really have an agent. Paul looks after me, Giggsy, Scholesy and the Nevs. He said, 'The manager will tell you tomorrow.'

"I told the lads that it was my last night and we went out for a drink in Chicago with them. I flew back the next day. My head was in a spin. I didn't know whether I'd done the right thing. I got home and said to my girlfriend Shelley, 'I'm not going.' That wasn't anything against Newcastle, but I was leaving the club I'd been at all my life. It felt horrible."

Despite his reservations, Butt travelled up to Newcastle the following morning and signed for a bargain £2.5 million as a replacement for Gary Speed. He had played 387 games for United, putting him 30th in the club's all time appearance chart, and scored 26 goals.

"I was desperate to do well at Newcastle and things started really good, but then I got an injury and played through it," says Butt. "I was so desperate to prove myself to the fans, coming as I had from Manchester United. Expectations were high and I wanted to match them. In the end I had had to stop. I was crap when I came back."

His performance for Newcastle against Manchester United in the 2005 FA Cup semi-final wasn't his finest hour. Butt's side lost 4–1 in Cardiff and the fans and media turned on him.

"It wasn't a good time and I went on loan for a season to Birmingham under Steve Bruce," he says. Butt departed from Birmingham of his own accord in February 2006 after finding out that Bruce had put his son Alex ahead of him in the squad. He was fined two weeks' wages.

"I had to go back to Newcastle – my contract is that good," admits Butt. "And I really wanted to prove myself."

He did. Butt was one of Newcastle's best players in the 2006/07 season.

"Things went much better in my second spell and I've enjoyed my time here. I get on with the fans and I think they rate me," he says. They do – he's appeared as the cover star of the Mancophile Newcastle fanzine *True Faith* under the strap line 'Technique'. And he's played with some excellent players.

"It's not an obvious one, but Patrick Kluivert was an unbelievable talent and is a very nice person," says Butt. "Problem was that he went out to bars every day. He didn't drink alcohol, but he got a bad press for it. What was he doing wrong when he wasn't drinking? What did fans want him to do? Stay at home? It's not easy when you live away from home. I have a place in Newcastle in the week but my family are in Manchester. I can't cook and you want to go out. Sometimes I end up at a kebab shop in the middle of Newcastle called Munchies!"

Butt and long-time partner Shelley married in 2008 in Portugal. "I've been with her since I was 18. She's from Wythenshawe and I met her in Royale's. My chat-up line was, 'Do you want a drink?' We slowly became more serious.

"We've got two great kids, Jersey who was born in 2004 and Reuben in 2007. We didn't want a big wedding, so our families and a few friends came to Portugal for three days. Giggsy came, Scholesy, Nev and Keaney came over. There were only about 50 people there and it was great. I'm not into the fame thing: I just want to be normal."

When 2008 dawned, Sam Allardyce was the manager. By the end of the year, Kevin Keegan had come and gone and Joe Kinnear stood as Butt's sixth Newcastle manager since he moved from Old Trafford four years ago.

"It's a frustrating club to play for," Butt says. "And it's much worse for the fans. Under Keegan I was thinking, 'Wow, we've got a great manager here in Keegan, who everybody loves –

players and fans – and we brought some good players in.' I was thinking, 'Buy one or two more decent players now and we'll definitely be up there.' But then, all of a sudden, bang, Kevin goes, and we get knocked straight back down and then there's another change. Coming from Manchester United, that's been an eye opener."

And he knows he'll have changes of his own in the near future. "I've been thinking about what I do after football," he says. "I don't want to play on and on for shit teams. I'll be done when I'm 35 so that's not long away. I could never sit at home doing nothing. I'm not really into doing the media thing, hanging onto the past and talking about it.

"I'd like to maybe do what Eric Harrison did at United and work with the kids. Know what time I have to be in every morning and what my hours are. I want to see my kids and I want to see them grow and I'd like to live in Manchester.

"I go out with my mates from football on a Saturday night and my mates from Gorton on a Sunday. It's always been that way. I was good friends with Scholesy, Nev and Ryan and still am. Same with Keaney. He lives at the bottom of my street where my family live in Manchester; our kids go to the same school. I see Incey now and then too.

"And I'm lucky that I've had such a good career," concludes Butt. "You appreciate that when you see so many people miss out for different reasons. If someone had said to me years ago that I'd be at United from 14 to 29 and win the trophies that I did, I would have taken that."

6
JESPER BLOMQVIST
The unlucky Swede

JESPER
BLOMQVIST
MANCHESTER UNITED

"You will be six feet away from the European Cup, but you won't be able to touch it, of course. And I want you to think about that fact that you'll have been so close to it and for many of you it will be the closest you'll ever get. And you will hate that thought for the rest of your lives. So just make sure you don't lose. Don't you dare come back in here without giving your all."

Half time in the United dressing room at the Camp Nou, 26th May 1999. Alex Ferguson leaves his players in no doubt about the personal consequences of failing to overturn the 0–1 scoreline in their Champions League final against Bayern.

Jesper Blomqvist, United's Swedish winger has, like most of the team, underperformed. Of all the players interviewed for this book who took part in the match, he is the one who is best able to reflect and explain why United failed to fire for most of the game.

Blomqvist remembers vividly how he felt the night before, waiting in his hotel room in Sitges. "I wrote a list to coach myself. It said, 'You can do it . . . You are faster than the rest

. . . You are in good shape . . .'" It was a tactic he had used before to self-motivate. Now he was using it to conquer his overpowering nerves. He had signed at the start of the treble season for a £4.4 million fee from Italian club Parma, but he was desperately low on confidence. Blomqvist had known for three weeks that he would play in Barcelona because of suspensions to Roy Keane and Paul Scholes. Ryan Giggs would be moved to the right wing, with Nicky Butt and David Beckham occupying the centre. Although Blomqvist played 38 games in the treble season, his own injuries had a debilitating effect in the final weeks of the season.

"They meant that I wasn't playing in the run-in. I hadn't played for three weeks so I wasn't feeling so sure of myself. I was the type of player who needed to feel the support of my teammates and coach, but I could understand if they were a little uneasy because I'd not been playing.

"I should have been enjoying the occasion," he goes on. "My parents had flown over from Sweden and the team had flown to Spain on Concorde, but I was not relaxed because I felt too much pressure. I didn't sleep very well the night before the game."

Blomqvist saw little of the preparations. He was too busy trying to get a grip on himself. He didn't see the great Catalan soprano Montserrat Caballé singing *Barcelona*, the anthem of the 1992 Olympics which she'd written with Freddie Mercury, in Barcelona's Ritz hotel. He missed the sun dip behind the towering tiers of the 98,600-capacity stadium and the mountain of Tibidabo, but remembers the thousands and thousands of Manchester United supporters who'd travelled to see the club's first European Cup final outside England. And he didn't want to let them down.

"My legs weren't responding as normal," he recalls. "I looked around the Camp Nou and they felt like jelly."

Ironically, in a game devoid of quality football and (for long periods) excitement, Blomqvist came closest to scoring.

"It was a half-chance, but it was our best chance to score," he recalls, "but I didn't. Bayern were a much better team."

Teddy Sheringham replaced Blomqvist after 67 minutes and had a greater impact on the game, making intelligent runs down the left side. Blomqvist was not to know it then, but he would never play competitively again for Manchester United. And it would be two years before he played another competitive game of football.

September 2008, Stockholm. I'd been speaking to Blomqvist for a month to arrange an interview in the beautiful Swedish capital, where he now lives. He was always helpful and is no different when I phone him from the bus from the airport to the city.

"I have training at 5pm and it's the Milan derby at 8.30pm," he says. "Perhaps we could meet about seven. We could have watched it at my house, but I've just moved and don't have the right channel."

He decides on Leary's, a big Irish bar close to Central Station which serves food and will be showing the game on several screens. The bar is full, with every table reserved and Blomqvist gets noticed immediately when he walks in the bar. A man comes over and says, "Are you Jesper?" He nods. Another approaches, interrupts the conversation and says bluntly, "Blomqvist – Milan or Inter?" In a country where the vast majority support their compatriot Zlatan Ibrahimov in his Inter colours, Blomqvist's choice of Milan is not the norm.

"I'm so busy," he says, ordering food and still looking exactly as he did a decade ago. "I've just agreed to go on the Swedish version of *Dancing On Ice*. I wanted to do something different from football, to meet new people . . ." His life is at something of a crossroads.

Blomqvist was born in February 1974 and grew up in Tavelsjö, a village of 247 people in the north of Sweden, 150 miles south of the Arctic Circle.

"I had a very happy childhood because I don't remember

any bad things from it," he recalls. "I was very sporty and did ice hockey, skiing, downhill slalom, football and athletics. I was pretty good at all of them."

His parents worked as academics at the university in the nearby town of Umeå and the family enjoyed a middle-class lifestyle. Dad also doubled up as a football coach in the village.

"I was small and I would play in goal or up front as a kid," smiles Blomqvist. "I was very quick and the best in the team, but not the region. I had to work very hard, I was not born with a God-given talent. I liked to train, to see my progress and to improve. I was very competitive at school and a terrible loser. If things were not going the team's way then I would try and dribble past everybody to score. I wanted to be first at everything. There was me and another boy who wanted to be first in maths – and we usually were. He was going on holiday and was allowed to get ahead before he went. I didn't like that so I hid his books. I was terrible. Some classmates didn't like me because I was so competitive."

Blomqvist dreamed of being an air steward because he wanted to travel, but by the age of 15 had been spotted by scouts from IFK Göteburg, then Sweden's leading club.

"They wanted me to move to Gothenburg, but I was still at school and didn't want to leave," he explains.

Instead, Blomqvist left his village side two years later to join Second Division Umeå FC in 1992. He continued his studies.

"When I was 17, I wrote an essay about what everyone in my class would be doing in the future. When I wrote about myself, I said that I would be a footballer and play in the Milan derby. I said that Fabio Capello would be my coach. I think the teachers thought I was a little bit crazy."

Though seemingly far-fetched, that dream moved a touch closer when he left to join Gothenburg's youth team after finishing his studies in 1993.

"My parents drove down to Gothenburg with me, a 12-hour drive, and we went to IKEA to buy some items for my new apartment. When they left to drive back, I thought, 'Oh no, this is for real. I'm on my own now.'"

Homesickness did not hamper Blomqvist's progress on the pitch. He was fast-tracked through the youth team and made his first team debut after just six weeks, playing a part in the side which won the championship. He was earning £600 a month.

"If that wasn't enough, I was also selected for the national team," he explains. "The timing was good because the World Cup finals were due to be held in 1994. I had always wanted to go to the United States and would have gone anyway if the football had not stopped me. Now I had a dream to go as a football player with the national team."

First, though, Blomqvist had to do compulsory national service. "I had to go the countryside and sleep in a tent for 40 nights," he explains. "We travelled around on jeeps with missiles, which we were taught to use to bring down enemy aircraft. That was my preparation for the World Cup!"

Blomqvist became Sweden's youngest ever player to appear in the World Cup finals when he played in their opening game against Cameroon in front of 93,194 in Pasadena. With Sweden trailing 2–1, Henrik Larsson replaced him after an hour.

"I didn't play well," he says. "I was too young." The game finished 2–2 and Blomqvist was on the bench for the following match, a 3–1 victory over Russia. He made a substitute appearance in the final group game, a 1–1 draw with Brazil, the team who knocked Sweden out 1–0 in the semi-finals.

"The World Cup was a good experience," says Blomqvist, "but I was still angry with myself for how I played which made me even more determined to do well in club football."

First though, he had to get to grips with a complex degree in technical physics which he'd enrolled on at university in Gothenburg.

"It was too much work so I had to leave after six months and swap it for a less technical degree in mathematics," he explains. "I've always liked numbers."

On the football field, everything clicked for Blomqvist. "We had a great team, with seven or eight players in the national side who had finished third in the World Cup. We had a fantastic manager, Roger Gustafsson, and were the most dominant team in Sweden, winning the league year after year. Gustafsson was barely 40, but he was an inspirational man in every way – he told us to treat the fans with respect, to always sign autographs. He turned down offers from abroad because he preferred to work with the youth players of Gothenburg. He never looked for the headlines or the money. Who else would do that? Nobody."

Winning the Swedish Allsvenskan for the fourth time in five years earned them a place in the Champions League qualifying round, where they beat Slavia Prague to reach the Champions League group stage alongside Manchester United, Galatasaray and Barcelona. IFK were favourites to finish bottom, a prediction which looked accurate after they lost 4–2 at Old Trafford in their opening game.

"That was my first game in a big European stadium with a special atmosphere," remembers Blomqvist. "We were timid and should have done better. We had too much respect and I remember thinking that we could beat United at home."

He thought right. Victories over Barcelona and Galatasaray (twice) saw IFK top the group by the time United visited in November 1994.

"It was an incredible evening," remembers Blomqvist. "I was on top of my game, confident of myself and my teammates. We didn't play the best football in Europe, but we worked so hard for each other. I scored one goal and had one assist."

The lightning-quick winger, now on a wage of £400 a week, which he supplemented by working in a bank, tore strips out of United. Just 20, his club's 3–1 victory ended the European ambitions of United's double winners.

"Everything was going my way," remembers Blomqvist. "I was in the zone. I feared no one. I had so much confidence in my game. I didn't know what failure was. We played Barcelona away and I felt like I could do whatever I wanted."

"He ripped me to bits," says David May, who tried to mark him. "I'd only played 15 games at right back for Blackburn and never for United. The manager warned me about Jesper and I thought, 'Here we go.' I'm six foot three, but I felt about three inches tall in the dressing room after. Jesper and I laughed years later, but I was still getting 'Blomqvist' abuse when I played at Burnley ten years later."

United crashed out of Europe, while Bayern Munich eliminated IFK on away goals in the quarter-finals, but interest in Blomqvist grew. His splendid performances helped elevate him to Sweden's Player of the Year and alert bigger clubs to the promising blond winger with shirt sleeves over his hands like an oversized pyjama top á la Denis Law. He'd done that since childhood to protect himself from the cold.

Blomqvist was flattered but unmoved. "I wanted to stay at IFK because there was more to learn and I wanted to be more secure in myself," he explains.

"The IFK players were the kings of the city," says journalist Johanna Gara, who was 17 and living in Gothenburg when Blomqvist played. "Jesper was one of many stars. We'd see them out a lot on The Avenue, everybody knew them. Jesper was quite shy, while all the girls fancied Niclas Alexandersson, who went to play for Sheffield Wednesday, Everton [where he played on the opposite wing to Blomqvist] and West Ham."

IFK won the league again and Blomqvist remained the outstanding young talent of Swedish football. In one game against Helsingborgs, he beat an offside trap and ran onto a through ball. The goalkeeper advanced out of his area, but was left confused and humiliated as Blomqvist ran around one side of him, leaving the ball to run past the other. The first time Blomqvist touched the ball was when he side-footed it into an open goal. It was awarded Goal of the Season in Sweden and the offers for Blomqvist continued to flood in.

"United called. And Kevin Keegan called from Newcastle, who had just lost out on the league to United. He said, 'Whatever you want, you'll get it.'"

By late 1996, Blomqvist, then 22, felt he was ready to take up an offer and move. He didn't have an agent.

"I wanted to join Milan and I said to any agents who were calling me, 'Bring me Milan and I will sign up with you.' I was so set on joining Milan. Nobody could have convinced me to do otherwise. They were the number-one club in the number-one football country," he says.

He was fortunate to have the choice, but people tried to persuade him against joining the Italian champions.

"Sven-Göran [Eriksson] called me from Sampdoria. He said, 'Think about this twice. Maybe it's better to come with me and play more at Sampdoria first.' I spoke to Jonas Thern, the Sweden captain who was at Roma and he told me to start at a smaller club. In hindsight they were correct, but I was convinced about Milan. I was very stubborn."

Blomqvist got the move he wanted and was transferred for £2 million.

"It was a huge story," recalls Henrik Ysten, editor of the respected Swedish football magazine *Offside*. "A boy from the north going to the biggest club in the world."

While Blomqvist had the luxury of choosing his club, other circumstances would be beyond his control.

"I wanted to sit back, grow into it, watch and learn the language, but I was thrown into the first team after nine days training. I came on as a substitute against Udinese. I did well and [Milan owner] Berlusconi said it was the best substitution he had seen. I then played every week in a struggling team. They changed coach. I came from little IFK in Sweden where everything went well. I didn't know how it worked with the big clubs."

There were some friendly faces. Paulo Maldini spoke English, so did Edgar Davids, Marcel Desailly and Zvonimir Boban. They all helped and encouraged their new teammate.

"Milan didn't have the team spirit of IFK. I was really shy and didn't speak Italian; I was single and living by myself. I was homesick and struggling. What must they have made of me, a country boy from Sweden coming into the dressing room in stonewashed jeans and white sports socks? I didn't even know what Parmesan cheese looked like."

Blomqvist also found subtle cultural differences. "I was brought up not to boast, not to believe that you are better than anyone else. I was speaking to Boban about tennis one day and he asked me if I was any good. I told him that I was OK. He replied that there was no point in us playing, because he was very good. He may have been better than me, but even if I had won Wimbledon I would have said that I was 'OK'. I had to learn to take other people's overconfidence into consideration."

Things got worse for Blomqvist. "I came on in one game and it was 1–1. We were going for a win, but I headed the ball to one of their players which led to a goal. I felt so bad and I was sat in the dressing room after, saying, 'It's my fault, it's my fault.' I started to cry and couldn't stop. Berlusconi [Milan owner and Italian President] started to speak. He was a good motivator and was telling people that we needed to regroup and focus on the next game. And I sat there crying. What must he have thought of me? What must the players have thought?"

The defending Italian champions finished 11th in 1996/97 and failed to qualify for Europe. Coach Arrigo Sacchi quit and Fabio Capello returned from a successful season at Real Madrid to coach Milan. But Blomqvist would soon find that he would never realise that student dream of playing in a Milan derby with Capello as coach.

"I started the 1997 pre-season at Milan. If something went wrong then Capello would blame the Dutch players or the Swedish players [Blomqvist's former IFK teammate Andreas Andersson had also joined Milan, though he played just 13 times before joining Newcastle]. After two months, Capello told me that I was his fifth choice for the left-wing position.

I told him that I wanted to fight for my place, but after a few days realised that I should leave."

After 20 appearances for the troubled *Rossoneri*, Blomqvist moved to Parma.

"Capello called and told me that he didn't want me to go because of injuries. I told him that he had no confidence in me and I had to leave. He said, 'I decide what's going on here and you are staying'.

"The problem was that Milan and Parma had already agreed a deal for me. Capello was really angry with me and I was angry with him too. I had envisaged being in Milan for ten years, not leaving after one. In hindsight, I took everything too personally."

One of the top Italian teams of the 1990s, Parma were bankrolled by the dairy giants Parmalat and had finished just a point behind champions Juventus the previous season under Carlo Ancellotti.

"It was a step down, but the coach believed in me and I played in every game. I became used to the tactical Italian game and had changed my style to be more defensive – even if that stopped me doing what I was best at, running at players."

Blomqvist's Italian improved as well as his football which helped him settle further.

"We met Milan in the Italian Cup and won 3–1. It was one of the best matches I have ever played and I was awarded Man of the Match. I was so happy, but Capello was still angry. He said some harsh things to me in the tunnel after the game. That only made me feel better."

Life was good at Parma, a compact, wealthy city between Milan and Bologna.

"It was easier for me at that club. It was much smaller and homely, but we had big names like Buffon, Thuram, Dino Baggio, Crespo and Cannavaro – a very good team. I came from Milan so I was well respected. I had a good year and enjoyed working with Ancellotti."

Then Parma sacked Ancellotti. "My agent said I didn't

feature in the new coach's plans," says Blomqvist. "I was shocked. I didn't want to leave Italy, I was preparing for the pre-season. Everything happened so quickly. Within days I was sat talking to Alex Ferguson at Mottram Hall. I formed a good impression of United from the minute I met him. He came to meet me at the airport personally and carried my bags. We had a long conversation over dinner. I asked him about Giggsy. I didn't want to be a reserve at United and Ferguson explained that he wanted us both in the team. I wasn't scared of competition because there had been a lot at Milan, but Giggs and I were very similar players and he was a hero in Manchester. Ferguson was impressive, but I didn't want to leave Italy. I'd found my feet. But it wasn't my choice."

United paid Parma £4.4 million for Blomqvist in July 1998 and he moved to Manchester.

"In my first night at Mottram Hall, where I lived for three months, I wrote in my diary: 'How did this happen? Do I really want to be here? I didn't want to leave Parma and I didn't want to leave Italy. How will this end? How can I find my joy in football again?'"

Blomqvist's mood began to lift in the conducive atmosphere of the United dressing room. "I felt that they respected me because I'd come from Italy. I felt the confidence of the coach too which was important. Having fellow Scandinavians like Henning Berg, Ronnie Johnsen and Ole Gunnar helped me settle. Raimond van der Gouw and Jordi Cruyff were friends too.

"I'm delighted that Ole Gunnar has legendary status among United fans. He had several offers to leave United and earn money and a guarantee of playing every week elsewhere, but always chose to stay at United. His experience was completely different from Massimo Taibi [the Sicilian goalkeeper United signed from Serie A side Venezia for £4.4 million in 1999] who I played with in Milan. He was a good goalkeeper, but there was always the problem of following Peter Schmeichel and several goalkeepers suffered from that. I could not believe it when United signed Massimo and I was nervous for him. Because he knew me and I spoke Italian, I really tried to help him out and we'd go to an Italian restaurant in Hale, but it was a disaster. He was out of his depth moving to play for a big club where he couldn't speak the language. United expected him to play straight away and it didn't work out. He played four games, made big mistakes in two of them and went back to Italy."

Another player who arrived at the same time as Blomqvist was Dwight Yorke. "He was a larger-than-life character who was always smiling. There's not many players who can arrive at a huge club like Manchester United and become an immediate star, but Yorke did. He was so at ease with everyone."

There were other ways you could improve your status in the dressing room. "You gained respect for having a nice car, a watch and a beautiful girlfriend." Although Blomqvist could never quite understand the fascination of British footballers with flash cars he caved in, though he found his own prudent Scandinavian way to avoid paying huge sums out on something which, after all, is only a watch.

"I drove an Opel [Vauxhall] when I started at Old Trafford, which stood out because it wasn't special or expensive. Before long, I'd succumbed to the pressure and bought a Jaguar.

"I had a Rolex too and several players commented to me that they liked it. I never did tell them that it was a fake."

Blomqvist also smartened up sartorially. "I went from being the worst dressed player at Milan and Parma to being the best dressed one at United. The likes of Maldini used to wear a suit for training every day. At United they wore T-shirts and jumpers. I had some competition with David Beckham though, he started to dress well, whereas Scholesy or Nicky Butt dressed like Manchester lads from the streets. Don't tell them that!"

Blomqvist often ran into Beckham and then-fiancée Victoria. "I went to hire a video in Wilmslow, saw this girl and thought, 'Wow, she looks like a Spice Girl.' Then David said, 'Hello Jesper, how are you?'"

There were obvious and important differences between Manchester and Milan.

"The training was more intense in Manchester than Milanello, where they would spend three days studying opponents. It was always more about tactics in Italy. Steve McClaren was more tactical and introduced Italian methods of training when he took over from Brian Kidd [in December 1999], where we'd look at opponents and study tactics. Kiddo was more about creating a good atmosphere. Everybody loved him and he made interesting training sessions. Manchester was a very different city to live in too, but as a professional the football was the most important thing, not the weather or food. There was a wonderful chicken sandwich at The Cliff, though, which I used to eat every day."

One of his new teammates particularly impressed him. "Paul Scholes was the most naturally talented footballer I ever came across. I don't think he ever set foot in the gym or touched a weight. He's done really well to play for so long, by cleverly tweaking his game. Henning Berg was a very good professional and now he's doing well as a coach in Norway.

"Ronny Johnsen was away on holiday and I wanted to get his satellite card so that I could watch a Swedish channel. He gave me a key and I went to his house. I went inside, but he didn't tell me that he had put the alarm on. I went in, got the card and left. When I drove away I saw police coming with flashing lights. I drove back to Ronny's place and explained the situation to the police. They didn't recognise me at first, but then one of them did and there was no problem. This story was printed in a newspaper in Sweden that I had been caught robbing Ronny Johnsen's house!"

Within a month of Blomqvist joining, United made the front pages when the club announced that they had accepted a bid to be bought out by the broadcaster BSkyB. Many fans protested at the prospect, but the mood was different among the players.

"It wasn't really an issue," says Blomqvist. "Nobody mentioned it much."

Blomqvist's girlfriend Tina, herself a Swedish international footballer, came to live in Manchester and they found a house in Wilmslow. By autumn he had found his feet in the English Premiership.

"I remember reading the programme and I was top of the OPTA stats for midfielders the previous month. I did well in the away games at Everton, Brondby and Southampton – these are the personal moments I remember. I felt invincible again, like I was at Gothenburg. I appreciated how big a club United were and it was a great club to play for. We played brilliant attacking and passing football."

"Jesper is emerging from his shell," said Ferguson at the time. "We would have won the league if we'd had him to play when Ryan Giggs was injured last season."

Blomqvist became a regular in United's greatest season. He played in most of the Champions League away games because Ferguson considered him more effective in defence than Giggs. And he played in all the key games in the run-in until he picked up an injury.

"The little injuries would hold me back, just as I was getting to my best point," he explains. "I was never able to put together a string of matches which would give me even more confidence.

"I found Roy Keane difficult to work out at first. I thought he was mad and annoying. I couldn't understand him and thought he was being egotistical. He shouted a lot, especially at players like Phil Neville, but I realised that he was always putting the team first. Ferguson let him go on because of this. He also stood up for the players, whether it was on the pitch or off it with commercial decisions. He was an excellent player, with vision of what was going on in the game. You always want a player like him in your team. Roy was number one in the dressing room."

Blomqvist incurred Keane's wrath in Turin after the 1999

"An inspired run from the full back on the far side… a chance… AND A GOAL!" Lee Martin becomes the first full back to score the winner in an FA Cup final.

Fergie's first trophy, the 1990 FA Cup. Back row L-R: Russell Beardsmore, Paul Ince, Lee Sharpe, Steve Bruce, Danny Wallace, Mark Robins, Les Sealey, Mike Phelan, Brian McClair, Clayton Blackmore. Front row L-R: Mark Hughes, Gary Pallister, Lee Martin, Bryan Robson, Neil Webb.

Gary Pallister becomes the final United player to score in the 1992/93 season during the last game against Blackburn Rovers as United lifted the title for the first time in 26 years.

Brian McClair, Paul Parker and Ryan Giggs celebrate United becoming champions in '93.

Lee Sharpe and Gary Pallister enjoy
a celebratory beer and sponsors Carling
get a wonderful advertisement.

United brightest young stars also triumphed
in a garish tie competition.

Eric wins his £100 bet with Dennis Wise that he'd score the penalty in the 1994 FA Cup final against Chelsea.

Pensive faces as the United coach attracts unwanted attention in Istanbul, 1993.

Mathew Simmonds, sporting a terrible leather jacket, decides it will be a good idea to abuse the dismissed Eric Cantona at Selhurst Park in January 1995. What happened next would make global headlines.

Having served his punishment, Eric returns from his ban with a goal against Liverpool.

"We've won the Football League again, down by the Riverside…" United overhaul Newcastle's 12 point lead to win the league at Middlesbrough in 1996. Local boy Gary Pallister, Andrew Cole and Roy Keane celebrate in perfect symmetry.

The sartorially sharp Cole and Giggs can't help but register their disgust at Ian Rush's white suit before the 1996 FA Cup final.

Robbie Fowler and Roy Keane don't necessarily agree. United v Liverpool at its finest.

Eric's late volley settles the 1996 FA Cup final as United's young stars make a mockery of Alan Hansen's, "You don't win anything with kids" quote to win the 1996 league and cup Double.

From Fergie Out to the double Double. The United players look relaxed as they celebrate, except for David May who looks like he's adding something of his own to the bath.

Chairman and manager. Martin Edwards and Sir Alex Ferguson.

Maybe he didn't think his move to United through fully, but the waif-like Jordi Cruyff usually performed well when selected.

The much fancied Porto side are dispatched 4-0 at Old Trafford in the 1997 Champions League quarter final first leg.

Champions again in 1997, but Eric Cantona would announce his retirement from football the day after this photo was taken.

Jesper Blomqvist enjoyed a good first season at Old Trafford before injuries robbed him of a decent career at the club.

Possibly the greatest-ever Manchester United performance and certainly the greatest-ever individual display as United come from 2-0 down to beat the mighty Juventus in Turin in the 1999 Champions League semi-final second leg. The peerless Roy Keane turns to celebrate after scoring. He reckons he did "alright."

"I think I've hit on something here," opined Ferguson when Andrew Cole and Dwight Yorke first played together. Here they celebrate winning the 1999 FA Cup final.

Part one of the Treble – David May gets the celebrations rocking as United win the league in 1999.

This is the one. Ole Gunnar Solskjaer celebrates after his extending toe clinched an injury time winner in the Camp Nou.

United's players begin celebrations which would last 75 minutes after winning the European Cup for the first time since 1968 in such dramatic circumstances. The Bayern Munich players, understandably, are destroyed.

Nicky Butt and David Beckham, two lads who had risen through the youth ranks, celebrate the Treble, the greatest moment in their football careers.

50,000 United fans look on in ecstasy from Camp Nou's towering stands as Peter Schmeichel grips the European Cup in his final game for United.

Andrew Cole after a four hour interview at Mottram Hall.

Lee Sharpe keeps wrapped up in an autumnal Leeds.

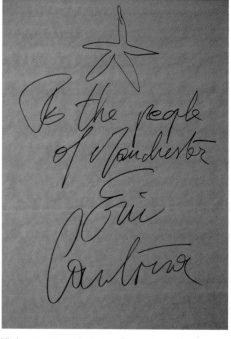

Eric wears the French Beach Soccer shirt
in a Marseille hotel room.

His impromptu squiggle on a flip chart would
go on to raise £2,500 in a Manchester auction.

Always good company. David May outside Urbis in Manchester.

It's November but Nicky Butt wears a t-shirt at Newcastle United's training ground.

An unlikely manager. Jesper Blomqvist back home in Sweden.

Paul Parker wear his Setanta work coat before a game at Grays in Essex.

Lee Martin, pictured at the 2009 Champions League final in Rome.

Jordi Cruyff looks relaxed in Barcelona.

Happy at home. Gary Pallister stands in front of photos of him scoring two at Anfield for United with his adoring daughters.

Martin Edwards stands in front of his impressive United book and trophy collection – including the author's prequel to this book.

Champions League semi-final second leg. "He blamed me for the pass I gave to him, which led to him being sent off. It wasn't the best ball in the world, but he had a bad first touch which lost possession."

Against a counter-attacking Juventus team, Keane made a challenge on Zinedine Zidane, received a yellow card and missed the European Cup final.

"He was really shouting at me in the dressing room after," recalls Blomqvist. "He was so angry and saying, 'It's your fucking fault that I'm going to miss the final.'" Blomqvist didn't reply.

"I think he's still mad at me! That was the way he worked. Things were never his fault. I didn't care much for that type of attitude. He went on about it for weeks and it became a bit of a joke in the dressing room."

He remembers Ferguson being at his best in Turin. "He told us that Juventus were a great team, but that they didn't have the players we did. He was talking about players like Davids, Zidane, Del Piero and Inzaghi! Ferguson really believed in the team, even though he exaggerated a little."

Another big character in the dressing room was Peter Schmeichel. "He tried hard to be the number one, but had to settle for number two behind Keane. Once, in training, he and I chased a loose ball. I went in hard and tackled him. He was furious and tried to punch me. It was close to being a real fight, which would not have been good for me as he was very big. He would have beaten me."

Blomqvist told Schmeichel that he wouldn't speak to him until he changed his attitude. "It was childish, but I didn't speak to him for two weeks and then he came up to me one day and asked how I was. I told him that I wouldn't speak to him unless he apologised. I had to stand up for myself. The other guys in the team appreciated that I had stood my ground with him. I was OK then with Schmeichel."

Blomqvist appreciates the part these big characters played

in United's success. "Ferguson, Keane and Schmeichel were all winners," he says. "Look how many games we won in the last five minutes. They never gave up. It wasn't the most talented team in the world, but it was the most determined."

Like Jordi Cruyff, Blomqvist responded to the particular ambiance, if not the culinary heritage, of English football. "I liked Italy more because of the food and weather, but I preferred English football because of the atmosphere in the stadiums and the intensity of the matches. The crowd were very encouraging so as long as you always tried. I've been to a lot of big derby games in the world, but the one game which sticks out to me was a Manchester derby game at Maine Road. The intensity of the fans was stronger than I've ever seen. Every attack was roared on. City really, really wanted to beat United."

Blomqvist was fit again for the last week of the 1998/99 season. With Jordi Cruyff on loan at Alaves and Giggs playing on the right, Ferguson would have been left with a selection nightmare in Barcelona if he wasn't.

"I was left out of the FA Cup final but the manager told me I was going to play in the European Cup final," he states. "But I'd lost my momentum and my confidence wasn't high." He tells me the story about his less than ideal preparations which resulted in his below-par performance. By the time he has finished, it's 1am in Stockholm. The pub is closing and the staff are asking us to leave.

"I feel that I need to give you more," says Blomqvist. "Can we speak tomorrow? I have an idea. Come to watch my team play. We have a very important game. We have to win. Then we can talk after the game and I can take you back to Stockholm. I can't do the interview before a match: it takes too much out of me."

Blomqvist is months into a managerial career at Second Division Enkoping, the team from a town of 37,000 an hour north of Stockholm.

The train station is a mile from the football ground and a spectator, upon hearing me ask directions from a bus driver, tells me to follow him the ground. We talk about Jesper.

"He's very popular," explains Magnus. "He has been playing a little bit recently too and his class really shows. In the last game, he came on as substitute and scored the only goal by chipping the goalkeeper from 40 metres. I don't think he'll play tonight, though. His knees are hurting."

The sun dips below the horizon, closing a bright and beautiful late September day. Overhead, birds migrate south in great flocks to warmer climes before the winter sets in. The scoreboard registers the temperature at five degrees, which drops to zero by full time. Such is the harsh climate, the league season starts in late March and finishes by October.

Fewer than 600 spectators are present to see Blomqvist's team in a relegation battle against IF Limhamn Bunkeflo, who have travelled nine hours by bus from their home near Malmo in southern Sweden. They've brought no fans to the stadium which surrounds an athletics track, is open at both ends and features a small open wooden terraced stand facing a tall main stand of 1,000 bright yellow seats. It's not a ground for the purists.

Exactly ten years ago, Blomqvist played for United away to Bayern Munich at the start of the treble season. Tonight, he watches from the bench as his goalkeeper is sent off after seven minutes. A penalty sees his team fall behind and the fans groan. In among the Andersons, Lindbers and Olssons are a Mohammed, Mtaka and Simba, evidence of the seven nationalities at Enkoping and football's globalisation – even at the lower end of Sweden's Second Division.

Enkoping battle and equalise through a penalty, but the visitors win yet another spot kick. The stand-in goalkeeper saves it. Blomqvist remains rooted to the bench throughout the drama.

The visitors take the lead again in the second half, but despite being down to ten men, the shattered Enkoping don't give up. Their fans appreciate it. After an hour, a man stands up and starts the first chant of the night. They equalise.

With 89 minutes and 44 seconds on the scoreboard, ten men Enkoping get a dramatic winner. Even Blomqvist, wearing a sweater, jogging bottoms and running trainers, leaves the dugout and punches the air.

I spot the fan I met before the game.

"I told you we like him!" he shouts from a cluster of cheering supporters.

After the game, Blomqvist invites me to eat with the players. He's happy, considerate and bright. The players like him, the club officials and journalists too. With his little-boy-lost looks, he might not seem an automatic shoe-in to be a manager, but he seems to be enjoying it. Enjoyment and fulfilment, rather than money, matter to Blomqvist.

We're the last people to leave the stadium and the flood-lights are switched off as we walk back to his Audi for the one-hour drive to Stockholm. We'd left the interview in the summer of 1999, with United the treble-winning champions of Europe and Blomqvist ready for the new season.

"I felt great that summer," he says. "Some players like Dwight Yorke can arrive at a club and settle straight away. I needed more time to build relationships with people. After the treble win I felt sure of myself and settled at United. I felt that the coach and the rest of the group believed in me. I was ready to move on another step because United fans had not seen the best of me. I was ready to have a great season. I went on a pre-season tour to Australia and scored a great goal. Then my knee swelled up in Hong Kong. That was the beginning of the troubles . . ." Blomqvist's voice trails off and he sighs.

"Everything was very difficult from then on. I had an operation, but I couldn't run properly. I just thought it was another little injury but it became a series of operations. After a while I became afraid."

"'Articular cartilage,'" pronounced the specialists, an injury which also affected Ole Gunnar and Jordi Cruyff, two players who Blomqvist remained close to – he last visited Manchester for the Norwegian's 2008 testimonial at Old Trafford.

"You don't hear so much about it and nobody knows the best solution," says Blomqvist. "I was seeing specialists in different countries. Each time I thought I'd make a recovery I'd push towards match fitness only to suffer another problem.

"Jordi Cruyff recommended a guy in Croatia and I had a good feeling for him so I spent a lot of time there. I spent so much time there that I ended up with a Croatian girlfriend, who I was with for four years. I always felt that I could come back and play for United, always held that belief. But by then it was too late for United."

Blomqvist's three-year contract expired in 2001 and United didn't renew it.

"I used to talk to Ferguson a lot about my situation," says Blomqvist. "I would hear him whistling and singing and he made me smile. I'd hear him more at The Cliff, which was much smaller, cosier and had more atmosphere than Carrington [the £14 million training centre on the south-west outskirts of the city which United moved to at the start of 2000]. But I cost United a lot of money and felt guilty. I told Ferguson that I was really sorry and he said, 'Jesper, football can be like this sometimes. You did very well for us in your first season.' I really appreciated his words."

Blomqvist was indeed expensive. Without taking his wages into account he cost just over £115,000 per appearance, making him United's priciest game-for-game signing. United treated the Swede well, allowing him to train at Carrington even after his contract had expired.

"Ferguson then talked to Walter Smith and helped me get a move to Everton in 2001, signing a six-month contract on a game-to-game basis. The money didn't matter, what was important was that I got back playing and felt part of a team." The Everton players soon saw to that.

"Duncan Ferguson stole my car keys and then my car on my first day of training," he says. "And Paul Gascoigne was at Everton too. A mobile phone belonging to Alan Stubbs buzzed when he was in the shower after training. Gascoigne read the message which said, 'My wife's just had a baby and it's called Jayne' or whatever. Gascoigne smiled, then typed in a reply which said, 'That's a fucking ugly name.' Stubbs didn't know anything about this. Gascoigne was always joking and doing stupid things, like asking waitresses for white milk. He told me that he'd once stolen a double-decker bus in London."

Blomqvist made his Everton debut against Manchester United on Boxing Day 2001, two and a half years after his last game for United in Barcelona. He did well for 73 minutes, attempting to expose weaknesses in the United defence. United only scored the game's two goals minutes after he left the field to a standing ovation from the travelling Reds.

"It was one of the highlights of my career," he says. "My former teammates were good with me and so were the United fans. Even though we got beat, I got Everton's Man of the Match."

He was recalled by Sweden, but then David Moyes replaced Walter Smith at Everton. "He's an excellent manager, but he didn't want to give me a contract." So after only 15 games with Everton, Blomqvist was on the move again.

"I went on trial to Middlesbrough, where I agreed a contract with manager Steve McClaren, who told me that we'd sign it when I got fit." Blomqvist did his pre-season, got very fit and went to sign the contract, only to be told it would be for half the wages they had agreed. "I was really angry," he says, "and they told me that the day before the transfer deadline which gave me no chance of finding a new club."

Charlton made a quick move for him, but his time there was also blighted by injury. "I had a really bad year because I had a recurrence of my knee problems," he explains. "It was horrible not being able to play. I only managed a couple of games for Charlton and I was going back and forward to Croatia all of the time."

He joined Djurgardens of Stockholm on a pay-as-you-play contract in 2003, for which he was bizarrely accused of being a 'Judas' by IFK fans. Djurgardens won the league in 2003 after he managed nine games, but Blomqvist's knee problems were not over and he spent much of the next two seasons in Croatia seeing a specialist.

"You cannot begin to understand how frustrated I was," he says. "I couldn't even wear shoes because I had to wear special types of footwear. I could not sit down for too long because my knee would swell up. I could not fly without putting an ice pack on my knee. I could not walk around a city because my knee would swell up. I would wake up in the morning and the first thing I would do was to touch my knee to see the swelling. I would then check it 40 times a day – again and again. I did that for three years. It drove me crazy and I became depressed. I finally realised that even though I wanted to come back, I couldn't spend my whole life concentrating on my knee. My family was very supportive, my girlfriend too. I cannot have been an easy person to live with, never wanting to go shopping or to the cinema."

Blomqvist announced his decision to retire from football, aged 31, in 2005.

"I decided that I couldn't go through life having knee problems. It hurt inside, but I quit playing. I know I was unlucky and it's sad because I've such a love for the game and felt I had so much to offer at the highest level. I never reached my true potential. It's a pity, but it's not the worst thing in the world. And unlike some footballers who had no money when their careers were cut short, at least I made some money from football. Yet it was frustrating to watch former teammates still playing long after I finished."

Blomqvist returned to Stockholm and began working on Swedish TV as a football analyst.

"I also started a university course for coaching, while helping out with the youth team at Djurgardens for free. I'd learnt so much from coaches like Ferguson and I thought I'd like to give that to the players. But not just Ferguson. My first coach in Gothenburg led by example. He treated everybody equally and respected players. And in Milan Sacchi was the best tactician I worked with. He knew exactly when I should time my runs and would shout instructions. Ancellotti was clever too. Capello, although I didn't have a great time with him, creates a very winning atmosphere.

"Ferguson's biggest asset is his belief in what he's doing. He really believes in his players and thinks that they are the best. The players start to believe that. In 1998, he told us that Inter were not a team, but a collection of individuals and we believed him."

Second Division Enkoping asked him to be assistant manager in 2007. "I worked very closely with the manager and was asked to become manager when he left in 2008. I've enjoyed it so far and I've really enjoyed playing a little, but I have to be careful with the knee. It's really hard being a manager at a struggling club. Everything is about results. You live with it every day and sometimes you ask yourself if it is worth it. But then you have a night like tonight and everything seems worth it. At the moment I am just enjoying being a coach, without having ambitions to work at the top level.

"I just wish I could have given United fans so much more too," he says. "I was criticised after my performance in the European Cup final and I can understand why. I wanted to prove people wrong, but I never played for United again. That saddens me."

7
PAUL PARKER
The reliable defender

PAUL
PARKER
MANCHESTER UNITED

"Trigger, trigger, trigger. Shoot that nigger. Which fucking nigger? That fucking nigger!" January 1989, and the Stretford End terrace, during an FA Cup third-round tie against Queens Park Rangers, single out defender Paul Parker for some special treatment. What followed next has become part of football legend.

Parker made a 'gun' with his fingers, pointed it at his head, looked up at the sea of 10,000 faces and pretended to shoot himself in the head. Those racists who thought they would humiliate and intimidate Rangers' England defender were silenced. Parker had confronted and outwitted them.

Parker had previously experienced plenty of such revolting bile from the terraces. "Black players used to get a lot of racist abuse when we travelled north," he recalls from the kitchen of his house in Billericay, Essex. "I would get a lot of abuse at Leeds United, where their fans would sing, 'There ain't no black in the Union Jack; send the bastards back'. Years later, when I was with United, it was a relief to go to Elland Road and get abuse because of the colour of my jersey rather than

163

the colour of my skin. I almost smiled when they called me a red bastard rather than a black one.

"Yorkshire was the worse place to go in the 1980s though," says the man who was known as 'Robocop' and 'Benny' (a raffish character in *Grange Hill*) by his United teammates. "I remember going to take a throw in at Barnsley when a bloke started shouting, 'You fucking nigger, you fucking wog.' When I looked, I saw that he had a small child with him. I said, 'You've got your opinions, but does he need to hear them?' He replied, 'He's going to hate you fucking niggers when he grows up as well.' I wasn't one to back down. I'd grown up in an area with the biggest National Front following in the country, but this man wasn't right in the head. I never let racist abuse get to me on the pitch but I had to say something. Then I took the throw and carried on."

He'd expected better from Manchester United fans. "I remember thinking that United had had black players in the past and being surprised. I thought Man United were a top club, their fans educated." So much for Manchester being an immigrant city with a high racial tolerance.

His response came partly from his understanding of the nuances of fan culture, and also from his personal philosophy on racism.

"I sometimes read black footballers saying that they would walk off the pitch if they heard racist abuse. Should you always walk away from people calling you names? I'd rather question people like that idiot in Barnsley, who paid to get in that ground to abuse me. He was the one with the problem, not me."

Since then, there have been positive changes, as Parker notes.

"Thankfully, football has changed a lot," he says. "There's three United fans with turbans who sit by the dugout every week. I was fearful for them when I first saw them, but now I'm happy that they feel safe going to football grounds. It wasn't always like that.

"The racism hasn't disappeared though. England supporters

still have racist elements and you still get it at lower level. Millwall have a big problem. I do radio work in London, but I'll never do games at Millwall. There's too much hate there, too much racism."

In 1989, Parker was already an England international, regarded as one of the best defenders in the league – fast, fit and brilliant in the air, despite only being 5' 7". The Queens Park Rangers side he played in were more than competent, too. It took two replays to separate them and United in the Cup that year. They had finished fifth in the first division the previous season and featured Parker, Clive Allen, David Seaman, Ray Wilkins and player/manager Trevor Francis.

Parker was also on the cusp of being one of England's players in a successful 1990 World Cup, where he set up Gary Lineker's equaliser in the semi-final against West Germany. Such performances got him noticed, with English coach Bobby Robson noting, "Parker leaps like a salmon and tackles like a ferret."

By 1991 he was a Manchester United player and those same fans on the Stretford End who had abused him, applauded him.

Parker was born in the shadow of Upton Park in 1964. "By rights I should have been a West Ham fan," he says, "but they meant nothing to me, as the son of Jamaican parents, because of their hostile attitude to black players."

That racist attitude extended to their fans.

"I remember making a rare visit to Upton Park when I was 13 to see West Ham against Manchester United. I was barely 5' tall but I was kicked and pushed by West Ham fans and told to get out of the way. There was non-stop chanting aimed at the few black players on the pitch, bananas were thrown and it was a frightening and unnerving experience. I went to Tottenham instead and stood on The Shelf to see players like Martin Chivers, Steve Perryman and my idol Pat Jennings."

The National Front tried to sell Parker's mum a magazine outside Upton Park and she told them where to go.

"There was always an undercurrent of racism which made life difficult for newcomers and their children," he says.

A few years later, Parker played against West Ham's youth team for Fulham. His opponent was Bobby Barnes, a promising black winger who would make the first team.

"One of the West Ham coaches kept shouting to Barnes, 'You can get past that coon.' I don't know how George Parris and other blacks coming through the West Ham youth system tolerated that atmosphere."

Parker was one of four children and the family eventually moved out of the East End to Romford and then Rainham in Essex. He attended school in Hornchurch, "with no enthusiasm because I lived only for football. I took English so that I could read road signs, maths to find out how far I had to go and geography so I knew where I was."

He represented Essex at 800 metres and basketball, but not football. "Representative football teams were full of big lads already built like adults and little guys like me were not considered."

Parker told the careers officer at school that he wanted to be a professional footballer, to be informed that he had a one-in-a-thousand chance. Aged eight, he had started out a striker, before switching to defence. As a tiny eleven-year-old he was taken to Romford Juniors, one of the best teams in the area. Fulham, despite being on the other side of London, had an excellent scouting network in the area and spotted him immediately. They signed him on affiliate forms in 1976.

"I came to regard Fulham as my club and became an associate schoolboy with them," he explains. "I was a right back and while I was tiny, what I lacked in height I made up for in pace, tenacity and tackling ability. I was also very determined."

Fulham were worried about Parker's size and sent him for a test on his bones. Specialists told the club that he could grow to 5' 8". That was enough for Fulham, whom Parker joined full time on an apprenticeship when he left school in 1980.

He was given the job of cleaning the boots of new manager Malcolm Macdonald, a man he describes as "strong physically and mentally. He liked brandy and short, stumpy cigars. There were always boxes of them on the back ledge of his Citroën Safari."

Macdonald led Fulham to promotion from the Third Division and gave Parker his first-team debut against Reading when he was just 16.

"I was up against a front line whose average height was six foot one, but my pace got me out of trouble. I liked Malcolm, but Ray Harford was a major reason behind Fulham's recovery. He was my mentor. I liked him and he liked me. He called me an 'enigma' which, until I was told what it meant, I thought was another way of calling me a nigger."

Parker was a poor trainer who found it difficult to concentrate unless he was playing a game.

"Ray told me in no uncertain terms," he recalls. "It was only when I began to take training more seriously that I was given a professional contract."

Life as an apprentice had its moments.

"We all had to go in the dressing room at Christmas, strip off and stand naked on a bench in front of the senior players and sing a song one by one. To 'help' we were given props, the wellington boots of the groundsman and a broom so that we could pretend to play air guitar. Then we had a string attached to our penises, which our audiences were not slow to pull. There were buckets of cold water ready to be thrown at us if our performances were considered poor. It didn't help that I am the only black man born without rhythm, so I don't think I covered myself in glory."

Parker played five times for Fulham in 1981/82 and was the only Third Division player chosen to play for England youth alongside Paul Elliott, Danny Wallace, Mark Walters and Stewart Robson. The majority of the other players in the team didn't go on to make a living from football. Parker established himself in Fulham's first team and earned rave reviews for a performance against Liverpool in the League Cup in 1983/84. Former Fulham player Bobby Robson compared Parker to Nobby Stiles.

"I found out that Bob Paisley had put in a £200,000 bid for me," Parker recalls. "But not having an agent there was nothing I could do as Fulham wanted to keep me."

Parker put his success down to several factors. "I was getting good coaching at Fulham as well as maturing as a player and a person. I had a good spring in my feet which meant I could compete with players much taller than myself. The secret was in the timing, but also in knowing how to block off the man. I was marking by positioning and used my brain and cunning. I was also not slow to get sympathy from referees who tended to favour me if there was a clash because I was so small for a central defender."

Parker's ambitions to play at the top level were not matched by Fulham's. "The best players were allowed to leave and I was made captain, aged 21," he recalls. Two years after being one point from the First Division, Fulham were relegated to the third.

"Perhaps I should have followed the others out of Craven Cottage, but I loved Fulham. I had to do something, though. I wanted to play in the First Division, not the Third. I was a regular for England Under 21s but earned just £80 a week, a third of what my teammates were getting. My problem was that I was trapped in a contract and I stayed at Fulham, playing in a very young side which finished 18th as attendances dwindled."

Fulham again drew Liverpool in the League Cup and were demolished 10–0. "It was one of the most embarrassing and humiliating experiences of my life," says Parker, "It would have been 20 had it not been for our goalkeeper. It wasn't like me, but I tore into my teammates. As we walked off the pitch, I realised that my Fulham days were over."

At the end of a miserable season, Parker was sold to QPR

alongside Dean Coney for £425,000, where Peter Shreeve, the assistant manager told him, "You're a good defender. You can head, tackle and recover. But you can't fucking pass the ball. Give it to someone who can."

"That hurt my pride," says Parker, "but it was the truth in one brutal sentence."

He considered QPR to be a huge club because they had six people working in the office – four more than Fulham, "And because they had a person employed to open the main door on match days. Manager Jim Smith was manager, a blunt Yorkshireman who was as volatile as any boss I came across – until Alex Ferguson. We played on plastic and my job was to man-mark. I soon came to realise that with my speed, if the ball was ever played over me it would run away and no-one could catch it."

Armed with that knowledge, Parker enjoyed some comfortable afternoons while opposition strikers ran themselves into the ground trying to catch the ball as it ran towards David Seaman. There were disadvantages to the plastic pitch. "My legs were like lead on a Sunday and Monday and my muscles felt they had been hit by sticks," attests Parker. "I ruined many a good pair of trousers on a Saturday night because any weeping wounds would stick to the material like glue. I've also got scars on my elbows."

Parker was one of QPR's best players as he made his club debut at West Ham, where he marked Tony Cottee out of the game in a 3–0 victory. In another game, Newcastle's Paul Gascoigne was sent off after landing several blows on him in frustration.

"We had a good side, but I needed my win bonuses to keep up my instalments on a Ford Capri I'd bought," smiles Parker, who was voted Player of the Year by Rangers' fans in his first two seasons at the club. He was happy, though not entirely free from the spectre of racism.

"I played one England B game in Iceland where I received

a lot of abuse from travelling members of the National Front. I was the only black player in the team and there was very little I could do about it."

Life was better at Loftus Road. "We had a team of funny characters. The black Andy Gray, Mark Dennis and Alan McDonald, three of the most uncouth footballers, shared a bedroom. McDonald used to have a fag at half time and one night, him and Dennis pissed all over Gray's bed when he wasn't in the room. When he came back, he climbed straight into bed. He soon realised that he was lying in a piss-soaked bed and started going absolutely mental. He was disgusted and threw the mattress out of the window. I heard the noise. Andy Gray was a character. He used to try and sell snide Ralph Lauren polo shirts on the team bus to matches. I can remember Don Howe, this statesman of football, just sitting at the front of the coach shaking his head."

Parker won his first England cap against Albania in 1989, aged 25. "I was as proud as any Englishman could be, even though I was in awe of the other players like Bryan Robson, Terry Butcher and Gary Lineker. The manager Bobby Robson wasn't in awe of me – he kept calling me Danny Thomas, which was amusing as he'd retired three years earlier."

Parker kept his place for the rest of the World Cup qualifiers ahead of Italia 90 and was named QPR's player of the Year for the third season in a row in 1989/90. He was earning £650 a week – less than a third of his England teammates.

"I was on England duty when Bryan Robson casually mentioned that Manchester United were interested in me," says Parker. "If that was today, an agent would have been right in my face pushing the move through. I was content at QPR, a club who did well against the big London clubs. I could live at home so I never did anything about United."

Parker had some knowledge of what Manchester had to offer already. "Peter Reid came to QPR and I got to know him very well. I'd go up to Manchester and enjoy nights out in the city. Reid then became Howard Kendall's assistant manager at City. I liked Manchester. Before that, I just thought that the north was a hard place to go and play football. The crowds were louder and they considered southern teams soft. Everything I had previously thought about the north was negative. We were so cocooned in London that we believed that there were places in the north which had no electricity. There are still people like that in London.

"Southerners who ask me what my favourite city is are surprised when I say Manchester. But it is. It's a small, friendly city and I enjoy walking around there. I was only there for five years but the city and the club get under your skin. A lot of players who move to Manchester to play for United end up staying."

Parker's thoughts were on Italy in the summer of 1990. He was in a squad of 26 which was to be whittled down to a final 22.

"I roomed with David Rocastle. I expected us to both make the cut, but when David sat crying his eyes out after speaking to Bobby Robson, I realised he wouldn't be going. I would. We flew to a training camp to Sardinia. An open training session meant that fans came in an abused me and John Barnes, two black players. For once we ignored it."

Parker played in all six of England's 1990 World Cup matches. "We had plenty of luck against Belgium and Cameroon, but not against West Germany in the semi-final. The Cameroon game in Naples was my highlight. We were surprised at how good they were, so it was something to beat them."

Parker was stunned by the jubilant public reaction to England reaching the semi-finals when he returned home, but he was brought down to earth when Bobby Gould, his new manager at QPR, greeted him for the first time by saying, "You're a big-time Charlie now and I don't like big-time Charlies."

The following season was not a good one, with injuries

restricting Parker to just 13 league games. Alex Ferguson later said that he would have tried to sign him much earlier if it wasn't for those injuries. Parker's relationship with Gould wasn't good because the QPR manager was convinced he wanted to leave.

"My year didn't improve when I was convicted for drink-driving which earned me the biggest rollocking I've ever had . . . from my mum."

Arsenal came in for Parker and agreed a fee of £1.8 million with QPR, but his wage would have remained unchanged. Howard Kendall said that he wanted Parker at Everton, which promoted half a dozen letters from racist Everton fans saying, "Don't join us", albeit not in such polite terms. Then Terry Venables called from Tottenham, who had also agreed a fee with QPR.

"I was a Spurs fan, I lived locally and had just opened a wine bar in Tottenham territory," says Parker. "I was delighted at the prospect of playing there. They were offering much better money [and far better than what he would get at Old Trafford] so I went to see Terry Venables with my agent at the Royal Lancaster Hotel in London to sign. Venables was in full flow when a barman interrupted and said that there had been a call for me from Maurice Watkins at Manchester United."

The mood of the meeting changed with Venables sensing that Parker wanted to speak to United.

"He said a phrase I will never forget: 'If you go up to see United, you won't come back.' Venables shook our hands, said the offer was still open and wished us well."

Parker and his agent drove north the following day.

"In fairness to El Tel, he never bore a grudge after I had signed for United. When I called him with the news he just said, 'OK, then,' and the line went quiet."

It was a hot summer day when Parker arrived at Old Trafford. "The car park was so busy that I thought there must be a game on," he says. "Alex Ferguson met me and he was the perfect tour guide. He knew everything about the club and how it worked. As we wandered around the pitch, a group of fans on a tour group were watching the grass grow and one shouted, 'Are you going to join us?' My wits had deserted me and I replied, 'Yes.' In retrospect, I should have kept my mouth shut, but Sir Alex said, 'Oh, you've decided then?' as he probably made a mental note to come up with less money."

Ferguson outlined his plans for his £1.8 million signing. "He was completely straight with me and told me where he wanted to play and his vision for the team in the future. He was a brilliant motivator who would get to know every positive and negative about me, just as he did with every player. Peter Schmeichel had signed on the same day. I moved into the Midland Hotel and my family initially stayed in Essex. I soon saw that everyone wanted to talk about football and United. It was hard to have a quiet drink because everyone wanted a bit of your time. It was possible to go out in London and not be recognised. Not in Manchester."

Parker flew to Austria to meet his new teammates. "They were at the end of a massive pre-season tour and I walked into a room of people who were sleepwalking. Austria Memphis beat United 5–1 the following day. A few days later I went to The Cliff and looked at all these big names I'd played against for QPR. Then I realised that I was one of them.

"As he was with England, Robbo was the main man at Old Trafford. He was the first person you saw when you went in the changing room at The Cliff. Brian McClair would sit just to his right. I'd try and get in without seeing Choccy. He was so clever, bright and dry that he could put anyone down. He would analyse people to see if they were right for Manchester United. It was always United first with Choccy. Unless you were Eric, you fitted in with the United way: working hard, not being big time.

"Eric once turned up at a function at Trafford Town Hall wearing a suit and red Nike trainers. Choccy was straight into him, saying, 'You can't do that.' Everyone was waiting for the manager to arrive. When he did, he looked at Eric and said, 'Only you could get away with dressing like that.' Everyone's chins hit the floor. It was brilliant of the manager and one reason why Eric didn't last at Leeds, where the management had been too strict and there was jealousy. There was a Yorkshire mentality, a resistance to change.

"Ferguson cut through all that because he knew that Eric could make United better. Eric was a maverick and you can't become a maverick. You have to be one. We'd been wearing the shirt with collars since July and nobody thought to turn the collars up. Eric arrived and turned his up. If Sharpey or Giggsy would have turned the collars up, they would have got away with it, but neither thought to do it. Whereas Eric . . ."

United won the League Cup and finished runners-up to Leeds in 1991/92

"We could see the team getting better," said Parker, "though you wouldn't have said that after watching us against my old team QPR on New Year's Day 1992. We were hammered 4–1."

Sir Alex Ferguson has had better birthdays. "A horrendous performance," was how he described the game. The result made it difficult for the United manager to enjoy turning 51, but QPR striker Dennis Bailey would have had no such problem celebrating.

Bailey scored a hat-trick as his 15th-placed side pulled off the biggest surprise of the season against a top-of-the-table United side chasing their first league title in 25 years.

"It was one of the low points of my career," recalls Parker. "How Rangers fans must have enjoyed my humiliation and who could blame them?"

Parker wanted to show his former teammates he'd made the right decision in joining United.

"It all started to go wrong for me the day before," continues Parker. "We stayed in a hotel on New Year's Eve even though the match, which was televised, didn't kick-off until 5pm.

"We trained in the morning when most sensible people were sleeping off their hangovers. It was a big game for me, but there was no time to relax and I could see that as a team we were lethargic. Rangers ran us ragged and my old team-mate Andy Sinton caught me as cold as I have ever been caught. Sinton was nicknamed 'the Rat' because of his scuttling running style. He scored, but the real Rangers hero was Dennis Bailey."

At the end of the game, the triumphant Bailey walked into the United dressing room holding the match ball. A devout Christian, Bailey wasn't one to gloat, but he wanted the ball signed by the United players.

"Steve Bruce, who had been his marker, got hold of the ball, fumed, 'Don't be silly' and threw it out through the door," recalls Parker.

It was the first time the Hoops had won at Old Trafford in their history. The tiny away following of 900 in a crowd of just 38,554 watched in as much disbelief as the home fans as QPR's incisive passing allowed them to dominate and seal United's worst home defeat since 1977.

"That was just unbelievable and we got what we deserved," said Ferguson after the match. "It was a lack of determination in clearing the ball and defending properly. We hadn't even got started when QPR were 2–0 up."

"This is a dream come true for me at Old Trafford," added Bailey. "My first ever hat-trick and at a ground I have only ever been to once before. That was eight years ago when I was a fan supporting Tottenham in a cup match."

Bailey, who still goes to the Pentecostal Church on Brixton Road every Sunday, had no doubt about who was behind the victory. "I could not quite believe what happened to me out there on the pitch against United. But I am convinced that I did it with God's assistance. God helped me do this – as he always helps me. I will be saying prayers of thanks for what has occurred here."

The defeat saw United slip to second behind Leeds United,

the team who would eventually pip Ferguson's men to the title. Their star player was Eric Cantona.

"I recall those last few weeks of the 1991/92 season with shame and guilt," says Parker. It was seen as a real achievement to win the League Cup, but I can't believe we let Leeds overtake us to win the league. Maybe we lost our collective bottle. Maybe we didn't have the resolve or could deal with the pressure of playing for Manchester United or just a bit naïve. We didn't change tactics in key matches and lost games we might have drawn. We didn't know how to handle big matches and the title seemed as far away as ever. I know how we felt at the end of that season had a huge effect on our manager."

The end of the 1992 season saw Norman Whiteside's testimonial attended by an appalling 7,434 crowd. A day later, demolition work started on the Stretford End terrace. The crash barriers had already been removed days later when United's Class of 92 won the FA Youth Cup.

"When we returned for pre-season training, Sir Alex Ferguson had a right go," says Parker. "His message was loud and clear: no losers, no sulkers and make sure you don't fail this time. We did not. We were already mentally stronger and filled with a collective determination to right the wrongs of the previous season."

United started well, but subsequent goalscoring problems saw the club sign Eric Cantona.

"People always ask me about Eric," says Parker. "And I say that he was one of us. We'd all throw £10 in the kitty when we went out, but Eric put a bit more money in because he wanted to drink champagne and not beer. And plenty of it.

"We'd go to Mulligans or the Amblehurst Hotel in Sale. Sometimes we'd meet on a Sunday afternoon and have lunch and Viv Anderson would pop in too. We'd go out on Tuesday night because we had Wednesdays off. We'd go in the bars around Manchester like Henry's and Lloyd's. Peter Schmeichel, who had a heart of gold, couldn't handle his drink and we'd often send him home early. Jimmy McGregor, our physio, would call him 'The German' to rile him. To a proud Dane, that was a strong insult. Later we'd go to Yesterdays in Alderley Edge. It wasn't an issue, but it would be now. Could you imagine most of the United players going out together twice a month? For us, it was about being out together as a team. That was Robbo's thinking and Brucey carried that on. If one of the lads was being a bit silly or had had too much to drink then they'd be told to calm down. But you didn't want to get into that situation. You know that you are going to get crap from the manager, but it hurts more if you get it from your teammates because they are the people who you work with. If they came down on you then it wouldn't be forgotten."

People would frequently approach Parker in Manchester, especially after a beer. "My mates would say, 'Why are you talking to that pisshead?' but if people came up, were civil and weren't abusive, I'd have no problem chatting a while. If they were abusive I'd try to quell it. I wouldn't be rude to anyone unless they were rude to me. I wasn't big enough to fight. If people started getting abusive then I'd just walk away. Being a footballer was a 24/7 job and I accepted that. Now, supporters have been pushed away from the players, but when you are a player you see things differently.

"Everyone wants a bit of your time so you retreat a bit. If I left Old Trafford after a game, I'd always go for the side door with 30 people outside, rather than the main door with 100. I regret that a bit, but I suppose I was being sensible then."

A lot was made of the decline in Old Trafford's atmosphere during Parker's time at United. "I noticed it in my second season when the Stretford End wasn't there and it got worse and worse over the years, more so when I went back to watch matches. There's too many corporate fans who are more concerned about being inside Old Trafford than supporting the team. I've always said that fans should make Old Trafford more of a fortress than it is. Expectations rose to the point that fans expected to win every game. When visiting teams got on top, fans should have got behind United more and not turned on the team because away teams knew the crowd would turn against United. The atmosphere was much better at away games, where United fans were very loud."

Parker was a key performer, playing at right back behind Andrei Kanchelskis. "Andrei was a good player to play behind," he recalls. "He was so quick and strong that nobody expected me to overlap him. I was bought to defend, which I was comfortable doing, but I didn't expect any help from Andrei. He could speak hardly any English and was a mad driver in his powerful A4. I got to know a policeman from Stretford quite well. He told me that there was a speed camera outside the Gorse Hill pub on Chester Road, and that it kept catching Andrei speeding. The policeman used to get Andrei off all the time. There was another one which used to catch him near The Cliff. Andrei used to say, 'Me no care.' He didn't have a care in the world and was always smiling. He would drink vodka for fun and remains the only person I've ever seen to do keepie uppie with a medicine ball. Sparky had strong thighs, but not in comparison with Andrei. The boss tried to ban him doing it, but he'd carry on."

United was a happy camp, though there were moments of tension.

"We returned to the dressing room at half time in one game which we were losing," reminisces Parker. "The manager was not happy, especially as someone's mobile phone was ringing. It was at a time when everyone had a similar ring tone so I was really hoping it wasn't my phone. I checked in my pocket and it wasn't. Other lads did the same and sat back relieved when it wasn't theirs. Then a very nervous Brucey answered his phone and switched it off almost immediately. The manager grabbed the phone as Brucey explained that he needed to keep it on as his wife Janet was in hospital having an operation as she had a bad back.

"'I know four bad backs,' screamed the gaffer. 'Four bad defenders at the back.' With that he smashed Bruce's mobile on the floor."

Training, however, was usually a joy. "I enjoyed Kiddo's training because it was so varied. He was the best coach I came across in 20 years of football. He kept things simple and basic in the knowledge that if you were a Manchester United player, you were there on merit. It was assumed that you were a top-class player. Brian liked short, sharp sessions, always different and stimulating and there was never any time to relax.

"If you were not right then he could sense it in how you trained. He knew that if your head wasn't right then you couldn't play football. Hunger, fitness and desire only come if your head is on right. If Kiddo knew that you had a gripe with the boss, he would be the conduit between you and the boss. That's not to say that you couldn't go to the boss – you could, but there were times when it was better to trust Kiddo not to talk to the boss if you didn't want him to, as he would also offer the boss's perspective. If you'd made a mistake and been spotted out on a night when you shouldn't have been, Kiddo would let you know that the boss knew and perhaps suggest that you had a decent excuse. He'd even give you an excuse to use. He tried to help the players who worked under him. As a result, players would have run through a brick wall for Kidd."

As champions Leeds slipped to 17th in 1993, United's title rivals were Aston Villa and Norwich City. A key game was away at Norwich in March.

"There was a fearsome clash at half time between the boss and Paul Ince," says Parker. "Ince was getting the hair-dryer treatment for what the manager thought was a poor first-half performance. As the rest of us winced in our seats, Ince bit back. They stood head-to-toe in a most amazing slanging match with Ince saying that he'd never play for United again. It needed the pacifying qualities of Brian Kidd to get him on the pitch for the second half, cajoling him quietly and telling him how much the team needed him. Ince was never afraid to stand up for himself. He was also comfortably our best player after the break. At the end of the game, the manager was first to congratulate him."

If Parker was ever on the receiving end of the manager's ire, he would adopt a different approach. "I would bide my time and approach the manager and say, 'Boss, can I have a word?' There were never any rows and he would listen to my point of view and, if he was wrong, he would be gracious enough to admit it."

United duly won the league, sparking the best celebrations Parker has experienced. "Steve Bruce and his wife Janet had a friendly and open house," says Parker. "I lived over the road and often popped around after training for a chat. It was the natural venue for a party to celebrate winning the league then. The big surprise came when Oldham beat Villa, meaning that we would play Blackburn the following day at home as champions. People began to gather at Brucey's – only a few at first, but one by one the whole team arrived. Eric came in a taxi from his hotel in town and Andrei was the last to show. Supporters gathered outside and there were some TV cameras and press photographers. For a little while, we forgot about the game the next day and the drink meant we didn't tend to worry about it too much.

"It took an age to get to Old Trafford the following day because supporters clamoured around our cars near the stadium, scratching them with their belts. The boss gave his pre-match speech and one picture shows me yawning so that shows how I felt. That was countered by the buzz of adrenalin and the fact that we could relax and play without fear. All the games before that had been tense because of their importance.

"I caught Kevin Gallacher in the match and he should have had a penalty. Maybe the ref didn't see it. A defeat would have taken the shine off our celebrations so we made sure we got our act together after going a goal behind.

"Me and Pally had a £100 bet about who would score the most goals in the season and I was leading with a solitary goal. When he scored near the end I was the only player who was gutted. I've never been so close to winning a goalscoring competition in my life! Then again, there was little chance of Pally paying up. He would have bought me a box of crisps or something.

"I played in the 1993/94 double-winning season, but the celebrations couldn't compare with '92 because everyone had waited so long. The ground was full of Cantona flags and it was one hell of an evening. It still means a lot to me that I was one of the few to win the first Premiership trophy."

That summer, United visited South Africa for a pre-season tour. "I'd heard so many bad things about South Africa and didn't know what to expect," remembers Parker, "so I was amazed to see such a beautiful country. We met Nelson Mandela but I didn't appreciate the significance of meeting him until much later."

United played against Arsenal at Ellis Park, Johannesburg and the Kaizer Chiefs at the FNB Stadium, Soweto. The difference between the crowds at the two games was stark, a predominantly white crowd at Ellis Park contrasting with an almost all black crowd.

"The games were tough and put us in good shape for the double-winning season," recalls Parker. "We attracted a lot of attention, some of it for sitting around the hotel pool in shorts – it was winter in South Africa.

"The gaffer let us out a couple of nights and beer was 40 pence," adds a value-conscious Parker, "yet our hosts wouldn't let us spend any money."

Parker considers the season that followed as his best as a professional. "I still think about it all the time," he says. "I get emotional when I think about it. I played 56 United matches, the most productive year in terms of appearances and, at 29, I felt on top of the world. I was even recalled by England.

There were so many great United moments that season, and some nervy ones too like Galatasaray away."

United's visits to Turkey are now commonplace, but you never forget your first time. In 1993 United travelled to Galatasaray after a 3–3 draw at home in the first leg – a game notable for Peter Schmeichel accosting a protesting Kurdish student burning a Turkish flag on the pitch. United effectively needed to win the away game to progress to the Champions League stage and whilst it was always going to be tough, few realised just how tough.

"To this day it's the most hostile atmosphere that I've ever known," reckoned Gary Neville of that trip to Istanbul. "As we walked out into the stadium it was the most incredible noise I'd experienced in my life. I was only a young lad, but I probably learned more in ten minutes that night than I had in two years playing for the reserves."

At least Neville and Co got to experience the febrile atmosphere in the notorious Ali Sami Yen stadium – 164 innocent United fans were locked up and deported after being held in prisons around Istanbul for 24 hours. They missed a 0–0 game and Eric Cantona fighting with Turkish police. Galatasaray went through.

"There was a calm before the storm because the weather was great, the hotel was beautiful with really friendly staff," recalls Parker. "Their mood changed on the day of the game. They started asking us for tickets and things became obviously tense. We got to the stadium two hours before kick-off. I've never heard a noise like it in my life. One side of the ground sang a song, then the opposite side, then each end followed by the whole ground. It got nastier when the game started. Tugay was a great footballer, but he was a nasty little shit. He had a self-assured arrogance because he knew how good he was. His passing was immaculate.

"After the game, the police were supposed to be protecting us, but one of them whacked me as I went down the tunnel.

I would have fallen right down the steps if Peter hadn't stopped me."

The United players felt no safer on the coach. "Jubilant Galatasaray fans banged on the side, attempted to rock it and threw anything they could get their hands on while the police made no attempt to intervene. At the airport there was no security and we had to wait the best part of three hours before they allowed our plane to leave. I am never going back to Turkey. Never."

That Christmas, the players enjoyed a night at the Hacienda nightclub. "Robbo got us in there," says Robson. "It was full of students and we wondered why we were there. We all left together. Sparky was getting in a taxi with Incey. In a complete jokey way, he said, 'Come on Incey you black twat, let's go.' It's not PC, but he was joking. A bouncer came over and whacked Sparky for calling Incey. In return, Incey jumped into the commotion and went mad, confronting the bouncer and saying, 'He's my mate, don't hit my mate.' The bouncer apologised. Everyone found it hilarious."

While 1993/94 was disappointing for United in Europe, the team won the league and cup double. Sir Matt Busby also passed away in January 1994.

"Even City fans bowed their heads for a man who personified all that was great and good about Manchester United," says Parker. "All the players and the backroom staff went to his funeral. Our first match afterwards was at home to Everton and, such was the emotion, there was no way they were going to beat us. We pummelled them from the first whistle but only got one goal. Everton did not want to win and knew they could not. I have never witnessed an emotion-charged match like it."

The spring of 1994 saw United visit Wembley three times. They reached the League Cup final, but were defeated 3–1 by Aston Villa.

"Schmeichel was banned and we missed him," says Parker, "Villa were soon two goals up, but when Mark Hughes pulled one back with seven minutes left there was a genuine feeling we could go on and win." Unfortunately, a Dean Saunders penalty won the game for Villa and their manager Ron Atkinson.

"Mark Hughes got us into the FA Cup final, though, and so I thank him." United were playing Oldham Athletic in the semi-final. In an act of greed, the Football Association chose Wembley as the venue, despite United and Oldham being neighbours 200 miles north.

"Under Joe Royle, Oldham were always tough opponents in their three top-flight years," says Parker. "They made sure we didn't get a goal and the game went into extra time when they scored. In the dying seconds of extra time, Mark Hughes hit a stunning trademark volley from outside the area to equalise."

United overcame Oldham 4–1 in the replay at Maine Road to set up a final with Glenn Hoddle's Chelsea. "Chelsea wore awful lilac suits. I spoke to Nigel Spackman, who I had played with at QPR, and he said, 'We look like a Welsh choir.' It started to rain and their suits went blotchy. Chelsea should have been ahead at half time, but we dominated in the second half. Maybe the 4–0 scoreline flattered us, but we were worthy winners."

Parker puts the success down to having a talented and settled squad. "Roy Keane was an inspired signing too. Bryan Robson was 36 and coming towards the end of his career. From day one Roy was loud, opinionated and lovable. For the next 12 years he was the heart, soul and driving force of Manchester United. He was vilified by opposing supporters and adored by United fans. Roy liked a drink in the early days, but being the individualist he was, used to insist on walking home. As the rest of us piled into taxis or got lifts, Roy would set off into the darkness on his own, spurning all offers. We never knew why, perhaps to walk himself sober.

"On one occasion Roy set off home from Yesterdays in Alderley Edge to his home seven miles away in Hale. He showed up to training the next day with his face covered in scratches.

He was a bit coy about the reason. Then the police turned up and chatted to Sir Alex, leaving with the problem apparently sorted. Only then did Roy reveal how on the way home he'd had a fight. With a passing German. In some bushes. The German had complained to the police, but the matter didn't develop and become public. That was Roy – abrasive, belligerent and competitive. We loved being around him because he was always interesting, always doing something or saying something provocative. Once you were playing, there was no one you would have rather had on your side."

If 1994/95 was Parker's highlight in red, then the following season was a low point.

"My head wasn't right in the 1994/95 season. I was injured, going through a divorce, drinking and socialising far too much because I was feeling sorry for myself. I would arrive at The Cliff for physiotherapy, spend much of the day on my own and leave late.

"I felt like I had nothing to aim for. The team was doing well without me. Part of you doesn't want the team to do well without you, because it shows just how indispensable you are. It's selfish and it's wrong, but you want your place back. Miss ten games in a season and people start to murmur that you are injury-prone – you don't want that so you start to cut corners and take too many anti-inflammatories."

Parker had suffered from pain in his right ankle for over a year.

"I should have sorted it out, but Alex Ferguson wanted winners and I desperately wanted to be a winner for him. I was 30 and supposedly at the top of my profession. I had a good relationship with the manager, apart from the time I called him 'Taggart' after the Glaswegian TV detective in training. I regretted that straight away. The other lads had egged me on. It was the type of thing a 13-year-old would say to a teacher. The manager looked at me and called me a 'little fucking pygmy' which I suppose was fair in the circumstances.

"I went over on my ankle in a pre-season game and again a month later. I was sent off on the opening day of the season after coming on as substitute, banned and held back for European games because I was English. That's why I played in Barcelona. I had an operation which I never properly recovered from, mentally or physically. There were unexpected complications because the ligaments in my ankle had ruptured so it was clear I faced a long lay-off."

The match in Barcelona was pivotal for Parker's future. It has left mental scars. Just how great I find out when, back in Spain, I receive a text from Paul. It reads: "I'm in Barcelona next week. Can you take my son to see the Camp Nou?"

"No problem. Are you not going to go? "

"No," comes the reply. "I'll stay in town. I don't ever want to see that place again."

Parker has not been to the Camp Nou since November 1994, when he played in the United side which was demolished 4–0 by Barcelona.

"Fergie dropped Steve Bruce so that I could mark Romario," recalls Parker later. Indeed, Ferguson had described Parker as "the best player we have in this country to mark the best striker in the world" at the time, adding that very few players had Parker's discipline and mental toughness.

Romario had just starred in Brazil's 1994 World Cup triumph and was playing alongside the mercurial Bulgarian Hristo Stoichkov. The three-foreigner rule meant that Eric Cantona and Peter Schmeichel sat marooned in the stands.

"We were demolished," recalls Parker. "Romario gave us the run-around. He was quick, strong and you would have thought that his foot was a cushion because his first touch was so soft. I couldn't get near him, but then we had a pattern of play which we couldn't keep because of the foreigner rule. From that moment, my career at United as a frontline performer was over."

Parker was desperate. "I would give myself a fitness test at home on Friday night by bouncing up and down. I wanted to play for United. There's a buzz playing for United and you chase that when you don't have it. I'd ruptured ligaments and couldn't play. Other lads just played on. Steve Bruce used to say, 'I'm strapping up and going out.' And with that he'd strap up wherever needed strapping and go on the pitch."

Unable to recover properly, confidence spiralled downwards. "I was filled with pessimism and doubt and even when I started to return to something resembling full fitness I knew I wasn't the player I had been at my best."

With a contract due to expire in 1996, Parker was determined to be playing regularly, but United had moved on and a new team was taking shape. Gary Neville was coming through and Parker's chances were limited.

"I played my last game in a 4–1 defeat at Tottenham on New Year's Day 1996. I was poor. I knew it and so did the manager."

Parker did play in an FA Cup third round tie at a snowbound Reading in which he scored a rare goal. "Was it a shot or a cross?" asked Parker. "To anyone who does not know me it was a lovely sweeping shot to the keeper's right hand. To anyone who knows me it was a cross."

Still just 32, Parker was summoned to Old Trafford to see Sir Alex.

"I knew why he wanted to speak to me, but as the stadium loomed in front of me, I still hoped. One more year would be about right, I thought. Right for United and me."

There was no reprieve.

"Sir Alex got straight to the point and was honest as he had always been with me. He explained that Gary Neville was his number-one right back. I could feel myself filling up but I was determined not to cry in his presence. I said, goodbye and shook hands as I left the room as silently as I had entered it. To this day, I have never got over that moment of rejection."

"I look upon Paul's time with us in two ways," said Sir Alex Ferguson. "I remember what a superb servant he was for our club, but there is also a fair element of sadness about his short but great career. He was an extremely fit, athletic player, but he was blighted by injuries that ultimately forced him to retire early."

"Leaving Manchester United was my hardest moment at the club," says Parker. "Everyone welcomes you and helps you when you arrive at a club like United, but nobody prepares you for leaving. It takes time to for your ego to get over it and your emotions are everywhere. I wanted to get out of Manchester, which wasn't me because I like Manchester."

One newspaper offered Parker £20,000 to "say something nasty" about the club and those who ran it, "and it was an easy decision to reject them. I wouldn't say anything detrimental about United because that's not how I feel about them."

Marseille came in for Parker and he went to the Velodrome for a few days. The money would be the same as United and his ankle stood up well.

"I left and with handshakes all around. Joel Cantona, Eric's brother, told me how keen Marseille were about signing me. I was really looking to getting away from Manchester and living by the Med. Suddenly it was all off. I found out that my agent at the time had asked for another £50,000 and Marseille, understandably, wouldn't comply. I felt let down by him."

Parker went instead to less sunny Derby, where he rejoined Jim Smith. He played just four games.

"Next stop was Sheffield United, another club and another hotel to live in. My problem was that I still considered myself a Manchester United player. I wasn't. Where Keane and Ince would once receive my five-yard passes, I was now being advised to lump the ball 40 yards to a big target man. Derby and Sheffield United were big opportunities for me and I did not take them."

He was given the chance to return to his first club Fulham in March 1997, where he played three games before being sacked by Micky Adams.

"I was at such a low ebb, a burden on my partner Nicola, when the phone went. It was Chelsea."

Ruud Gullit, the manager, was straight to the point. "There were no promises, just that I was needed to cover for key defensive injuries until the end of the season. I played four games, but was cold-shouldered by Gullit, who had the worst man-management skills of anyone I had worked with."

Parker played his 404th and final league match for Chelsea against Middlesbrough in April 1997.

"A month later, Chelsea didn't want to give me a ticket for the 1997 Cup final when I was still on their books. I had to sneak on the players' coach and persuade an official to find me a seat. I felt so embarrassed. I finished playing at 33, but my passion and enthusiasm for the game died after I left Chelsea and I just wanted to get away from it all."

Chelsea won their first trophy in 26 years and, out of contract, Parker considered his future.

"I made a big decision in 1997 to pack football in," he says. "My ankle wasn't perfect. It still isn't and I know I'm going to have big problems in the future. Back then, I didn't want to let a club down by not being 100 per cent. I didn't want to go from club to club picking up a wage that I didn't deserve. I regret that now, I should have taken the money while I could. It hurt me to see my good friends playing on and on and winning trophies."

He managed, without distinction, at Chelmsford City and Welling United, while earning a name as an honest, informed analyst on television. He covered non-league for Setanta from 2007 until their demise in 2009 and found similarities with the top game.

"Players are the same at every level in that they don't like criticism – I didn't when I played. It's only when you stop playing that you realise constructive criticism is valid and part of the game.

"A lot of the players watch our coverage and some don't speak to me at games because they don't like what I've said."

Like one former York player who said he didn't like Setanta and didn't like Paul Parker.

"Their friends and family are often watching on television, sometimes for the first time and they don't like or expect to hear anything critical, no matter how constructively it's put.

"That's only the same as Rio Ferdinand, who completely blanked me and stared at the wall at Old Trafford after I made some comments on MUTV while Paul Scholes said 'Hello'. . . I would have done the same when I played.

"I still get asked for my autograph when I got to watch United," Parker says. "Then all of a sudden half of them will disappear because a current player has showed up. That hurts – when you realise that there's someone in front of you who is doing it now whereas you're history.

"Even though there is more media coverage, footballers have less personality than when I played. Interviews have become colour by numbers and clichéd. I'm tired of hearing players repeating, 'Wigan's a tough place to go.' I'd have more respect for a player saying, 'We're going to Wigan to win because we're a better side than them.'"

Parker has mainly fond memories of his five years at United.

"I'm proud when I look back at my time at Manchester United. Sometimes I'm a little bit jealous of others who were there longer. I should have saved some more money when I was at the height of my earning power at United, but I frittered it away on cars and a hectic social life.

"I should have realised that it was not going to last forever, but when you are young and fit you don't think further than the next day. A divorce didn't help my bank balance, either.

"I was fortunate though that I played for a successful Manchester United, because I've heard other very good players complain that they played for a great club at the wrong time. I was in the team which won the league for the first time in 26 years, the first United team to win the double. I'll never forget that."

Author's postscript

In June 2009, Setanta went bust. In August, I was woken at 5am by the following text message from Parker. "Hello Andy. At this moment [11am] I'm sitting on a beach in Bali! I'm just letting you know that from 25th August I will be abroad for at least eight months. Firstly in Darwin, where I will be coaching in the aboriginal communities and then in New Zealand where I'll work for SKY NZ and coach in two schools. Let me know when you are in the area."

8
LEE MARTIN
The unlikely hero

**LEE
MARTIN**
MANCHESTER UNITED

Passengers on the local train to the Cheshire town of Hyde one Saturday evening in 1990 had more to talk about than United's indifferent form. They were treated to the sight of emerging first-team defender Lee Martin, resplendent in his club tie and blazer, exercising in the aisle. "I started cramping up so I had to jump out of my seat and stretch just after Gorton. People looked at me, but what could I do? I'd just played 90 minutes. I couldn't see it happening today.

"I had an Escort Mark II which I had to park on a hill as it needed a jump start every morning. It was knackered for a few weeks so I used public transport to get to Old Trafford."

It was a very familiar journey. Martin had been travelling to watch United from his home in Hyde since the age of 12, taking a train to Piccadilly Station and switching to a bus from Piccadilly Gardens to Old Trafford to complete the hour-long trip. But now he was a first-teamer.

"I went to the game early so the bus wasn't full of fans," he remembers, "and I got off the bus outside the Lou Macari chippy and walked down Warwick Road with my boots in a bag."

It was very different after the game.

"I left the lads in the players' lounge afterwards and walked to the bus stop by the Dog and Partridge pub. This time the bus and train was full of fans. Even though we weren't playing that well, the fans were fine and just asked me about the match."

Martin was born in the pleasant and, on the surface at least, quiet working-class town of Hyde in 1968.

"I had a good upbringing. Mum was the secretary at the school I went to until I was 11, so I was always very settled there. My dad was an engineer who worked really hard all his life for little money. He grafted 12 hours a day, six days a week from 14 until 65. Dad would be coming home from work as I went to bed. They're both still in Hyde, happy as ever."

Hyde, on the edge of the Pennines, achieved unwanted notoriety twice in the last century from its associations with gruesome murder cases. Britain's most prolific serial killer Harold Shipman had his doctor's surgery in the town and murdered most of his suspected hundreds of victims there. And during the 1960s, the Moors murderers Myra Hindley and Ian Brady lived on the town's Hattersley Estate, where police found the remains of 17-year-old Edward Evans.

Boxer Ricky Hatton lives in Hyde but the town has also earned its place in football history. An explosion in a local coal mine in 1889 saw Ardwick and Newton Heath, the teams which would become Manchester City and Manchester United, play a charity game to raise money for the victims' families. It was the first time that either had played under lights and 10,000 watched the game – 9,900 of them Ardwick fans, underlining how they were considered the biggest club in the world around that time.

Two years earlier, the local team Hyde FC lost 26–0 to Preston North End in an FA Cup game – still the largest defeat in English professional football. In recent years, United's reserves have played at Hyde's Ewen Fields ground.

"Hyde was a good place to grow up," says Martin. "It was close to Manchester and Old Trafford. There was a big field behind our street and I spent hours playing football there. I was a good child. Once, my older sister crayoned all around the walls. I was accused and pasted for it, but then my parents realised that I wasn't tall enough to crayon so far up the wall.

"My dad took me to United reserve games from the age of six or seven because it was very cheap to watch. From the age of 11 or 12 I would go with friends and watch the first team – players like Steve Coppell, Gordon Hill and Sammy McIlroy. The buses to the ground were full of young lads from all over Manchester. Hill was my idol, a great player in an exciting team. United didn't have much success, but they were great to watch."

Martin would arrive early at Old Trafford. "I would queue to get into the Stretford End and then stand at the front of the terrace for two hours until the game started. Once you had your spot, you could not leave it. Mine was right behind the goal in the open, so I'd get wet but I didn't care. The atmosphere used to build slowly and we'd all sing songs. By kick-off time the noise would be really loud, especially against Liverpool or City. It was great."

Martin was showing signs of having an above-average football talent, though he would find it tough to impress those who might promote his career. Throughout it, he had to struggle against an often lukewarm assessment of his potential to make it as a professional. Naturally diffident about his own achievements and also disarmingly modest, it must have taken some effort to force himself forward.

"I was a striker who scored a lot of goals for the school team, around 50 a season including my Sunday team. But when it came to the county trials I was always on the bench. The man who ran it pulled me to one side and told me to concentrate on my schoolwork because I'd never make it as a footballer.

It was a strange thing to say; I thought coaches were meant to encourage people. I always looked back to that comment to inspire me."

Martin made the most of one 30-minute substitute appearance against Oldham. "I scored a hat-trick," he recounts, with his usual understatement. "Talk about right place at the right time because there were four or five scouts there. One of them was from United so that was that."

Martin was asked to go to The Cliff training ground for a week. He duly got on a bus with a suitcase containing enough clothes for seven days.

"They read everyone's name out to say which rooms we were sleeping in, but not mine. They'd wanted me to travel each day from home, but changed their mind when they saw me with my suitcase and put me in accommodation with the other lads behind the old Manchester racecourse in Salford. The trial was a success and I started training three times a week. We received two complimentary tickets for each home game, so that was a bonus for a match-going fan like me."

Although Martin is remembered as one of first crop of 'Fergie's Fledglings', who were the initial products of Alex Ferguson's reorganisation of United's youth set-up, he actually first came to United when Ron Atkinson was in charge. Training took place on the shale pitch at The Cliff in Salford, a place noted for its accessibility to the public, a world away from the tight security of the new facility at Carrington.

"There would be all kinds of people turning up to train. People like Mike Sweeney [a Salford Red and local media personality], who would throw himself into challenges against the young lads."

Martin continued there until he finished school where he picked up one O level in PE. Only recently has he finally passed more GCSEs, returning to education to gain the qualifications to pursue a second career in teaching. He also (demonstrating once again his lack of arrogance) went for an interview at British Aerospace in Woodford in case United didn't offer him a contract, but didn't get the job.

"Even up to the age of 16, I didn't see myself as a future Manchester United player," he explains. "I didn't consider myself special and that was brought home to me when I was only offered a one-year Youth Training Scheme contract, while all the other young players apart from the goalkeeper Gary Walsh were offered two-year apprenticeships. I was on £27 a week – I gave my mum £15 for rent and my bus pass was £7 so I had a fiver spare each week. It actually seemed like enough."

Walsh, who would go on to enjoy a long career as a goalkeeper, had grown up in Wigan and played rugby for Wigan and Lancashire. He claimed that if United hadn't approached him at 14, he would probably would have played rugby league professionally.

United had also signed Walsh in bizarre circumstances. "I went to watch my mate play for Wigan under-14s but the goalkeeper didn't turn up and I was asked to go in net," said Walsh. "By chance, United's scouts were watching and they returned two games later and asked me to sign."

Again, Lee refused to be discouraged by the implied lack of faith in the shorter contract: both he and Gary Walsh used it to motivate them – they were the only two from that 32 whoever made the first team.

"I've got happy memories of playing in the youth team," says Martin. "The camaraderie in the team was superb and we'd sing on the bus to matches. We went on a tour to Switzerland aged 16, where we were allowed two pints one night after the competition had finished. Only we drank for four hours and played terribly the next day. Our coach Eric Harrison looked me in the eye at half time and told me that I wouldn't be at the club much longer. We were brilliant in the second half and won the game . . ."

Despite the oft-repeated assertions that manager Ron Atkinson neglected the youth set-up at Old Trafford, United had an accomplished youth side and reached the Youth Cup final against Manchester City in 1986.

"We drew 1–1 at Old Trafford and lost at Maine Road. City had a very good side containing players like Paul Lake, Andy Hinchcliffe, Steve Redmond and David White. They were our big rivals, but we respected them because we knew that they were decent players."

Harrison, the coach largely credited with developing United's class of '92, was in charge.

"He was tough to play for, but he was a great man," says Martin. "Training was hard every day and we knew that we would get a bollocking if we didn't put the effort in. We trained twice a day every day. The environment was tough and competitive, but it created first-team players for Manchester United so it was going to be."

When Alex Ferguson took over in November 1986, he had served notice that there would be a significant shift from the Atkinson regime.

"He got every player at the club together at the start and told them that things were going to change," recalls Martin. "He said that training would be changing and that there would be new people coming to the club like a dietician. He was very impressive."

Harrison also switched Martin, still far off the first team, to left back, a position into which he would settle and establish himself in United's reserves.

"I was more than happy with that," he says. "We had a good group of lads who were slightly mischievous. Because he was small, we once put Russell Beardsmore in a kit bag and carried him into the middle of a busy road. Cars were having to drive around the bag, with no idea that there was someone inside."

Beardsmore, who would enjoy fleeting success with United's first team, was not averse to playing the odd practical joke himself. "He once threw a snowball at Sir Alex at the training ground. He hit him on the head and Fergie was fuming, but had no idea where it had come from. Russell hid behind a car and the manager never found out who had thrown it. It was a good job because it was like a ball of ice with stones in it.

"We used to lock people in the sauna at The Cliff. I've been locked in there for an hour many a time, before staggering out dizzy and confused. We once put Billy Garton in for over two hours. He was stumbling around when he came out and about three stones lighter."

Martin was pulled away from his reserve teammates when he was asked to go on tour with the first team to Scandinavia in 1988. "I thought it was to carry the kit bag and help out," he recalls. "I actually played every game on the tour in several positions. I was only 19, but I got a couple of man of the match awards."

This was not his first team debut, however. "I came on for the last ten minutes in the last game of the previous season against Wimbledon at home. I replaced Remi Moses and United were leading, but it was all a bit of a blur and Old Trafford was far from full – there were less than 30,000 in there.

"Wimbledon were a physical team and I remember watching the match from the bench in trepidation because they were clattering all the United players. Wimbledon were very aggressive and played a lot of little mind games too – they had a stereo on full blast in their dressing room and left the door open in an attempt to unnerve opponents. Millwall were the same, as if they wanted to live up to their hard-man image."

After appearing in a few more friendly games in England, Lee was called into Sir Alex Ferguson's office before the first league game of the 1988/89 season against Queen Park Rangers. United had finished the previous season strongly and surged up to second place behind champions Liverpool, so optimism was high.

"The manager told me matter-of-factly that I'd be playing the next day. I nodded and then ran out of his office to the bus stop, travelled home and ran from the bus stop to tell my mum and dad. I was so excited that I was going to play. My parents were delighted and told me to stay calm, but I could see that my dad wasn't calm. He was pacing around and smoked a lot. He hardly ever smoked, but he was very nervous for me. I hardly slept that night."

The following day was one of the hottest of the year. "I was absolutely terrified that I would have to talk to people like Bryan Robson in the dressing room," he says. United drew 0–0 and the £100-a-week full back from Hyde performed well.

"I did all right," Martin says, once again very modestly, of his role in a line-up which featured Leighton, Blackmore, Bruce, McGrath, McClair, Robson, Strachan, Davenport, Hughes and Olsen. Martin didn't keep his place for the following week and was limited to a couple of appearances as United suffered from a poor start to the season.

"I didn't even want to move from the reserve-team dressing room. When I did, I didn't speak for a month. As I played more games and got to know people better, I relaxed and came out of my shell. Gary Pallister probably brought me out of my shell more than anyone – and he didn't sign for a year after my first-team debut." Bryan Robson once commented that there was a joke among the other players that Lee Martin had a one piece zip-up suit because he was always showered and dressed and ready to leave before anyone else – Robbo wasn't to know that this speed probably came from shyness.

Lee was selected to start against Liverpool on New Year's Day 1989, a game which surpassed all expectations, and which started the 'Fergie's Fledglings' bandwagon rolling in the media. "I had to mark John Barnes, who was arguably the best player in the league," says Martin. "He was at his peak, but I did well and contained him and my teammates did even better. We were expected to lose, but we won 3–1 with a really young side, which included Russell Beardsmore among the goalscorers." Martin still has a video of the game, which he pulls out from his collection as we speak and promises to watch again.

A week later, United played Queens Park Rangers in an FA Cup third-round tie. Injuries meant Ferguson fielded another very young side, including Martin.

"Again, we were the underdogs," explains Martin, "I remember reading in one newspaper that we didn't have a chance, but we finally went through after three games. There was a real buzz about us at that time and I loved it because I'd played with all these lads in the reserves. All of a sudden, I was playing with my mates for United."

The team included Tony Gill, the Bradford-born defender, who would make 14 appearances for the first team until injury would force him to retire at 22. "Tony was the first one of us to get into the first team, when he played against Southampton away at the start of 1987. When we saw him in the team, it showed all the other young lads that we could reach it too."

Alex Ferguson was later to regret that United's parlous problems with injuries – which critics were quick to point out hit hard as there was a lack of cover in the squad – forced him to press promising youngsters into service too early, with a damaging effect on their careers. He saw the fate of many of these 'Fledglings' as a repeat of what had happened when he was put in the same situation when managing at Aberdeen. It is the case that some of these young players suffered physically, but there were also consequences for their confidence and self-belief. Nor were they allowed the luxury of making their mistakes in a successful team, given time to find their feet and mature like Ferguson's later protégés.

Tony Gill, for example, broke his leg in an away game against Nottingham Forest in 1989. Lee remembers what happened vividly. "I was playing left back and he was playing left midfield. I saw the tackle from Brian Laws: it was awful. He came straight through him and shattered his ankle. Tony never played again after that. He was taken to hospital in Nottingham and then we picked him up on the coach on the way home. It was a shame because he had the potential to go on and become one of the top players."

Two of those who did prosper made very different first impressions. "I can remember Lee Sharpe on his first day training with the first team. He was totally overawed and didn't want to get involved because the standard was so high after coming from Torquay.

"But I knew after watching Ryan Giggs at 13 that he would be a great Manchester United player. He's the only player I've ever said that about, but I watched him most weeks when he was a youngster at United and he stood out a mile. Scholesy had something special, but Giggs was guaranteed to become a star. In later years I would mark him in training and he would destroy me. Andrei Kanchelskis was also a nightmare to mark because his feet were so quick. I can remember the manager fuming with Andrei during one game. The only problem was that Andrei couldn't speak English, so the manager had a real go at his interpreter [George Scanlon, the former captain of the Cambridge University team who went on to become a Dean of Faculty at Liverpool University]. Fergie was shouting, 'Tell him that he's fucking useless.' Andrei was just sat there smirking."

By this time, Martin had bought his own flat in Glossop. He preferred the odd drink in a pub in the Derbyshire market town to the glitzier city centre and Cheshire scenes preferred by the more established first-teamers.

"There was a drinking culture which Sir Alex Ferguson addressed," says Martin, "but I've got to say that the lads who drank the most were also Manchester United's best players and never let us down on the pitch. It was what teams did then – Liverpool drank a lot and it created more camaraderie than problems."

There was further pressure on Martin. As a home-grown player, he felt that he had to be the perfect professional because the manager would come down harder on the players who had come through the youth system.

"There were many times when he came up to my face and had a go. I didn't reply, because ultimately I knew that he wanted me to do well. Sometimes he was looking for a reaction – not direct back to him, but in my game. It wasn't nice at times. There were some Saturdays when I went home doubting that I'd ever play for United again, but on Monday morning the manager would say 'Hello' and everything would be forgotten. You'd then look forward to seeing the team sheet pinned up again to see if you were in the first team."

There were plenty of wise old sages on hand to offer advice if Martin was left out.

"Jim Ryan [a coach and later Ferguson's assistant] would tell me that if I worked hard then I'd get back into the first team and he was usually right." Martin played more games for United in 1989/90 than any other season.

"I know everyone remembers it for the FA Cup win, but we really struggled that season in the league," he recalls. "We were 16th at one point and the fans were not happy. That was understandable. We were struggling to score goals and sometimes we were that bad that we struggled to put three passes together. Personally, I would put myself under too much pressure because I wanted to succeed, but there are times when you need to be relaxed and not tense if you are going to be on the top of your game."

Martin had seen some of his former reserve mates progress to the first team, like striker Mark Robins. "I was sharing a room with Mark Robins before one away game at Nottingham Forest," he recalls. "The players were not allowed to use room service, but me and Mark ordered a pint of milk each. They were delivered, but the manager saw what was happening. He took the milk and poured it down the sink and told us never to order from room service again. Then he stormed out."

Robins and Martin were close. "Like me, he'd trained at United since he was 12 so we became good mates. Mark wasn't great outside the box, but he was a great goalscorer in it."

Martin also roomed with Neil Webb, who was signed from Nottingham Forest with great expectations, but who never seemed to fit in at Old Trafford. "He had a bottle of wine in the room the night before one game in London, which you were not supposed to do. Later that night, I saw him crawling around the room on his hands and knees. I don't know if he was sleepwalking or not, but it was strange. Neil was a nice bloke. He had a tough time with injuries and I don't think that he saw eye to eye with the manager, but I'll always remember him for the ball he played to me in the 1990 FA Cup final."

United were desperate by the time the 1990 FA Cup started, with speculation rife that Ferguson was about to be sacked. A tough draw away to Nottingham Forest didn't lift the mood, but 7,000 Reds travelled across the Peak District to support their hapless heroes.

"All the talk was about the manager being sacked. I saw the banners calling for him to be sacked and realised that he'd already had three years in charge but it was a crunch time for the players too," recalls Martin. "Our reputations and careers were on the line. We'd had a crap season and it would not have been acceptable to be knocked out at the first stage."

United won 1–0 and were drawn against Fourth Division Hereford United in the next round.

"The manager wasn't there that day, so the assistant manager Archie Knox took control. He got us together in a tiny dressing room and said, 'I don't care how you play: I just want to see us in the next round.' We walked out onto the pitch and there was a big bull on it, some kind of mascot. The pitch was dreadful. There had been floods locally and I remember the car park being under water. It was touch and go whether the game would be played. We were desperate to play, because we were desperate."

With five minutes to go, the score was 0–0. As the home fans in the 13,777 crowd sang *You'll Never Walk Alone*, captain Mike Duxbury set up Clayton Blackmore for the only goal of the game. "It was a tight one," says Martin. "And I remember someone blowing a whistle in the crowd during the game and everyone stopped. One of their players carried on and took a shot. Luckily, Jim Leighton was more alert and he saved it. If ever we ground a result out, that was it. We returned to the dressing room and Archie congratulated us. He said, 'You did what I asked: you're in the hat for the next round.'"

In the fifth round United drew Newcastle United away. "The game was on a Sunday and I went out for a few beers on the Friday for a mate's birthday. I had five or six pints during the day and boarded the coach to Newcastle the next day with a slightly thick head."

It was also one of Mike Duxbury's final outings for United, the Lancashire-born defender making 378 appearances between 1980 and 1990, as well as earning seven England caps.

"Mike was a lovely, gentle guy," recalls Lee. "He was a great player who really helped me out and encouraged me. He never got flustered about anything and never called anybody.

"I started the game on Sunday, but didn't play well. The manager went for me at half time and I fell backwards into the piles of clothes. He said, 'You've got five minutes to improve or you are off.' I did much better in the second half and we won 3–2 – a great result at Newcastle. Fergie apologised to me after the game, explaining once again that it was all said in the heat of the moment.

"Mark Robins, Brian McClair and Danny Wallace scored that day and Danny's goal was an absolute cracker." Martin speaks warmly of Danny Wallace, another of those whose career at United never developed as expected, though for very different reasons.

Wallace, a pacey winger, was given his debut at Southampton aged only 16. He was signed by Ferguson in 1989 and scored on his United debut. He played a pivotal role in the 1990 FA Cup campaign, though his finest performance in a United shirt probably came in the 6–2 League Cup win at Arsenal in the same year where he scored one goal and was involved in another four, shining on the left as Lee Sharpe ran riot on the right.

Wallace left United to go to Birmingham City in 1993 after suffering several debilitating injuries – and these continued. He thought he was just unlucky, but it was the beginnings of multiple sclerosis. After diagnosis, it took him five years to talk publicly about his disease. "I don't know why," he said, "but I was embarrassed. People used to see me playing football, running up and down beating players. I didn't want to become known as the man who needed a cane to walk." A reticence about injury and illness pervades British football, and professionals often prefer to try to go on, frequently aggravating conditions, rather than appearing weak or work-shy or risk losing their place.

Despite continuing poor form in the league, United continued to progress in the Cup. "We beat Sheffield United away in the sixth round, meaning that we didn't play a single game at Old Trafford in the 1990 FA Cup run and met Oldham in the semi-final at Maine Road," continues Martin.

Oldham Athletic, under manager Joe Royle, were good enough to reach the top flight at the start of the 1990s. They were also an outstanding cup side, as United would find out. Players like Frankie Bunn, Roger Palmer and Earl Barrett sound as if they should be *Viz* characters, but they were Paul Scholes's childhood heroes who provided great excitement in the town of chimneys as average gates surged from 5,000 to 13,000.

"The gaffer called me in before the semi-final and told me that I would be playing. Colin Gibson was dropped and he wasn't happy. We drew 3–3 in the first game at Maine Road and Oldham were excellent. Denis Irwin was there and other top players like Mike Milligan and Rick Holden. Mark Robins came on for me and gave the ball away soon after, which led to a goal. He came back into the dressing room to a huge bollocking."

Robins would have a better replay, when he again replaced Martin as Ferguson looked for a winning goal. "When Mark replaced me, he didn't give the ball away that time, but scored the winner which put us through to the final. Some United fans invaded the pitch and carried him off like a hero. We sat in the bath with the other lads celebrating and Mark and I couldn't believe it. We'd played together as kids, in youth and then reserve teams. And now we were going to Wembley to play in the FA Cup final."

The build-up to the 1990 FA Cup final was intense. For the first time in five years, the country's biggest club had a chance of winning a trophy.

"It was non-stop with the media," says Martin. "There were countless interviews and photos after training, especially with the bigger players, where we talked about what we thought would happen in the final against Crystal Palace. I enjoyed it all."

He was inundated with requests for cup final tickets.

"People I'd not seen for years came out of the woodwork and were asking me. The players were supposed to be getting 100 tickets each, but were told that our allocation was being cut to 25 each. I had to tell a lot of people to whom I'd promised tickets that I couldn't get them."

United's cup final base was at Burnham Beeches, a four-star hotel west of London that was favoured by final teams.

"We travelled down on Thursday and the team was read out by the manager the day before the game. When my name was read out, Mark Hughes pulled me to one side and said, 'Make sure you enjoy it because you might never be lucky enough to come back.' That was very good advice and I listened. Mark was a quiet lad, completely different to how he was on the pitch, but he'd chip in with odd bits of advice which I appreciated.

"Walking out at Wembley Stadium before the cup final remains the greatest memory in my life," he says. "The excitement, the expectation and the sense of achievement all came together. My friends and family were all there. It was sunny and the noise from 80,000 was really loud. There were flags and royalty to meet, plus the national anthem and *Abide With Me*. It was everything that I ever dreamed of and it was coming true."

Martin was anxious as the game started. "I was so nervous in the first five minutes of the game, but then I hit a long cross-field ball which found the man and I relaxed. We were 3–2 down after Ian Wright had scored in extra time and we needed something special. We were shattered, gone. The grass was long, the pitch big. I came off in extra time with cramp and my legs were absolutely shot. Luckily, we had players in our side like Mark Hughes and Bryan Robson who could save us and that's what Hughes did."

The United party had reserved a London hotel for a possible celebration dinner. "We went there after the draw but it was quite low-key as we had nothing to celebrate." They flew back to Manchester on Sunday morning and returned to London on Wednesday, the day before the replay. "The manager pulled me to one side and asked if I was going to be OK for the game," says Martin. "My legs were shattered and I was worried that I was going to get cramp, but I said I was fine."

Martin had never scored for United and was quoted as a 60/1 outsider to do so by the bookies. Even the United goalkeeper's odds were 50/1 – but that position was a source of fresh contention.

"Jim Leighton was told that he was dropped after his performance on Saturday and he didn't take it well," says Martin. "I saw Jim's face as he walked away from the meeting in which the team was to be named. He was crushed, but you would be, wouldn't you? I'd roomed with Jim and he was a good lad. I personally thought that he didn't deserve to be dropped, but in hindsight it was the right decision. Les Sealey was to replace him and that was a surprise because he was only on loan from Luton. All of a sudden he was going to play in the FA Cup final."

The 1990 FA Cup final replay provided Martin with his greatest moment. "It was a totally different game to the first one," he says. "Palace tried to kick us into the stands, which I didn't expect from one of Steve Coppell's teams. In the second half, with the score at 0–0, Archie Knox shouted from the bench 'Get forward!' I presumed that he meant me, so I moved forward. Neil Webb got the ball in midfield and picked a great ball out onto my chest. I half-volleyed it and it went into the top corner. Get in! As I hit the ball, I got cramp."

The television commentary summed it up thus: "An inspired run from the full back on the far side . . . a chance . . . AND A GOAL!"

Martin remembers, "The goal came after 61 minutes but by then I was really struggling. It was my 41st first-team game of the season. I'm sure they were thinking of bringing me off and there were a few times when Palace players got behind me. I was just waiting and praying for the final whistle. When it came, that was it; that was the moment when I first began to celebrate properly.

"Viv Anderson came to me and had me in a headlock, which actually hurt. All the lads were jumping on top of me, before I was rushed off into the tunnel to do a television interview live on BBC. It's probably the worst interview I've done, I was 21 and not really used to the media and so all my answers were really short."

Martin returned from the interview to walk up the steps to the Royal Box and lift the FA Cup.

"All the fans were congratulating us and throwing scarves for us to wear," he recalls. "Then we did a lap of honour; it was brilliant. That was my only proper goal for Manchester United. There was another one which was credited to me against West Ham, but Alvin Martin played it onto my knee and it ricocheted into the goal." He had made history of a sort, becoming the first left back to score the winner in an FA Cup final.

After winning their first trophy of what would be a hugely successful 1990s, the United party had chartered a train to take them straight back to Manchester. "We got to Euston Station and were told that it was to be a dry train, but Bryan Robson was not having any of that. He managed to acquire several crates of beer from somewhere, which we drank all the way back to Manchester. Everybody was celebrating and Bobby Charlton congratulated me. My parents were with me and I could see that they were so proud. We got back to Manchester about 2am. A few of the lads carried on the celebrations, but I went home. Some of the neighbours had written messages of congratulations in chalk on the driveway."

Lee, whose dressing room nickname was 'Schnozzer', was given ample opportunity to display his prominent schnoz on the front page of several national newspapers the following day from *The Times* to *The Sun*. The media descended on his Glossop flat at the crack of dawn. "They were taking pictures of everything, my car and my dog, a Doberman."

Although he wasn't used to commanding attention, Martin enjoyed the moment. The goal which sealed Sir Alex's Ferguson's first trophy was rewarded by the United manager, who told him to come to his office to talk about a new contract the following Monday.

"I was on £300 a week when I scored that goal, so me and my dad talked about what I should ask for," recalls Martin. "I didn't have an agent. We agreed that we'd ask for £1,000 a week and a car. We walked into see the manager, who said, 'I'm going to give you £600 a week for three years.' Me and my dad just nodded and agreed. Dad was a bit in awe of him and he didn't want to jeopardise my chances by asking for more money. There was appearance money on top of that, so I would earn over £1,000 a week if I was in the first team."

The future looked very bright and Martin enjoyed the summer of 1990 and returned for pre-season training.

"Everything was going well pre-season. I honestly thought that I was going to play for Manchester United for ten years. Then I felt a pain in my back during a match against Waterford in Ireland. I came off, but I was still in pain the next day and I had no idea what I'd done. I was sent back to Manchester for treatment the next day, but I continued to struggle."

That seemingly innocuous twinge against the £20-a-week part-timers of Waterford United, in front of 4,750 people at Kilcohan Park, would be the first time Martin suffered the injury which would define his future football career and, by default, his life.

"I came back to play against City away nearly three months later and I didn't do too well." Despite Martin's uncomfortable memories, United fans have a happier recollection of that game. City raced into a 3–1 lead, with their fans thinking that they were on the way to repeat the 5–1 scoreline of 1989, before two late Brian McClair goals levelled the score and led United fans to sing, to the tune of *Blue Moon*, "Blue Moon, you started singing too soon; You thought you'd beat us 3–1, now Howard Kendall has gone."

For Lee, there was no great celebration as he faced an operation in which two discs were taken out of his back. "They said it was wear and tear, which was worrying at 22," he states. "I'd be able to play for six months and then my back would seize up and I wouldn't be able to move for a couple of weeks."

Although Martin came back into the side for a spell midway through the 1990/91 season and was a regular in United's 1991 European Cup Winners' Cup success, injuries continued to hamper him – that and the fact that Clayton Blackmore was having an outstanding season at left back. Ferguson later singled out an error he made in a European tie as a turning point in his development. "Lee Martin," he wrote, "was terribly unlucky in presenting Montpellier with their equaliser. There seemed to be no danger when he freakishly sliced the ball past Les Sealey. Lee was not the most confident of people and that blunder was the last thing he needed in a season already blighted by injury." The manager had predicted that Martin would develop into a defender of international calibre, but now opined that his progress had worryingly ground to a halt.

"I think the manager wanted to keep me because I was English," is Lee's verdict. Indeed, the full back had played for England under-21s. "I went with people like Paul Merson to places like Albania, where soldiers with guns sat on street corners. That was a bit different from Hyde."

United then bought Denis Irwin from Oldham Athletic for a £625,000 fee in the summer of 1991, and other competition for the full-back slots followed. "Irwin was in my position and I could understand why he was bought. There was no rivalry between me and Denis: I really liked him, though obviously I wanted to be playing myself. Paul Parker arrived too, another full back and another great player."

Striker Dion Dublin also came from Cambridge United to beef up United's forward line. "Dion was very unlucky," says Martin. "He was a big gentle giant and I had a lot of time for him. We played a lot of reserve-team games together. It was such a shame that he broke his leg after so few United performances."

Martin remained positive about his own future. "I'm an optimistic person and always thought that I would get back in the first team. Jim Ryan kept encouraging me and told me that I was playing well and close to getting back in. I knew that myself. If you're good enough at United, then you play – the manager is very fair like that. Hearing that encouragement from Jim Ryan kept me going."

Martin became a reserve-team regular. He featured just three times in the first team in 1991/92 and twice in 1992/93, against Torpedo Moscow at home in the UEFA Cup and Brighton away in the League Cup in what was David Beckham's debut. The following season, 1993/94, he started five games for United, three in the League Cup and in the European Cup in the 3–3 draw against Galatasary at Old Trafford, a match which saw arguably the loudest away fans at Old Trafford and Peter Schmeichel apprehend a Kurdish protestor on the pitch.

"One thing I noticed was the research which the manager had done on the opponents." Martin adds. "Every time I played, he told me in depth about the player I was to play against. The manager's attention to detail was staggering."

In 1993/94, Martin also appeared in his only Premiership game, a 1–0 win at Goodison Park. "It felt great to be part of that great squad which went on to win the double."

When it came, Martin's departure from United, after 104 first-team appearances, in January 1994 was swift.

"I was on a weekly contract when Lou Macari, who had just been made Celtic manager, called me and asked me to sign. I thought it was Gary Walsh winding me up and I hung up, but it was Lou and he called me straight back. I agreed to join over the phone and explained that I would tell the manager the following day. I thought that would be a formality, but the manager went mad and said, 'Who do you think you are? You're going nowhere: you've got a reserve-team game tomorrow and you'll be reporting for it at five o'clock.'"

Half an hour later, the phone went. It was Sir Alex. "'Sorry about that,' he said. 'If you need any help with the move then I can give it to you. If you want me to come up to Glasgow with you then I will.' I was happy again and appreciated his offer of help – he's a busy man."

Martin flew north to Glasgow, where Celtic offered him £1,000 a week and a £50,000 signing-on fee. Celtic proposed a £250,000 transfer fee, but United asked for £500,000 before a fee of £350,000 was decided by tribunal.

"It was the first time I'd ever made a chunk of money in my career," Martin explains. "I put a bit into a pension and bought a car. I should have put it all away, but when you're young you don't think about the future."

He played his first Celtic game against Aberdeen the day after signing. "I played really well and set a couple of goals up for Charlie Nicholas," he explains. "Then I played every game until the end of the season. We had a decent side with Pat Bonner and Paul McStay."

Life as a footballer in Glasgow was an eye-opener, even for someone who had been at one of the top English clubs.

"I had a few phone calls in the middle of the night where people said, 'Fuck off back, you English bastard.' It was probably Rangers fans and when I arrived I was given information about certain areas and pubs to stay away from. I never told anyone at the club about the calls, I just thought that it was part and parcel of being an Old Firm player. Living in Cumbernauld outside Glasgow, I also felt quite safe and out of the Glasgow goldfish bowl."

That summer, Celtic went on a tour to Canada, where Macari found out that he was being dismissed, to be replaced by Tommy Burns. "Tommy told me that I was part of his plans, but then I broke my leg after getting my studs caught in the turf at Hampden Park. That ruined 1994/95."

Martin got himself fit by the next pre-season. "I was flying and we went on tour to Hamburg, but I broke my arm during a game against St Pauli.

"That ruined that season. I was so frustrated, but when I got fit I went on loan to Huddersfield and Coventry, where Gordon Strachan was manager. I had a really good run down there."

He returned to Celtic, where the back problems returned. "I went for more surgery and was told I would be able to play in two months. By that time my contract was up at Celtic, but I was told that I would go onto a weekly contract once I was fit again. Fair enough. I returned to Manchester for the summer, where I received a letter from Celtic saying that they no longer required my services. There was no phone call or anything. It was a nightmare: I was without a club or contract and with a dodgy back."

Martin sat down and wrote a letter, which he posted to all 92 league clubs in England. "I'd played for two of the biggest clubs in the world and it was demeaning, but what could I do? These days, an agent would fix clubs. I received a few letters back and before I knew it I was driving down to Mansfield, who offered me £600 a week. Then I went to Leyton Orient, who offered me a trial, which I wasn't keen on. I felt I was worth a contract. I had a call from Bristol Rovers and started to drive there from Leyton. I arrived late and took a hotel. The following morning, I met the Rovers manager Ian Holloway at the training ground. He said, 'We definitely want to sign you. Come and train with us for a week and see how you like it. If it feels right, then sign.' I liked him straight away and he remains the most enthusiastic man I've ever come across."

Martin enjoyed his week with Bristol. His back was "OK", but not 100 per cent.

"Ian called me into his office and offered me a three year contract worth £1,100 a week, plus bonuses, plus perks. I'd never earned that much money, but in the back of my mind I was worrying about whether to tell Ian about my back. I had my medical and that went fine. They knew the history with my back too. In the end, I told Ian that I would sign for two years and take it from there."

Martin started the first 16 games of the season. "I liked the club and the players. I love Ian Holloway: he was fun to be around, great in training and his team talks were inspirational. You would leave the dressing room convinced that you could beat anyone. My problem was that my back was giving me so much pain that I needed to take a lot of painkillers. I could barely move the day after matches. I then finally explained to Ian that I was struggling. He suggested that I went back to Glasgow to the last surgeon I'd seen. He suggested another big operation, but added that I might not be able to play again. I didn't want to go through it. I saw different specialists and tried different methods with my back. The physio at Bristol Rovers was very helpful, but I was struggling."

Lee Martin finally retired from football in 1998. "Ian Holloway helped me organise a testimonial game and Sir Alex Ferguson promised to send a side. We sold all 10,000 tickets out quickly and it didn't matter to me and I expected a reserve side from Old Trafford."

Squeezed in between a tour of the Far East and the Charity Shield, United sent a formidable group which included David Beckham, Ole Gunnar Solskjær, Paul Scholes, David May and John O'Shea. Ferguson came with them to Bristol.

"It was a lovely night, really warm and sunny and Sir Alex sent a very strong squad down. The team had won the treble and they brought all the trophies. I was really impressed that the manager came too. It was the perfect way to bow out of football."

Martin was 30. While in Bristol, he passed an HGV licence so that he could become a lorry driver.

"A friend in Glossop had offered me work, but before he offered me a job he told me to spend a week with one of his drivers. I did and it was the hardest thing I've ever done. We would drive until 7pm and would wake up at 6am to start the first deliveries. Day after day. I couldn't do it."

Then MUTV, which had started broadcasting in 1997, approached him. "I did the kids' show and I've worked for MUTV ever since. I enjoyed it and the money was decent. I would also help out, teaching kids football at a youth club back near home and they offered me a part-time job on a youth project."

The father of two teenagers – Ryan and Amelia – then separated from his wife, studied for teaching qualifications and met a new girl who lived in the Wirral, where he moved to. "I'm enjoying my life. It's a nice part of the world and I'm close enough to Old Trafford to do my MUTV work."

Yet Martin and playing were not finished. A six-year hiatus followed before he played competitive football again. "Peter

Davenport was Bangor City manager," he says. "And he asked me to go down there in the Welsh Premier League. I enjoyed it. I played as a centre back and tried to read the game. My back held up OK. The money was good too – £200 a week. Then Dav got sacked and Clayton Blackmore took over and I didn't really feature."

Martin signed for NEWI Cefn Druids in the Welsh Premier League. "I had a good six months and enjoyed playing, but with my commitments at Old Trafford I had to stop because United sometimes play on a Saturday."

He now is part of a United veterans' team. "It takes me around the world and I play with lads like David May, Lee Sharpe, Denis Irwin, Bryan Robson, Russell Beardsmore, Andy Ritchie and Clayton Blackmore. We get paid because we played for Manchester United 20 years ago, but we all love playing football. It's great to be away with the lads and Maysie keeps us all entertained."

Martin is also the youngest committee member at the Association of Former Manchester United Players. "I see a lot of the older players like Paddy Crerand and David Sadler, which I enjoy."

But he will for ever be remembered as the scorer of that goal in 1990, of which he is still, justifiably, very proud.

"People still come up to me all the time and talk about it. It might drive some people crazy, but not me. I'll never tire of talking about volleying the winner in an FA Cup final. Not a week goes past without someone pointing and saying: 'That's the guy who scored the winner in the FA Cup final' and I get invited to so many events because of that goal – like the 2007 FA Cup final. I just wish I'd enjoyed my United career a bit more and played more games because, at the time, you don't realise how lucky you are."

9
JORDI CRUYFF
The nomad

JORDI CRUYFF
MANCHESTER UNITED

F lags celebrating Barcelona's 2009 treble flutter outside the bar at Francesc Macia, a large roundabout named after a former Catalan president and local icon. A moped screeches to a halt outside, its rider takes off his helmet and ruffles his receding hairline as immaculately dressed uptown girls saunter past in the Catalan sun.

"Barça sent me very mixed messages," he explains. "On one hand I had no future, on the other they said they wanted to keep me. I was one of the best young talents in Spain at that moment and when they found out that United and Madrid were interested, Barça offered me a five-year contract. It was all a game they played with my career, but deep down I knew I didn't have a future at Barça.

"Bobby Robson had come in as manager, with José Mourinho as his assistant. I knew Barça would throw money at them to buy players. It was Mourinho who did the talking in the media and it became clear that I didn't feature in their plans."

It can't have been easy for Jordi, the son of the recently

dismissed manager who was still a Barça legend for his contribution as a player and for leading the Catalans to four successive league titles and their first ever European Cup in 1992. And it can't have been easy for new manager Bobby Robson, who wasn't versed in the language, Catalan politics or the mystifying club nuances.

Robson was acutely aware that, "Johan was always there at the back of the stand", even though he never criticised the new man in public. And Cruyff was something of a figurehead for an opposition group called Elephant Blue led by Joan Laporta, who is now Barcelona president, who wanted Cruyff reinstated. Robson felt Cruyff senior complicated matters by regularly attending games, but he was there mainly to watch his son, who became Robson's 'second Cruyff problem'.

Jordi tried to draw a line between his own position as a Barcelona player and the politics surrounding his father. He phoned Robson to reassure him that he wanted to stay and play for the new manager and would do all he could to make his tenure successful. In return he hoped that Robson would be fair to him, making any decision about his future as a Barcelona player on the basis of his abilities rather than politics.

In the end, Robson was unable to do this. He said later that Jordi had to move. Robson couldn't have someone in his dressing room who would, in the natural conversations between father and son, have been feeding back information to an opponent and would have been the prime suspect for any leaks.

There was an excess of talent – Ronaldo, Stoichkov and Figo were all fighting with Jordi for a place in the starting line-up – and it was unlikely that Cruyff would be selected ahead of these stars. But the suspicion would always be there that Jordi hadn't been selected because of who he was.

Others view the situation more starkly.

"Johan Cruyff's final two years at Barcelona were a disaster," said Antonio Franco, editor of the Barcelona daily *El Periodico*, "He had to go because he was unwilling to rebuild. Mainly because his hands were tied by his son. If he'd signed the quality of forwards the team needed, Jordi would have been relegated to the bench like a shot."

He's being harsh, for Jordi recalls that he had many suitors once his availability was made apparent.

"I had offers to go to Ajax, and Real Madrid were interested," reminisces Jordi. "Capello called me and told me to go to the Bernabéu, but I was not mentally strong enough or prepared for the abuse which would have come after joining Madrid from Barcelona. I would have been hammered all over the place. Radomir Antic called from Athletico Madrid, who had just won the double in Spain, but I didn't consider them a stable club. I was very close to signing with Ajax. Louis van Gaal was manager and I'd played there as a boy. The Ajax players in the Dutch team at Euro '96 had all been briefed to say that I should join them. I was keen, but Ajax had three different types of contract: A, B and C. They wanted to put me in a B, which I didn't think was right coming from Barcelona. They then offered me an A contract and explained that Patrick Kluivert would play for one more year and then the number 9 would be mine. I was about to sign, but then United came out to see me in Barcelona, the first people who had bothered to come to see me face to face."

Alex Ferguson, Martin Edwards and the club's director/ solicitor Maurice Watkins were the posse who flew to the city.

"I was very impressed that they had made the effort," recalls Jordi. "I went with my dad to pick them up at the airport and returned to my parents' house, where I was living. My mother made drinks and went to do her things, while my father and I talked to United. Ferguson reassured us and said that he would take personal care of me, almost like a son. He explained that a lot of young players were coming through the ranks and that joining United would be the right step. I liked the idea of playing for a manager who had been at a club a long time. United had a young team and, aged 21, I thought I could fit in. Ferguson told my father, 'I'll take good care of your son.' My father liked that.

"The contract was good and Ferguson had got under my skin. United left for the airport. When they'd gone, my father and I knew that United was the right choice. But it still surprised me when he advised me to join United, not Ajax – he knew everyone at Ajax and people would have watched out for me. I called Ajax and said, 'I know we have a verbal agreement but I'm joining United.'

Cruyff caught a plane to Manchester the next day.

"I think that every player joining United would be delighted, but I felt that I was coming from a far bigger club and better city. I thought it was a step down. I didn't realise or appreciate how big United was. Barcelona was the biggest club in the world and I didn't want to change that perception. My feelings were always for Barça. Over time I realised that United are bigger in some ways – but still Barça is more than a football club. A player shouldn't have that attitude when he joins a new club. I wasn't mentally ready for United."

Cruyff didn't have the typical footballer's background, though football dominated because of his father.

"My birth date was decided because of a Real Madrid v Barcelona game," he explains. "My mum wanted to have me by Caesarean section in Amsterdam by the same doctor who delivered my sisters. I was due to be born the week of the game, but Barça's coach Rinus Michels told my dad that he had to play in Madrid as they were chasing a first league title in 14 years. Rinus then decided that I could also be born after the game and on his birthday, 9th February 1974."

Jordi was duly born in Amsterdam, but there were further complications. The Catalan language was outlawed by General Franco and Jordi was a Catalan name – the name of their patron saint. The streetwise Johan had always grasped Barça's political dimension. He knew that the name Jordi was outlawed, but Franco's influence couldn't be extended to Holland, so his son became Jordi. Johan soon tried to register the boy with the Catalan authorities, but officials refused, telling him that his son's name was illegal.

"My dad said, 'My son has a Dutch passport, I can call him what I like and his name is Jordi.'"

They replied, "That is illegal. It has to be the Spanish version, Jorge."

"Then my dad said, 'I'm not going to make a scandal, but tell your bosses it will become a scandal.' They had to accept me because I was Dutch."

Jordi thus became the first 'legal' Jordi in decades, a gesture which sealed Johan's place in Catalan hearts. It also helped that he was man of the match as Barça slaughtered Madrid 5–0 away – a night which is still known as 'the Black Night' by Madrilenos – and pushed towards the title. Unlike Barça, Johan was used to success: he'd won three successive European Cups with Ajax before joining the Catalans for £1 million.

Jordi was a chubby baby in a wealthy family in Barcelona's Zona Alta on the foothills at the back of the city where they still live. Johan's legend grew at the 1974 World Cup finals as the Rinus Michels coached Dutch team changed football's landscape with their Total Football.

"I just saw that people came up to my dad and asked him to write on paper all the time," recalls Jordi. "But after a while I realised that he was very respected and important."

Jordi grew up in Barcelona, a childhood he describes as being "full of affection". He admits he was often stubborn, saying, "When people spoke Spanish to me I replied in Dutch. And when I went to Holland I spoke Spanish."

Being Johan's son meant other restrictions. "I wasn't allowed to sleep over at friends' houses after my dad had been forced to miss the 1978 World Cup finals. I never knew why, until much later."

The loss of Cruyff to the Argentina finals was a talking point even bigger than the actions of the army leaders presiding over Argentina at the time. Speculation was rife that the forward did not get on with the then Dutch coach, Ernst Happel, while others claimed Cruyff and his wife were making a stance against the human rights issues within Argentina under the brutal regime of Jorge Videla. Holland lost 3–1 to the host nation in the final in Buenos Aires after extra time.

"My dad never spoke about what happened until recently," says Jordi.

Thirty years later, Johan revealed the shocking truth about why he made his decision: "To play a World Cup you have to be 200 per cent. Someone came and pointed a rifle at my head and tied up my wife while the children were in the flat. There are times when there are more important things in life. For four months my home was watched by the police and my children had to be protected when they went to school."

The Cruyffs moved to Los Angeles in 1979 when Johan signed for the Aztecs, before going to Washington a year later.

"I loved the shirts which the NASL teams wore and still collect them to this day," says Jordi. "And I can remember playing football in the street with two stones. We had two Dobermans which all the neighbours were afraid of."

After a brief spell with Levante in Spain, Johan moved back to play for Ajax for two years. "Then my dad joined Feyenoord, which really pissed everyone off at Ajax," remembers Cruyff. "I knew that because I played at Ajax."

Johan had restructured Ajax's youth system, so that every youth team had to play in the same formation as the first team, and youth coaches had to develop players rather than win leagues. Jordi was sometimes asked to play in defence, to learn how defenders think. To this day, Ajax's youth system operates on Cruyff's lines.

"My dad still came to watch me play, which was a little bit strange," recalls Jordi. "It's not the done thing to move from Ajax to Feyenoord, like it's not to go from Barça to Madrid or United to Liverpool."

Jordi found out about the latter when a story during his time at Old Trafford linked him with a move to Anfield. "There was no truth in it, but Gary Neville came in the dressing room to confront me about it, telling me that I couldn't sign for 'them'. I was winding him up a little bit and he was furious."

At 13, Jordi was playing for Ajax and his regional team in Holland alongside Clarence Seedorf, Edgar Davids and Patrick Kluivert. Then his father got offered the Barcelona job.

"The family moved to Spain, but I didn't want to leave Holland. I was happy and wanted to stay with my grandparents. My father told me to get my things together and get on the plane – no arguments. I had to relearn Spanish."

Jordi joined the youth ranks at Barça. He had a good touch, but he was still tiny and a future in professional football looked unlikely. At 17, however, a growth spurt saw him catch up with his peers. He was promoted to Barça's reserve team at 19, where he continued to excel. Meanwhile his father had also revolutionised the way Barça played, a philosophy the Catalans have remained true to.

"Everything was about the ball at Barça, even the physical part," says Jordi. "It's all about possession and my father always drilled the importance of your first touch into me. Then it was the 'receive, offer, move' mantra."

He was offered the best contract in the reserve team, worth the equivalent of £300,000 a year, but Johan blocked the move and insisted that he received 25 per cent *less* than any of the reserve players, stating, "Don't worry about money. If you're good enough then the money will come."

"He felt that he was protecting me from accusations of nepotism," says Jordi, who was on the equivalent of £40,000 a year when he made the step up to the first team in 1994, joining a side which included Hristo Stoichkov, Romario and Pep Guardiola.

"I scored on my debut against Santander and everything

went well. I scored nine goals that season, including one against United."

Having a father as manager is not easy. Darren Ferguson, the gifted midfielder who played 30 games for United between 1991 and 1993, once reflected, "It was fine with Dad at first. The players respected my ability and if anything Dad was harder on me than them. I remember he dropped me for one game and made a joke about it in the team talk saying, 'Cathy will kill me.' I didn't think that was right and decided it would be best to move. I think Dad found the situation awkward too. I did feel part of it at United, but I was more relieved for my dad than myself when I left because I knew how much the club meant to him."

Jordi nods when I tell him this. "My father's only advice was, 'See, hear and don't speak'," he explains. "In other words he was telling me not to talk to him about what other players were saying. He wanted me to work my balls off and see how far I went. I knew that some players would be pissed off if I made the squad and they didn't, but only once did I see anything. I went into the showers after training one day and two players – Stoichkov and Beguristain [Barça's current director of football] were having a chat. I saw one give the signal to the other to be quiet. Eventually, I said, 'Look, if you have a problem go and speak to him; it's nothing to do with me.' I had to be ultra-careful. If I was mates with a player then we couldn't be seen socialising in public, because the media would have thought that the player was trying to get in my – and therefore my dad's – good books. It wasn't an easy position because if a player is not playing, they will search for any excuse."

Jordi claims that he learned a lot from the experience. "It actually changed my personality," he explains. "I used to be very extrovert, but I became quiet, serious and I would retreat inside myself. There's not a lot of things that can get to me nowadays; I can overcome things quickly."

Life could be equally hard for Jordi on the training field.

"If I made a mistake then my father would have a go at me more than anyone else. He wanted to show that he wasn't doing me any favours. I think the players respected that, but they also felt sorry for me because my father could be really mean, he could kill any player with his put-downs."

His resolve stayed intact. "More than anything, I knew that I was good enough to play for Barça. And so did my father. He would never have played me if I wasn't because he would have made us both look stupid. He would have killed our relationship if he would have put me into a high-pressure position which I couldn't handle."

Jordi was peripheral and needing experience, so father and son considered Jordi's future. "Santander wanted me on loan for two years and I wanted to go, but my dad told me to stay at Barça," he says.

Life at home, where Jordi still lived with his parents, wasn't conventional. "My dad and I wouldn't speak about football at home. Mum would ask me how things were, but never in front of dad. She wanted me to go on loan. She was already suffering when she went to games because my father was under pressure. She suffered even more when she watched her son play for a team managed by her husband."

In November 1994, Manchester United were Barça's opponents in the Champions League. The teams drew 2–2 at Old Trafford and 8,000 Reds travelled to the Camp Nou.

"Tonnie Bruins-Slot was the Barça scout who watched United," recalls Jordi. "He did an analysis of United where he explained to all the players that United were struggling with the foreigner rule, because the Irish players like Roy Keane and Denis Irwin were classed as foreigners. He predicted that Schmeichel would not play. All the players started laughing at him. I'd never seen that before, the players laughing at him. But he was right, he correctly predicted United's line up."

The depleted Reds went down 4–0 in front of 114,432, the third highest crowd ever to witness a United game. Cruyff set up Stoichkov to score Barça's first goal. "We respected United and knew that they had some good players, but we hammered them," he recalls.

While Barça were sublime that night, Cruyff's reign as coach had already seen its best times and memories of his European Cup-winning Dream Team of 1992 were fading fast in a club which demands continual success.

"By 1996, my dad had seen enough," Jordi says. "I already knew that my father wanted to leave Barça and he confirmed it when he told me, 'I'm sick and tired of this club and I'm going.'"

Being the son of the under-pressure coach seemed untenable, but Jordi's mood was lifted in the spring of 1996 when Guus Hiddink selected him to play for the Dutch national team.

"There was a lot of problems in the Dutch camp between the black and white players from Ajax," he recalls. "It was all about money, because the black lads felt they were not getting paid the same. Hiddink, who I've always really liked, just needed to weed out the problem players. He did it with Edgar Davids and sent him home. Hiddink learned a lot from that situation because his man management these days is excellent. You almost have to be better at that than being a technical coach."

Euro '96 was a success for Cruyff and he scored a sublime chip for Holland against Switzerland at Villa Park. "That goal really lifted me because it came at a time when I was in the middle of a media fight in Barcelona. They wanted me to leave and yet they were playing a game offering me new contracts. That goal made me realise that I could do well wherever I was at the highest level."

It was while rooming with the Anglophile Denis Bergkamp on that trip that Cruyff first thought about playing in England, starting a chain of events which led to him signing for United.

Cruyff was not bought as a reserve and Ferguson started him in the opening game of the 1996/97 season against

Wimbledon at Selhurst Park. The team that day was: Schmeichel; Irwin, P Neville, May, Pallister; Keane, Butt, Scholes,
Beckham; Cantona, Cruyff. United won 3–0 in front of 25,786
– around 16,000 of those being Manchester United supporters.
David Beckham's world may have changed on that sunny afternoon with one swing of a boot after he famously scored from
beyond the halfway line, but minutes earlier Cruyff had tried
something similar.

"Jordi tried to chip the Wimbledon keeper, Neil Sullivan,
from outside the box," said Beckham. "And I'm sure if the shot
would have been on target, Jordi might have scored."

Cruyff started the first five games that season, scoring twice.
The £800,000 transfer fee looked astute and his mood began
to lift.

"The atmosphere inside English stadiums was far better
than in Spain," he says. "Plus you had thousands of away fans.
I'll never forget that roar you get just before kick-off at an
English game."

But Jordi was soon injured and unable to make himself a
regular in United's starting XI.

"I struggled with English football. I wasn't used to
defending my own box. I was used to 4-3-3, playing as the
midline forward, creating and crossing. My best position was
off the striker. I could come from midfield and dribble both
ways. I could use my head, but I felt uncomfortable starting
with my back to the goal, alone and marked by two enormous
central defenders. If there's a striker keeping them busy then
I was fine, but if you have Cantona that wasn't going to happen
for me."

Jordi's waif-like frame struggled to stand up to the rigours
of English football. "The football in England was a lot more
physical and the injuries killed me," he says. "I had three operations in the first three years, which stopped me getting into
a rhythm.

"I can't complain about my first two years at Old Trafford.

I started my pre-seasons well but got injured in the first two seasons in September. I had to look at myself. I was a little bit too young and wasn't prepared to understand that I had signed for such a fantastic club. When you are 21 or 22 you are not too bright or experienced."

The winger who could also play behind the forwards was unsettled off the field too. "I had a lot of problems adjusting to the weather and lifestyle. I was a city boy and wanted to live in a city, to walk to restaurants or to take a coffee. I couldn't get used to having dinner at six. I shouldn't have lived on the outskirts in a big house in Bramhall surrounded by older neighbours."

Wigan Athletic's Roberto Martinez, a fellow Catalan, was a positive influence.

"He stopped me getting too depressed by showing me how lucky I was," says Cruyff.

"He was my confidant, who would always lift me. He'd say, 'What are you moaning about? You're at Manchester United winning leagues. I have to wash my own kit at Wigan.'

"He also enrolled us on a postgraduate degree in marketing in Manchester and made sure that I started doing my coaching badges. A few of the students' eyebrows were raised when I turned up a Maserati, but they were fine with me."

The pair would go to Manchester's El Rincon Spanish restaurant most days after training, where they would play cards and eat. "They had two fridges, one for us special customers," he remembers. "One of the owners would go to Galicia once a week and bring back the freshest fish for us."

The players also frequented Harpers, a Spanish tapas restaurant which exists because of George Best. Best spent every summer in Majorca and became friends with Felix, who ran a bar there. When George started getting involved with bars in Manchester in the early 1970s he asked Felix to come over and he still lives in Manchester, running Harpers, which has stayed popular with the football community.

"We'd occasionally see Best in there," recalls Jordi. "And he'd ask about my dad."

In his first season, Cruyff was close friends with Cantona. "I think he understood my situation and really tried to take care of me. He'd pick me up for training. I was one of the first people who he told he was going to retire.

Sir Alex Ferguson had guessed that correctly. In his autobiography he later revealed that Eric had changed, becoming subdued and giving the impression that he was not enjoying his football. The air of commitment he had always generated quietly in the dressing room had gone, as had his customary spark. Ferguson sees the charity game he played in Barcelona alongside Jordi as a pivotal moment – cementing the friendship between the two men and implanting the idea of going to live in Barcelona in Eric's mind.

Jordi tells it slightly differently. "Eric came to Barcelona with me, but then he disappeared for two and a half days with a former Espanyol player he'd played with in France. On the plane home, Eric looked at me and said, 'I'll make a bet that I leave United before you do.'

"'Not a chance,' I replied. 'And I'll bet you a meal at the most expensive restaurant in Europe.'

"A week or so later, when we were having a meal with Ole Gunnar, who I was very close mates with, and our partners, Eric said the same thing. We told him that he was being crazy and I wasn't sure whether to take him seriously, but once Eric has made his mind up . . ."

Cantona left and Cruyff became close friends with Ronny Johnsen, Raimond van der Gouw and others in United's foreign contingent.

"Jaap Stam joined a year later and stayed at my house for the first month," recalls Cruyff. "I smile when I think of Jaap. In one of the first training sessions he went right through me. I looked at him and said, 'Jaap, I'm feeding you and giving you a bed, what the fuck are you doing?' Jaap just gave me a look which meant that anything went in training. I knew then that he was going to succeed at United."

Cruyff got on fine with the English lads too. "David May used to walk in the dressing room each morning, look at me and say, 'Dos San Miguels, you dago bastard!' Occasionally he would change it to: 'Una margarita.' That would lift me because he always kept me part of the group. I should have pulled two beers from my bag or a bottle of tequila, that would have shut him up. May was a good player who was unlucky with injuries. And if you get injuries at a big club you get eaten up and fall behind. May was a good guy for the team though, he lifted sprits.

"Then you had Gary Neville, who thought that England was the best. He didn't like outside influences. He thought that English food was superior and I considered him close minded. Phil was completely different and very open. We'd speak for hours about football. He was fascinated about tactics on the continent and different styles of play. Phil made me feel very welcome and I'm grateful for that."

Cruyff, unsurprisingly, identified Roy Keane as the dominant figure in the United changing room. "I really started to respect Roy when he became the top-paid player. He got a new contract and his performances soared. United could have put Keane in goal and he would have been the best goalkeeper in England, or he could have played up front and he would have been the best striker. He had an incredible drive and I really respected that. Roy also tried to help me. He had a go at me a few times, a real go where he said, 'You should be ashamed of yourself. It's a fucking scandal with your talent that you are not playing in this team.' He told me to look into the mirror. He said it in front of everyone, so I felt that I had to save face by answering him back, but I knew where he was coming from. And I knew that he only wanted what was best for the team.

"Roy was in a very fortunate position though – which of

course he'd earned. He gave the ball away against Fiorentina in 1999 which led to a goal. Henning Berg also gave a bad ball away in the same game. Henning was dropped from the squad for a month and nothing happened to Roy."

Another friend was David Beckham, though the pressures of celebrity would leave their mark. "David was very normal, friendly and open until his relationship with his wife became serious. More people started getting involved in his private life, the newspapers became very interested in them and he started to protect himself by becoming more reserved.

"I loved Denis Irwin too; what a player he was. He was so small and yet he won everything in the air. A left back who takes Manchester United's penalties – that said it all. You don't see that anywhere in the world.

"Peter Schmeichel could have a very aggressive way of speaking," says Jordi. "He was quite a serious person but he was fine with me, a fellow foreigner. And he was one hell of a goalkeeper. I used to chip him in training and he would go absolutely mad. If he caught the ball he'd be so delighted that he'd kick it far away towards the river, knowing that you'd have to go and get it.

"The only player who would consistently score past Schmeichel was Solskjær. He was like a player in a computer game and would hit every shot with incredible accuracy. Solskjær was Schmeichel's nightmare."

Czech winger Karel Poborsky had signed at the same time as Cruyff, one of five foreign signings in the summer of 1996 alongside Ole Gunnar Solskjær, Ronny Johnsen and Raimond van der Gouw. Like Cruyff, Poborsky had scored an exquisite lob in Euro '96 and there was great hope that he could justify the £3.5 million fee which United paid Slavia Prague. He couldn't. David Beckham's progress limited Poborsky to 48 appearances before he was sold to Benfica 18 months after he arrived for a £1 million loss. Benfica also took a year to pay United.

"It was difficult for Karel because he didn't speak English," says Jordi. "I didn't understand Ferguson in the dressing room for two years either, though I'd pick out occasional words. If I heard the word 'Jordi' then I'd jump up and take notice. Karel also had the added pressure of having to play in 70 per cent of games because of the visa requirements. He wasn't the most technical player, but he was lightning fast and had a good shot."

Despite some good times, Cruyff shared Poborsky's unhappiness. "My mindset became very negative," he says. "English food was, is and will always be terrible. I hate beans, which is what you all eat. I tried a bean once and spat it out. Even on match days the pasta was dreadful. I used to bring my own olive oil to put on the pasta! These things should not have been a big thing to me yet they became important issues because I wasn't playing."

Like others, Cruyff found Brian Kidd's training sessions a joy. "Brian Kidd was really good and there was a large pool of young players. I think Kidd's heart was with his young players, the Manchester lads he'd helped to bring through, but I can understand that. Steve McClaren was excellent too and I can see why he's now doing so well in Holland."

Jordi also had his moments indulging in Manchester's nightlife. "I went to see The Cure live at the Arena. They are huge in Spain, but there were barely 1,000 people in the Arena which holds 20,000. The lead singer Robert Smith was disgusted and I could understand why."

Back at work, Cruyff went to see Ferguson where they had a frank discussion.

"We exchanged views of football. English people preferred a Keane tackle to a Giggs dribble. That surprised me because I was used to the opposite. Any player can tackle, few can dribble, and I explained to the manager that it is more difficult to create than destroy. Ferguson was shocked – his face said it all – but I was only being honest. I like open, creative, passing football. And I've also got a strong character. When something is unfair I rebel and that's what I was doing. I did feel at times that I wasn't being treated fairly. I hated it when he said to me, 'You're not going to play in the next two games, but you'll play in two weeks.' I'd reply, 'But what if the strikers score?' He'd promise to mix things up, but I wasn't convinced.

"I also don't want to sound disrespectful, because he's been a magnificent manager. He's been successful time and time again. And I can see why Ferguson didn't count on me because I was always injured. But at 21 I didn't think like a coach and I was probably difficult to work with."

Cruyff was happier with his attitude in his third season, 1998/99. "By that time I had started to see how big Manchester United were. I'd been on pre-season tours where 25,000 fans watched the team train in Bangkok. Not even Barça could pull in those crowds. Five thousand people were waiting for us at airports at 6am and I said to myself, 'Jordi, wake up. You're at an incredible club.'"

All seemed rosy at the start of the treble season, though something was still missing. "I was playing well, but I wasn't allowed to show it on the pitch. I needed that little push, that bit of confidence that comes with playing in the first team. When I didn't get that, there was nothing left for me, even though I had a good feeling that the season was going to be a very successful one for United.

"The situation became so bad that I didn't want my team-mates to do well because I wanted to be in the team. I was tired of sitting in the stand eating carrot cake. When you get to that point you have to go, because you become a problem. I looked forward to the international weeks, just so that I could go back to see my family in Barcelona. On one occasion, I wasn't allowed back. That really upset me and it became a battle of wills, me against Ferguson. One weekend, Ferguson asked me to do extra training. I was convinced it was because he didn't want me to go back to Barcelona, but just to prove

a point I went for 15 hours. I hated Ferguson for months, it became personal."

Cruyff eventually told the United manager that he had to leave to play football and knew that Celta Vigo were interested in taking him back on loan. "He didn't want me to go but I insisted," says Cruyff. "I told him that I wanted to be a footballer, not someone who looked at different stadiums from a bench each week. Ferguson acquiesced, saying, 'If it's going to be that way then I'll have to consider the situation.'

"Just let me go, I have to go," Cruyff insisted. "I know you have a brilliant team who can win everything, but I'm not part of it." Ferguson finally relented, but there was a small problem. In Spain, clubs had the right to buy a player they took on loan. United didn't want to sell Jordi and told him to return for the next pre-season.

He moved to Vigo, Europe's biggest fishing port on Galicia's wild Atlantic coast, in January 1999, where he became one of their most important performers.

"I played in a fantastic side with Alexander Mostovoi, Valery Karpin, Michel Salgado, Claude Makelele and Mazinho [the Brazilian who rocked the baby in the 1994 World Cup finals]," reminisces Jordi.

Months later, on one of the greatest night in United's history, the club won the treble in Cruyff's home city.

"United invited me to the final which was a nice gesture. The team had injuries and I would have played in the final, I'm sure of that. Playing in the European Cup final in the Camp Nou would have been amazing.

"I watched from the stands, leaving my seat a few minutes before the end. I knew my way around the stadium and went towards the changing rooms, hoping to cheer everyone up after the defeat. I took Roberto Martinez as my guest. Then I heard a lot of noise. I went back to see the pitch. United had equalised. Then they scored again. Incredible. There is a picture of me, Roberto and Ferguson with the Champions League trophy."

Not every memory of that night is positive for Jordi. "There were players who won a Champions League medal without playing a minute that season, but I featured in three or four games and didn't get anything. I would have liked a replica."

Jordi had made the 10 starts necessary to win a Premiership medal in 1997 but missed out in the seasons after. "I have no idea where that medal is," he says of the 1997 version. "But if you think that's bad, my father has lost two of his three European Footballer of the Year awards."

They'll doubtless be in Barcelona somewhere, where Cruyff made sure that some of the victorious players became acquainted with the Catalan nightlife on 26th May 1999, before returning to Old Trafford to rejoin his teammates a few months later.

"I really wanted to go for it," he says. "I had a really good pre-season. Ferguson saw how well I was doing and how well I'd done at Celta. He got me in one day to talk about Celta. He knew that Celta were a great team and said, 'If you could take two players from Celta, who would it be?' I told him that Makelele was the best, but also recommended Salgado and Mostovoi, explaining that he was a little older. I was pleased that he respected my football opinion. United did nothing, but Makelele and Salgado moved to Madrid that summer."

Cruyff made his fourth consecutive Charity Shield appearance in August 1999. He always did well pre-season. "And I always started the season well," he says. "I'm like a bear. I sleep in the winter and I'm wide awake and hungry in the summer. I always got injured in November. The winter months were always difficult in a physical and strong league like England and I always got injured in November."

Cruyff earned praise from his manager in the 1999 pre-season as he played some of the best football of his career. Then he was dropped for the opening game of the season at Everton.

"Being left out of the opening game was the final straw,"

he says. "Nicky Butt started on the left ahead of me away to Everton. And because I'm an impulsive bastard, I decided there and then to leave. I'd done really well pre-season and deserved a lot more opportunities in my fourth year. The players would agree. I was 100 per cent adapted to English football and wanted to succeed."

Some said that the slender Jordi wasn't strong enough to play in the Premiership. "That's rubbish," he protests. "My strong point was not playing with my back to the goal, but dribbling towards goal. I could compensate in other ways.

"I was prepared to be part of a squad, but not playing ten times a season. There's nothing worse than a footballer who doesn't play. I was helped by Jim Ryan though, who was like a father figure to me. He made me think, laugh and work. I needed that when I was playing in the reserves, but my confidence was broken. Playing for Celta had made me realise that I was better playing at a smaller club. I was the tail of the elephant at United. At a smaller club I could be the head."

West Ham came in for Cruyff, but Ferguson wasn't keen on him playing for an English team.

"He said, 'Let me speak to the board about you staying.' That wasn't an option for me. He also said, and I respect him for this, 'I've made a mistake with you because you have the winner's mentality that I didn't see.' He was fine and it wasn't even his fault that I left because he had a fantastic team, but I wasn't even getting minutes as a sub and that killed my ego."

Cruyff left Manchester in 2000, wishing everyone well as he went by pinning a note in the dressing room. He joined Alaves, the team from the pretty Basque capital city of Vitoria who had been promoted to the Primera Liga after a 42-year hiatus in 1998 and finished a highest-ever sixth in 2000, earning a place in the UEFA Cup.

"Their manager Mane came to me and said he needed a number nine," says Jordi. "I told him that I wasn't a nine, but a striker best used playing off the front man. He said, 'I need one of those as well.' He wanted me and that felt good. I was paid half what I was on at United, but I did a deal whereby they would pay me more money if Alaves did well."

Alaves did very well.

"They gave me freedom and I fell back in love with football. I was so determined to prove myself and I prospered. I loved being back in Spain and in the Basque country, which has the best food in Spain. You'd get a better meal for €10 than you would in the best restaurant in Manchester."

Alaves held their own in the Primera Liga, while excelling in Europe, where they knocked out some far grander names.

"We had a great team, a couple of mean bastards – Argentinians," comments Jordi, with relish. "If I received a kick then one of them would get revenge for me. Javi Moreno scored a lot of goals in front of me and earned a big transfer to Milan. The spirit in that team was superb."

Vitoria is more often associated with basketball than football. Tau, the basketball side, is consistently one of the best in Europe.

"We'd go out every Thursday night and get really pissed with the basketball lads, most of who had played in the NBA," says Cruyff. "We'd go to training from the disco at eight in the morning. There was a queue for the physio, who would put drops in our eyes to whiten them up a bit. The coach would see us and say, 'I can get pissed off with you or I can look the other way, see that we are having a good season and give you some light training to get the poison [alcohol] out of your bodies.' We always left the tactics until the Saturday."

Alaves met Inter in the last eight of the UEFA Cup and drew 3–3 in the home leg. "We travelled to Milan for the away game in our own clothes because there were no club suits," says Cruyff. "The Italian media were waiting for us at the airport, but they didn't recognise any of our players so we sent fans to do interviews with them and pretend they were players."

Alaves won 2–0 in the San Siro, with Cruyff putting his side ahead after 77 minutes. The Kaiserslautern side of Mario Basler, who'd scored Bayern Munich's goal against United in the Camp Nou, Youri Djorkaeff and Miroslav Klose were next in the semi-finals. "We absolutely hammered them, beat them 5–1 at home and 4–1 away."

Liverpool were their opponents in the final in Dortmund. "People reading this won't believe it, but we thought we were favourites to beat Liverpool," says Cruyff. "We'd beaten Real Madrid and Barcelona that season, plus big teams in Europe."

In one of the most dramatic European finals, Cruyff scored an 88th-minute goal to make it 4–4 and push the game into extra time, where they lost. "I'm sorry I couldn't help United fans by beating Liverpool, but we came close."

Cruyff continued to enjoy his time at Alaves until injuries again began to affect him.

"I only left Alaves when they were relegated in 2003 because I didn't want to play in the second division. I admit that I wasn't much use to them in that season."

He'd still speak with Ferguson occasionally. "He asked me about the defender Collocini when he was only 17 and asked how he compared with Rio Ferdinand of Leeds. Collocini was superb but still emerging and I told him Ferdinand was better."

Jordi also saw another former United player excel in Spain after struggling at Old Trafford.

"Diego Forlan has done well in Spain but is that a surprise?" he asks. "He needed a run of full games at United. Latin players have a different mentality and it needs to be understood and supported. They are used to different weather, food and eating hours. It you can't make allowances then you won't get the best out of Latin players."

Cruyff played for Espanyol in Barcelona. "My wife [Noemi, a fashion photographer] was about to give birth and I wanted our baby to be born in Catalonia," he explains. "I was paid a third of what I earned at Alaves. It was a problem with my

Barcelona links at the start, but then I played 31 games and my first season was good."

Jordi had remained in contact with Barcelona throughout and they would seek his opinion on all things Manchester United. When Joan Laporta, an outsider in the race for Barça's president in 2003, asked Cruyff to get in touch with David Beckham, Cruyff called with the news that Barça wanted to sign him.

"Beckham didn't call me back because the deal with Real Madrid had already been done," he says. "And I spoke with Barça about Ryan Giggs around 2004. I told them that Giggs would have been perfect for them. In fact I said, 'He'll be even better in Spain because he's a brilliant player.' There was not one other player at United who I thought would have made it for Barça, that's how highly I rated him. I think Barça were nervous about creating too much competition for Ronaldinho."

Injuries again hampered Cruyff's career. "I had virtually no cartilage in my knee. Sam Allardyce wanted me at Bolton and I did a pre-season there but failed the medical."

He returned to Barcelona where a doctor told him that he'd be out for one year, and that there was only a 50 per cent chance he'd play football again.

"The injury was similar to the one that Ole Gunnar Solskjær had," he states. "And at my age you either come back from this injury or you don't. There was no chance of a two-year rehabilitation."

After a few starts in which "training was so painful that I cried," Cruyff became despondent.

"I went skiing with my family, but just sat there as they were on the slopes. My father said, 'Go ski. You already have pain, what have you got to lose?' I went skiing and had no problems. I skied for three days and decided that I could play 30 games a season, but I wanted a team where I would play and have an understanding relationship with my manager about training."

Cruyff joined Metalurh Donetsk in Ukraine, who had a Spanish manager.

"I like strange countries," Cruyff explains. "I was going to play in Jordan, but went instead to Ukraine, where the football isn't bad and I was treated well there. I enjoyed two years before returning to Barcelona to be a father to my two kids and a husband again."

As the interview draws to a close, Cruyff says, "I know I've sounded negative at times, but my time in Manchester wasn't my happiest, I have to be honest."

He also reveals his plans for the future which involve yet another country where the suns shines. "I'm going to Malta tomorrow, where I'll be a player and assistant manager for Valletta. I'm not sure whether I want to go more into coaching, or more into the player-spotting role – maybe as a director of football at a club."

10
GARY PALLISTER
The big man

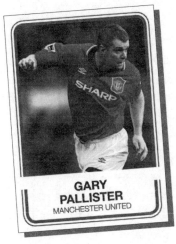

GARY PALLISTER
MANCHESTER UNITED

Gary Pallister had only been in Manchester a month and things were not going well. Britain's most expensive footballer was living alone in the Ramada Hotel overlooking Deansgate. "After training I would go back to the hotel room and pop to Pizza Hut for lunch by myself like some saddo," he recalls. "Paul Ince soon arrived and we spent most afternoons in the bookies. It wasn't ideal."

Things were even worse in the day job. Pallister had been desperate to get out of relegated Middlesbrough, where he didn't get on with boss Bruce Rioch, but the huge £2.3 million transfer fee put him under added pressure. He made his United debut in a 2–0 home defeat by Norwich City at the start of the 1989/90 season, but his performance was panned by the tabloids. "I wanted the fans on my side and losing at home to Norwich wasn't the best way to do it. But I was blamed for a goal which wasn't my fault."

A few weeks later City beat United 5–1 at Maine Road. "The roof fell in," says Pallister, "We actually started that game really well, playing lovely football. Then everything City hit went in. I didn't have the best of games and knew that I should have done better. To lose like that to City wasn't good enough and I'd say it was the lowest point in my whole career.

"The *Red Issue* fanzine made a point which many fans were thinking by publishing *Fergie's Takeaway Menu*. On it were two black puddings and a dumpling, complete with extortionate prices. They were talking about Danny Wallace, Paul Ince and myself. It was one of the funniest observations I'd seen and we had a laugh about it, but we knew the situation was serious."

It was. Pallister drove back to Middlesbrough after "the 5–1" with his family. "Thank God I had them around me," he says. "I sought solace at home that weekend, but I was confronted with a menacing situation when I returned to training at The Cliff on Monday. There was no security at The Cliff and fans were free to wander in. When I walked back to my car after training, three or four big United fans were waiting for me. As I moved towards my car, they approached me. They didn't look like they wanted an autograph. Instead, they told me that I wasn't fit to wear the shirt, that United shouldn't have sold Paul McGrath and that I was a fucking disgrace. It was very intimidating. I said nothing. What could I say? We'd just been whopped 5–1 by City. A few of the other players got abuse from the same lads. With all the security at Carrington, players now wouldn't believe that was possible, but it was a very real threat."

Pallister is recounting the story from his home in Yarm, a prosperous market town on the banks of the River Tees near Middlesbrough. Former teammates will not be surprised to read that no matter how dramatic the story, Pallister does not shift his six foot four inch frame from the horizontal position on his favourite sofa for the three hours of the interview. Thankfully his long-term partner Mary and their two girls Lauren and Eve are on hand to ferry cups of tea from the kitchen, past the snooker table and photos showing Pallister scoring twice at Anfield, playing with Cantona, marking former teammate Bernie Slaven at Old Trafford, wearing an England shirt and appearing on *A Question of Sport*.

Pallister enjoys the trappings of a top-level footballer who played in the 1990s boom. He played nearly 700 competitive matches, including 437 at United, putting him 18th overall for appearances in the history of the club. He won numerous trophies with the club and was also capped 22 times by England between 1988 and 1996. Sir Alex Ferguson described him as the best footballing centre half in the country, bar none. Such achievements would have appeared improbable as he took to the field in front of 170 as a 19-year-old for Billingham Town in the shadow of the giant ICI chemical works.

"My route into football was different from most," he says. "I didn't get into the professional game until I was 19, after coming from non-league. I never stopped believing that I could make it, even if trials at Grimsby and Leicester didn't go well for me. By the time I was 19, people thought I was a bit crazy, but I always kept that belief. I would have been happy to reach the lower reaches of the Football League at that point, but once I left Billingham Town in the Northern League for Middlesbrough everything spiralled on from there."

Pallister grew up in the North-East, but he was born in Margate, Kent.

"My father, who was from Billingham, was working down there as a fitter," he explains. "We came back north when I was five months old and settled in Norton, a working-class area. Mum went to work in a tax office and Dad stayed as a fitter. Most footballers had a tougher upbringing than me. We didn't get everything we wanted, but if I wanted some new football boots or my sister needed something then we would get it."

Pallister was a keen sportsman, while his older sister had the brains.

"She was very intelligent," he says. "I had to follow in her footsteps at school, which was difficult as she was very clever. I was more interested in sport, much to my mother's concern."

Pallister loved football, but refuses to admit which team he supported as a kid.

"I can't tell you," he says.

"You supported Liverpool?" I suggest.

"I can't tell you!"

"Leeds?"

"I can't tell you."

"So it wasn't Middlesbrough, your local team?"

"I can't tell you. But I did watch Middlesbrough. I went to Ayresome Park from the age of six and watched Jack Charlton's promotion-winning side of 1972, which conceded the least amount of goals. Nobby Stiles was there, Bobby Murdoch and Graeme Souness – some great players. My Uncle Malcolm would take me. We'd stand in the Holgate End, the Chicken Run or in the Boys' End. I loved football. I loved sport. I played basketball for the county and cricket too. I was a hurdles champion. The only sport I didn't get honours in was football – and that was probably because I was a centre forward until I was 15."

Pallister's conversion to centre half came about because of skating. "We had a very good school football team and we played a team who were getting destroyed every week," he explains. "Our centre half had been out on an all-night skate marathon for charity. We went one up but they equalised, two up and they equalised, then three up. Our teacher was furious and ordered the centre half off, before shouting, 'Pallister, centre half.' We won 9–3 and he kept me in that position for the next game. I was gutted because I liked scoring goals. Had that not have happened, I would have stayed a centre forward and probably remained in that position playing semi-pro all my career, a frustrated centre forward. But because of skating, I switched and Billingham Town eventually came in for me."

Pallister left school with no qualifications, and did a year at college before signing on the dole. "I was on £21.50 a week, which wasn't bad money for me at that time. I was playing for Billingham Town when the treasurer there helped me get a job. I was going to be a teaboy for the riggers and welders on the docks. I arrived for the interview, where a man showed me how to make a cup of tea. Next thing, the treasurer from Billingham, who worked there, said, 'Follow me and lie through your teeth.' He walked into where the clerks worked and said, 'This is Gary. He's very intelligent, has got three A-levels and six O levels.' I just nodded my head. After ten minutes as tea maker I was promoted to being a clerk's assistant in a nicer cabin. I was there for six months. I'd get up at five in the morning and work until ten at night if necessary."

Middlesbrough is hardly rated one of the best regions in Britain, yet it has a fine industrial heritage. "I'm proud of that and proud of where I'm from," says Pallister. "This area takes a lot of stick. Even the United players used to call it Miserableboro. Whenever Middlesbrough try and sign a big player, the media poke fun at the area and show pictures of the old iron and steel works. But those works helped this place survive. It's not a flash area and will never be as cosmopolitan as Manchester or London, but there's a lot of good to be said of Northern people. It's a bit tougher up here, but very friendly and people have more time for you. And there's some beautiful countryside close by."

Pallister was offered a trial for Middlesbrough in 1984. "Malcolm Allison was the Middlesbrough manager and Willie Maddren the reserve boss when I played for the reserves that night. I don't think that would happen these days. Players are harvested and very few escape the net. Yet me, Ian Wright, Stuart Pearce, Les Ferdinand and Chris Waddle all came from non-league football and went on to be England internationals."

He did enough to be given a three-month contract with the reserves, playing for expenses.

"It was not glamorous and when a lot of valuables started

going missing in the changing rooms, all eyes were on me, the new boy who was still on the dole," he says. "I was very relieved when they caught the thief. There were constant arguments and I didn't enjoy the environment. Most of the other players knew each other well and maybe felt that I was taking the place of one of their mates. At the end of the three months, Willie Maddren told me that they wanted me on a month-to-month contract, but that there was no money. Billingham received a couple of goal nets and a bag of balls for me."

Maddren devised a scheme to pay Pallister's wages. "He spoke to a wealthy local businessman called Dick Corden, who agreed to sponsor my wages of £50 a week. I came off the dole but was no better off financially. Corden's son Steve was also playing and we made our first-team debuts together at Plough Lane against Wimbledon. What a place to make your debut. It was a horrible, intimidating place to go and play the Crazy Gang. We got humped 3–0 and Steve broke his leg and never played first-team football again. I got good reviews in the papers."

The crowd that day was 2,844, including Pallister's parents, who watched him mark Alan Cork. After getting the bus to training each day, Pallister had established himself in a struggling second division side by the time Boro were relegated to the old Third Division in 1986. He was briefly loaned out to Darlington for seven games, an experience which toughened him up, before returning to Boro, where crowds were down to 4,000 and the financial situation was dire.

"The club were unable to pay the players' wages and Middlesbrough folded that summer," he explains. "The receivers padlocked the gates of the club's assets – Ayresome Park and our training ground on Hutton Road."

There was talk of resurrecting the once-proud club, but the players were in limbo. When they returned for unpaid pre-season training, it was on park pitches. On two occasions the local council paid them some money. Out-of-contract men were allowed to leave for free. Talented winger Peter Beagrie left for Sheffield United. Crystal Palace approached Pallister. "I went down and could have ended up there with Steve Coppell and Ian Wright, but I didn't really want to move down to the Smoke."

For a while, it looked like Middlesbrough wouldn't be allowed to start the 1986/87 season, until a rescue package was put together that would save the club from extinction. Representatives from ICI, a major local employer, and a 26-year-old haulage businessman called Steve Gibson were responsible for saving the club ten minutes before the final deadline for the 1986/87 season but, with Ayresome Park still padlocked, Middlesbrough began the season playing at Hartlepool's Victoria Park.

With emerging talents like Pallister, Stuart Ripley, Tony Mowbray and Colin Cooper, an experienced goalkeeper in the former United stopper Stephen Pears and a cult hero goalscorer in Bernie Slaven, Boro had plenty to draw on under new manager Bruce Rioch.

"Tony was a natural leader, an inspirational figure and was made captain at 21," says Pallister. "He was always going to make a good manager. Bernie was eccentric. I still keep in touch with them both. Bernie didn't take a shine to me at first and I couldn't understand his Scottish accent. When I was sent on loan to Darlington for seven games in 1985 I think he was quite happy about it. When I came back we became friends and would socialise together – though he didn't drink. He's the only Scotsman I've ever met who doesn't drink, and was a fantastic taxi service – travel didn't cost me a bean. Bernie would ring his wife from away games and she'd pass the phone over to his dog. He'd then communicate with his dog.

"I roomed with Bernie. We used to load up with chocolate, crisps and Coke – we'd have to protect our room and all the sweets in it. When I started football there was no insight into diets. You could eat what you liked during the week – so

I did. I could easily buy a large box of Milk Tray and polish the whole box off. I was still skinny as a rake though because I did so much sport. I've never been a great eater and I'm a dietician's nightmare. I would have fish and chips as my pre-match meal at Middlesbrough."

Although generally expected to be relegated again in 1986/87, Boro instead were promoted after finishing second, gaining a reputation for their attractive football. They were promoted again 12 months later to the First Division. Pallister played 57 games in 1987/88 and his good form was sufficient for Bobby Robson to award him his first England cap against Hungary in Budapest in 1988. A watching Brian Clough, who had also played for Billingham and Middlesbrough, said on television, "He looks like a million dollars, and he's worth a million pounds!"

Pallister's career enjoyed an upwards trajectory from then on. Manchester United watched him in a Freight Rover Trophy game at Rochdale and Alex Ferguson likened him to Alan Hansen for the manner in which he carried the ball from defence, but chief scout Tony Collins, who had watched Pallister several times, said that he was lazy and lacked concentration. United didn't bid and Pallister's demeanour also caused problems with his manager Rioch.

"Bruce Rioch and I were like chalk and cheese," he says. "I'm a laid-back kind of guy. I can look lackadaisical or even lazy. He was completely the opposite. His father was a sergeant major and he'd lived on an army camp in a very disciplined environment. I didn't respond to that and he didn't manage me like Fergie later did. We clashed all the time. It got to the stage where I didn't want to go into training in the morning."

Pallister felt persecuted by Rioch. "He would single me out," he says. "I was two minutes late for a bus and got fined. When Tony Mowbray was five minutes late soon after, that was laughed off. I felt he was disrespectful and I wanted to get away. If I saw Bruce now I'd shake his hand and I had no problems with him about his ideas and the type of football he wanted to play, but we just clashed, and words were often said."

Middlesbrough could not stay up and were relegated in 1989, though they beat Manchester United 1–0 on 2nd January, with former United striker Peter Davenport scoring. United could be forgiven – they had played and beaten Liverpool the day before.

Pallister and Mowbray continued to impress and were virtual ever-presents in the Boro defence, but Pallister felt he had a decision to make.

"I'd played for England and didn't want to play in the Second Division. And the situation with the manager was getting worse."

Middlesbrough didn't want to let him leave. "Bruce tried to bully me into signing a new contract and threatened to play me in the reserves. I stood up for myself. I might have been scared and easily manipulated at 18, but not at 21."

The situation quickly deteriorated.

"Bruce was quoted in the local press saying that I didn't want to play for the club. People thought that I only wanted to leave for money. It wasn't good – my family lived locally and it was unpleasant for them. Yet the people couldn't see how difficult it was behind the scenes with Bruce. I'd always said that as long as Middlesbrough were going forward I'd be happy to stay, but then we were relegated . . ."

Liverpool were the first club who got in touch with Pallister's agent in the summer of 1989. Given that I suspect Pallister supported them as a kid, it would have been an easy choice, but they baulked at the asking price. However, after getting rid of Gordon Strachan, Jesper Olsen, Chris Turner, Graeme Hogg, Norman Whiteside, Kevin Moran and Paul McGrath in the summer of 1989, United needed several new players, including a centre half.

Swedish international defender Glenn Hysen was a target and even stayed with Bryan Robson. Ferguson flew to Florence to do the groundwork, but were met by two very smug Liverpool officials on the way home. Hysen had already decided on Liverpool.

"I wasn't happy when Hysen moved to Liverpool, because at that time they were the team to go to in terms of winning things," says Pallister.

His agent called him two days later. "I know you're disappointed about Liverpool," he said, "but how would Man United grab you?"

"I thought 'Christ!'" recalls Pallister.

Middlesbrough wanted £2.3 million, a British record transfer fee, a price United considered excessive. But they reckoned without Middlesbrough chairman Colin Henderson, a shrewd negotiator and ICI executive.

"I turned up to the service station on the A19 where the talks were taking place in my sponsored car and Bruce Rioch saw me," he recalls. "Rioch said that if I went anywhere near then the move would be off."

Pallister spent the evening waiting in his agent's Rolls Royce in the car park. It was four am when the deal was finally concluded, with Ferguson maintaining that Henderson was the toughest negotiator he ever faced.

"The huge fee was bad because it put me under a lot of pressure, but I was glad to get away from Middlesbrough," says Pallister.

Ferguson later observed that Pallister arrived as a 24-year-old beanpole with a rich talent that was flawed at times by rawness.

"When I saw him stripped for his medical," recalled the United manager. "I thought: Jesus Christ, he's a bag of bones, a matchstick man. Those skinny thighs, there's nothing there."

But, after Pallister had cemented his place at Old Trafford Ferguson's assessment was that, 'his physique and football matured rapidly and, unusually blessed with balance and pace, he became the centre half which I wouldn't have swapped for any in the game."

Pallister moved immediately and lived in the Ramada Hotel on Deansgate for the first six months. Fellow new United signings Danny Wallace and Mike Phelan were also there. Burnley-born Phelan had signed from Norwich for £750,000, Wallace from Southampton for £1.2 million. Pallister was alone for the first two months in the hotel before his partner Mary moved south. Wallace moved with his family and dog, a Rottweiler. The hotel weren't too impressed with the dog, especially when he took it for walks around the car park.

While winger Wallace scored on his United debut at Portsmouth and settled into the side, Pallister took time to settle. He'd signed for United on Monday, trained on Tuesday and made his debut in that defeat by Norwich on Wednesday.

Pallister and Mary found a place in Wilmslow opposite Brian McClair's and his fortunes picked up on the pitch.

"I really enjoyed the 1990 Cup run. Jimmy Hill's comment that we looked a beaten team before the match inspired us to beat Forest in the third round. We played Hereford in the next round and I got a whack on the head, suffered mild concussion and had a migraine all the way back to Manchester. Newcastle away were next. Walking out that day remains the only time in my entire career when the hairs on the back of my neck stood up because of the atmosphere. I've played in cup finals and big European games, but I've never been shocked by the noise like that day at Newcastle. It was a great place to play football and we were worthy winners. We beat Sheffield United in the sixth round and had Webby and Robbo back from long-term injuries for the semi-final matches against Oldham. I played in the final, but wasn't fit for the replay until Jim McGregor got me there by using a stirrup strap for support to my swollen ankle." Goalkeeper Jim Leighton was dropped for the replay and replaced by Les Sealey.

"Jezza took it really badly," says Pallister. "We had a lot of sympathy for him, but Les had a great game and we won the cup – my first trophy. This is why I joined United."

United were getting stronger and there was the added bonus of European football – though Pallister didn't like flying.

"It's not natural is it, being 30,000 feet up in the air? I had a morbid fear of it from an early age. On my second ever flight we had a bomb scare on a school trip to Majorca and made an unscheduled stop in Barcelona. As we taxied, the captain said, 'We've had call saying there's a bomb on board.' I was near the back of the plane, but I was third off it after knocking people out of the way to reach the exit. Later, we had to identify our suitcases on the tarmac. I took mine inside. A bit later, my teacher shouted, 'Pallister, get out there, you've left your suitcase.' I'd picked up the wrong case, which looked the same as mine. I walked out and saw my case was surrounded by ten angry police officers with pistols and machine guns, concerned it was a bomb."

Pallister retrieved his suitcase, packed with sweets rather than Semtex, but the fear of flying never went away.

"We flew to Norwich one year with United and the plane was hit by a freak gust of wind. Me and Giggsy didn't like flying. The lads were winding us up shouting, 'Pally, we're going down.' The plane flipped as we landed and everyone screamed. I was petrified, but shouted, 'You're not laughing now, are you?' Ken Merrett [United's club secretary throughout the 1990s] spoke to the pilot, who told him that was the closest a plane could come to crashing."

Pallister still managed to fly to United's European Cup Winners' Cup games in 1990/91, including the final in Rotterdam against Barcelona.

"That Cup Winners' Cup victory was the best buzz of my football career. Barça were strong favourites. They didn't have Stoichkov and as I found out a few years later, he wasn't bad. I was uncharacteristically nervous on the way to the ground. Barça's coach Johan Cruyff had said that Brucey and I couldn't pass the ball so I was determined to prove him wrong. I set Choccy up with a chance in the first half. It was one of the best passes I've ever made and I felt like running up and saying, 'Who can't pass the fucking ball, Johan?' But Choccy blasted it over the bar.

"It was like a Manchester evening, dank and wet. We were the better team for 75 minutes of the game and deserved to win. I felt really proud. We had three-quarters of the stadium and celebrated for ages after.

"My roommate Micky Phelan had to do a drugs test, but he couldn't pass urine so I agreed to wait with him. So did Paul Ince. We didn't want to leave him alone and agreed to get a taxi back to the hotel. We waited for ages, then saw television pictures of the players celebrating on the bus back to the hotel. We couldn't believe we were missing the party."

Phelan is now United's assistant manager. "He has a very easy-going manner and I enjoyed his company. There's no edges to him, he's a genuine lad and I was sorry when he left United to join West Brom."

Pallister, Phelan and Ince soon rejoined their team-mates.

"We had four parties to celebrate over the next 48 hours. I remember Alex Ferguson walking around with a box of cigars at one point and wondered later if I had been hallucinating. It was brilliant and I slept for a week after. Incey was a character, very brash. He always had something to say and said it very loudly.

"Clayton Blackmore was our best player that season, with keys goals in Montpellier. He used to put a condom over his head and blow it up."

Clayton was a good friend and came to his aid when Pallister was assaulted in Manchester's Midland hotel, where the team were staying the night before a game. The initial cause of the incident was Pallister's craving for chocolate. Along with Mark Hughes and Blackmore he went to the hotel shop for supplies but in the packed lobby he accidentally nudged a large bloke in the back. Blackmore mistakenly got the idea that the gentleman was a friend of Pallister's as he followed him to the lift. Then the man knocked a carton of Ribena out of Pallister's hand, kicking it away when he tried to retrieve it. Hughes and Blackmore still didn't cotton on that this was an assault, until Pallister faced up to the aggressor who was trying to get into the lift with them. A fight broke out and the two tumbled into a glass case. Blackmore jumped on the stranger from behind and tried to restrain him just as Pallister hit him with a terrific punch which won the Welshman's respect. Blackmore remembers, "The manager came down to see what was happening. The lad then claimed that we started it. Security kicked him out of the hotel. I respected Pally more after that – it was a belting punch."

"It was all hands to the pumps," says Pallister, "but while Clayton helped me out, Sparky just stood there and watched it. People came over and the guy was saying, 'They attacked me, they attacked me.' Clayton was very sensible and said, 'Get the hotel manager and get our manager.' The man's wife came over and was saying, 'My husband is not like that: these guys must have attacked him.' Fergie just said, 'Either he's out of this hotel in the next two minutes or I'm taking the whole team out.'

"The guy was thrown out, just as his eye was coming up a treat. I walked into the pre-match the next day a little bit late and all the lads were sat there singing the *Rocky* theme tune."

This was par for the course in the United dressing room.

"Giggsy used to do rapping when we were out celebrating trophy wins. I can remember seeing him dancing Cossack-style in Mulligan's one night. He was worth millions and could have done his cruciate any minute, but that was no worry to him as he danced with his feet kicking.

"Paul Parker spent all of his money on clothes and mobile phones. We called him Busby because he was never off the phone.

"Schmikes was a big arrogant Danish guy who was the best goalkeeper in the world for five years. We'd fight on the pitch but it would be forgotten about after. Me and Brucey would have stand-up barneys out on the pitch, but we'd sit in the bath after and laugh about it.

"Scholesy was funny with a beer down him, Denis Irwin too – he could be cutting. Butty, Giggsy and Scholesy were a right trio, all good lads. We loved having a session on a Tuesday afternoon knowing that we had Wednesday off for training. We'd spend the afternoon and night in a pub and it was great for the team spirit. If you didn't want to go then you didn't, but everybody would turn up because they loved the atmosphere and social spirit in the team. Eric certainly approved and the only difference between Eric and the rest of the lads was that it got to a point where he had to have a security man with him, but that was just a reality he had to accept and it didn't affect the way he was. Basically I think he found happiness at United because he realised that the players we had would help him get the best out of himself and achieve what he wanted to achieve."

Pallister admitted that he was often the butt of the jokes. "I'd get a bit of stick, they'd pick on the big guy and they'd hammer me about my clothes," he smile. "But the spirit was superb. That alone didn't win us trophies, but it gave us a few more percentage points towards making us a great team."

1991/92 was a season dominated by the Uniteds of Leeds and Manchester. "We played Leeds early in the season and the manager asked me and Brucey what we thought about Eric after the game. I said that he was a player who had something about him. It was that arrogance and self-belief. You get a feeling for people when you play against them and he had something. It was like playing against Alan Shearer. He came to Old Trafford and played up front on his own. He was 18 and I thought, 'Wow, this kid can play!' He was a real handful. You recognise special talents straight away. Eric was in that category, but I didn't think he'd later end up at Manchester United."

Cantona's Leeds would pip United to the title. "I don't

want to take anything away from Leeds, but we were hamstrung by the FA who made us play four games in seven days, five in 11. We couldn't recover in time."

United drew with Luton and lost at home to Nottingham Forest, away to West Ham and Liverpool. The team didn't finish the season empty-handed, winning the League Cup against Nottingham Forest. In the semi-finals of that competition, United had been drawn against Pallister's old club Middlesbrough.

Following FA Cup and European Cup Winners' Cup success in the previous two years, United had a solid cup reputation, but Atlético Madrid ended United's European hopes in November 1991 and defeat in a first ever FA Cup penalty shoot-out at home to Southampton followed months later.

This left the League Cup, a competition United had reached the final of a year earlier, losing to Sheffield Wednesday and a single John Sheridan goal. "A serious disappointment . . . he was a Manchester lad and United fan," rued Sir Alex Ferguson after that one.

Unlike now, European competition didn't warrant exemption from the third round and the 1991/92 League Cup campaign commenced with victory over two legs against Cambridge United before Portsmouth were beaten at Old Trafford in front of just 29,543. Neighbours Oldham Athletic were defeated 2–0 at home in the next round before United drew title rivals Leeds United away in the final eight – part of a trilogy of away games to Leeds, in the league and both cups, in two weeks after Christmas. United drew the league match, but won both cup games, the League Cup game 3–1.

Lennie Lawrence's Middlesbrough were their opponents in the semi-final, a Second Division side on their way to promotion.

"It was a hard situation because, as an old Boro boy, I wanted my former club to win a major competition for the first time in their history.

"I was facing a lot of my old mates, and inevitably there

was banter between Bernie Slaven and myself. I went home for one weekend and wound up with Bern and defender Curtis Fleming on a night out in Yarm. Flem and I had had a drink, though teetotaller Bernie hadn't. Deliberately provoking them, I said, 'How can you boys expect to beat Manchester United?' They both got a bit tetchy until I calmed them down. Bernie kept telling me that he was going to score against me."

Slaven, the Scottish striker, scored nearly 150 goals in an eight-year spell with the Teesiders. In 1999, he said he would bare his backside in Binns Department Store window if Boro beat United in a league game at Old Trafford. They won 3–2 and he was true to his word, with the score etched on each cheek.

Ayresome Park was a forbidding place for any visiting fans and on police advice virtually all the 6,000 travelling United fans opted for the relative safety of coach travel for the semi-final first leg. One hundred and six coaches were lined up in the cold, dimly lit terraced streets behind the away end – the highest number of coaches for a United away game aside from a final.

A capacity crowd of 25,572, Boro's biggest for years, prompted the impish public address announcer to give a tongue-in-cheek reminder that: "Middlesbrough play at home every two weeks, not just when Manchester United come to town." The United fans jeered, singing "part-time supporters".

Such trivialities were soon forgotten as an engrossing and evenly contested game unravelled, with both goalkeepers in splendid form to keep the score goalless. Boro's keeper Stephen Pears knew all about United – he'd played five first-team games under Ron Atkinson in 1985 after spending six years as under-study to Gary Bailey at Old Trafford. Under the headline, 'Fruitless for United as Pears flourishes,' *The Independent* concluded, "This was a semi-final worth 10 goals in the chances created. At least five could have been scored, with a slight bias in United's favour."

Over 9,000 Boro fans travelled to Old Trafford for the second leg a week later, filling their allocation of 5,000 K-Stand seats and 4,000 standing places in the Scoreboard End. Loud enough to be heard back in Redcar, they remained so even after Lee Sharpe scored the first goal of the tie after 30 minutes, shooting low past Pears after impressive build-up play involved Ince, Robson, Giggs and McClair. Boro refused to bow to United's reputation and deserved their 50th minute equaliser when Slaven – it had to be – smashed home a cross from winger Stuart Ripley. The momentum carried them forward and, with 12 minutes left, most in the 45,875 Old Trafford crowd became increasingly nervous as John Hendrie chipped over Schmeichel towards an open goal.

"Just as it was about to bobble over the line, I managed to hack it away," recalls Pallister, who would win the PFA Player of the Year award a month later. "The Boro supporters have reminded me of the incident many times over the years."

Boro came close again in the final minute, when Willie Falconer headed toward the United goal. "Then Peter Schmeichel made one of the best saves I've ever seen, pushing his header around the post," adds Pallister.

The 90 minutes up, the players reconvened in the Mancunian rain. Writing in the *Manchester Evening News*, veteran United reporter David Meek said, "It rained throughout and the already notorious pitch had the added difficulty of a coating of energy-sapping glue on it."

Meek didn't mention the atmosphere, which many remember as one of Old Trafford's finest and certainly the Stretford End's last stand before demolition started two months later.

The game moved into extra time. If neither team scored then a replay was scheduled for Hillsborough – not what United needed with an already busy fixture list from a 22-team top flight.

Yet the Reds looked spent and Robson, the driving force, had a pained expression. Giggs sported one shin pad and a sock around his ankle. Boro had climbed into the ring with the heavyweights and they had United on the ropes.

The players needed support. They got it. Slowly, a rendition of "Ferguson's red and white army" rippled out from the centre of the Stretford End. After five minutes the whole terrace and the Stretford Paddock were singing. The momentum built steadily. After ten, F Stand were on their feet, then G and H along the sides joined in: "Ferguson's red and white army!"

It could not break the impasse, with Boro every bit at good as United. Giggs, 18, seemed the only red with any energy: time and time again Robson fed him balls. Some fans had criticised Ferguson for not playing Giggs every week. Now, the decision was paying off. In the 108th minute, Robson again fed Giggs and the youngster struck a volley into the top corner beyond the imperious Pears.

"I don't know whether he does that all the time or whether it was a fluke," offered the shattered goalkeeper after the final whistle, "but he hit it perfectly high into a corner. I never really saw it."

"I was a much relieved individual," added Pallister, "because I would never have lived it down if we'd have lost. United fans believed it would be an easy task against a Second Division team, but Boro were a good team, well organised by Lennie Lawrence and they stretched us all the way. I did feel for them after the game . . ."

Victory meant a place in the League Cup final for the second successive year, where the disappointment of losing to Sheffield Wednesday the previous year was tempered by Brian McClair's goal in a victory over Nottingham Forest.

Despite missing out on the league, United were improving. The club was also changing.

"When I arrived at Old Trafford, I would park in front of the ground and walk across the forecourt, have a picture taken with fans and sign some autographs. The fans were working class. That has changed and needs to be looked at because watching football isn't within their limits. The wages and status of footballers have changed a lot since I played. Players have a lot of security. But their status brings some negatives – there are worries that criminal activity might be attracted to them, that their houses will be robbed when they are away from home."

Although it didn't always please his manager, Pallister used to return to Middlesbrough to see his mates.

"Fergie didn't really like it. I'd go to Tall Trees and The Mall in Stockton. I was comfortable in what I knew. You have to be aware of what people want from you, who is sincere and who is not. Some people like the association of Manchester United footballers. I've had the same group of friends that I've had all my life. Giggsy is the same."

Pallister could also see that in Manchester, United players attracted some characters who were known to the police.

"We were aware that they were around us at times," he says. "But there were elements who were United fans. You felt that you were OK and wouldn't be targeted. I saw Man City players getting targeted in places where we drank."

Pallister had no such problems. "The only time I got annoyed with a fan was at a United Christmas party in the Moon Under the Water [a giant former cinema which was turned into a pub in Manchester city centre]. I was talking to Giggsy and Nicky Butt. An ignorant guy came between us and put a pad in front of Giggsy and asked him to sign it. He didn't say 'please' or 'excuse me'. I said, 'Excuse me, we're talking.' He replied, 'Well, I'm not after your autograph.' So I grabbed his pen, threw it away and told him where to go."

Manchester United became champions for the first time in 26 years in 1993. Pallister, Bruce and Schmeichel were the only ever-presents, appearing in all 42 league games, the final one against Blackburn with the league already won.

"It was a really special night at Old Trafford when we

celebrated against Blackburn," says Pallister. "You could almost touch the relief inside the stadium. The biggest club in the country had not won the league for 26 years so a lot of it had built up. We'd reached the promised land. We'd had a party at Brucey's the night before the game and I wasn't alone in having a thick head when I arrived at Old Trafford. We met in the grill room and the manager came in, looked at us, smelt the alcohol, and shook his head. He probably feared the worst when the ball came across me and Blackburn took the lead. It took us a while to sober up, then we started to play."

Pallister was the only United player who had not scored in 1992/93. "The lads decided that I would take any free kicks and we got one in injury time, which I hit and it went in. I loved that."

Pallister's partnership with Steve Bruce was one reason for United's success.

"We were both North-East lads so we had a good under-standing," he says. "I liked him from the first time I met him and we socialised off the pitch with our partners. He became my roommate in my later years at United too.

"We played together for long periods without injury and developed a great partnership. We were different types of players. Steve had a reputation for being an old-style centre half, but he was more than that. You wouldn't see anybody time a tackle better than Steve, which was useful as he didn't have any pace. He was a terrific passer of the ball as well, which he never got credit for. Like Tony Mowbray at Middlesbrough, Steve would have run through a brick wall. He was a great foil for me and I enjoyed playing alongside him."

Ferguson referred to the Pallister-Bruce central defensive pairing as 'Dolly and Daisy'. "I really don't know where the manager got that from, or who was who. It was something he just came out with in an interview one day and we never found out what he meant but we were mortified by it! It's not exactly the most intimidating of nicknames for centre backs, is it?"

Few could challenge their hegemony in the United back four.

"You see players coming through as a threat and you always knew that the gaffer was going to do what was best for the club. He was hard, but fair. I've seen his decisions really hurt some players. They weren't happy being left out of big games, but few bear grudges long term."

Pat McGibbon was a promising centre half from Northern Ireland who made his debut in a League Cup tie against York City at Old Trafford. A young United side were beaten 3–0 at home and McGibbon was sent off. He never played for the club again.

United won the double in 1993/94, with Pallister playing a career-best 61 matches that season.

"Roy Keane joined the club and from the earliest training sessions it was apparent that he was a fantastic player. He gave off the same kind of aura as Robbo. Off the field he was a mad Irishman with a short fuse. We had a few temporary differences [the pair actually didn't speak for a year between 1997 and Pallister leaving in 1998] where we didn't speak for periods, but there was always an essential respect and we had some great times."

Pallister remembers one dramatic game over all others that season. "It wasn't even a game we won, but we infuriated the manager by giving away a three-goal lead at Anfield. The manager and Schmeichel had a massive argument which at one time looked like costing Peter his job. The gaffer was ranting about his kicking in the game until Peter reacted by exploding back at him. It culminated in the gaffer telling Peter that he was out of the club because no manager could take that kind of abuse in front of his players. In the end, Peter apologised to the lads and the gaffer, which saved him."

Despite the enormous respect that he has for his former manager, Pallister and Ferguson had their moments. "We came in at half time in one game and he called me a name which I thought stepped over the line. We were going hammer and tongs in the dressing room and had to be separated. Fergie went on, telling me to take my boots off because I wouldn't be needed in the second half. We went for each other again. Archie Knox separated us, then I took my boots off and walked towards the bath. Archie told me that I'd be playing, and Fergie told me to put them on as I wasn't getting away with it that easily. I told him where to go and that I wouldn't play for him. It was only the lads and Kiddo saying, 'Come on, play for yourself.' I went out and we won 2–1. I came back into the dressing room thinking that my United career was over."

Pallister conceded that Ferguson read the situation very well. "We were off the next day, but when we returned to training he asked me to come into his office. I was ready for him and whatever he said. He sat me down and said, 'I just want to apologise for what I said.' I was like, 'Wow, knock me down with a feather.' It was outstanding man-management. He knew that he had pushed me too far to the point that I felt I had to protect my own pride. We shook hands; it was forgotten and never mentioned again. It was dealt with straight away. I've still got the greatest respect for him. He was fantastic for me as a player."

The respect was mutual. When the sprinter Usain Bolt asked Ferguson who the quickest player he'd worked with was, he replied, 'If you're talking over certain distances, then Gary Pallister would have taken some beating in a sprint. I think he was the quickest in the 100 metres – we once had a race and he murdered Giggs, Ince, Parker and Kanchelskis, who were all very quick. But speed in football isn't about running 100 metres on a football pitch. So you've also got to consider Kanchelskis, Ronaldo, Giggs, Cole, Paul Parker – he was very, very quick – Anderson, Ferdinand, Lee Sharpe as a young kid was quick."

And it's not as if Pallister didn't know about the manager's temper. "We had a card school at the back of the coach with

me, Eric, Robbo, Denis, Jim McGregor. The manager sometimes played and would throw his cards across the bus like a
naughty schoolboy if he lost. This was the manager of
Manchester United!

"I'd walk down the bus saying asking if anyone had seen
the jack of hearts that the manager had thrown away." Brian
McClair commented later that Ferguson wasn't to know that
his apparent awful luck at cards actually stemmed from a delib-
erate plot amongst the other members of the 'school' to ensure
he lost.

Despite the success of the team, United fans didn't always
do their part. "United's away support at games was fantastic,"
says Pallister. "Fans would follow us around the world. We'd
go to Volgograd in Russia and there would be a few hundred
fans who must have made huge sacrifices. I always made sure
that I showed my appreciation to them after a game. It was
different at Old Trafford and there were many times when we
said in the privacy of the dressing room, 'It was quiet out there
today, that was tough.' I played sometimes when it was like a
morgue. If the crowd is quiet and apprehensive then it makes
you apprehensive. Passes start getting misplaced and you make
the wrong decisions. Sometimes teams come to Old Trafford
and you face a blanket defence. There were some very comfortable afternoons at Old Trafford where the opposition just came
and stuck everyone behind the ball so all I had to do was sit
back and watch all our great players do their thing.

"They can take time to break down. It's so much easier to
play a game when you feel like that fans are behind you and
responding. I don't think the fans understand how much of a
difference they can make because it's huge."

Pallister cites Barcelona's Hristo Stoichkov and Romario
as the most difficult players he's played against. "They were
like puppet masters pulling all the strings all night long," he
says of the 4–0 defeat in 1994. "Romario was the best player
I came up against. I left the field and it's the only time in my

career where I thought, 'I couldn't get near the man I was supposed to be marking.' It was his movement, his speed and, most of all, his awareness. Fergie had given us instructions, with Paul Parker to mark Romario. A few times, when we thought that the manager didn't quite get it right, Brucey and I would play as we saw fit. So I said to Parks, 'You stay right and I'll stay left.' If you start chasing one player then you lose your structure, balance and discipline. We got it wrong – as Fergie has pointed out. But he also thought that we could go to the Camp Nou and attack them."

"What infuriated me," said Ferguson, " is that we'd spent three days adjusting our zonal defending method to incorporate man-for-man marking of Romario. I wouldn't have taken such pains if I didn't think the change was necessary."

United got over that defeat in Barcelona by demolishing City 5–0. "Andrei ran them ragged and scored a hat-trick in the bargain. That stopped City fans taunting us about that 5–1 game from 1989."

Pallister was in the United side which won the league at his former club Middlesbrough in 1996.

"I'd always got a bit of stick going back to Ayresome Park," says Pallister. "After we won the league at Middlesbrough, a lot of their fans stayed behind to applaud us. We had the trophy and Fergie shouted me over and said, 'Pally, go over to the [Boro] fans and show them the trophy.' I thought he was mad, but he insisted. I walked over nervously – and got a great ovation. That was a huge relief for me, very emotional and a real cleansing of the soul. I'd been forgiven."

United retained the league. In April 1997, they beat title rivals Liverpool 3–1 at Anfield, with Pallister scoring twice. "The funny thing was Fergie's reaction to those goals," says Pallister. "He turned around to [United director] Mike Edelson and said, incredulously, 'Pally's scored two!' as if he couldn't believe it. I got a bollocking after that game, too. It was before the European Cup semi-final against Borussia

Dortmund and I was asked if we'd been working on set pieces. I told the truth, that we'd been working on them all week. Fergie was then asked the same question and said, 'No, the goal was off the cuff.' Then he came to see me and gave me a back-handed slap."

United looked like winning the league for a third successive year in 1998. Thirteen points clear of Arsenal in February, the loss of Roy Keane, who had suffered a cruciate injury the previous September, started to affect United. A Marc Overmars goal was enough to give the Gunners victory at Old Trafford in March as United started to slip. Worryingly for Pallister, he was starting to suffer ongoing back problems, which caused him to miss both games against Monaco as United were again eliminated from the Champions League.

"I slipped coming out of the shower before our game against Chelsea and my back went into spasm a few hours later."

United bought Jaap Stam in the summer of 1998, when Pallister was 33.

"We played Leeds at home in our last home game of the season. I had no reason to think this, but as I walked off the field I wondered if it would be my last game at Old Trafford." It was.

Ferguson called Pallister into his office the next week and explained that there had been a bid from Middlesbrough (for £2.5 million), which had been accepted.

"He told me that I didn't have to go, but that I couldn't be guaranteed a place – not that you were anyway. I'd seen players get bitter and I didn't want to go down that route. And the team coming in for me were Boro, managed by Robbo, the best player I'd ever played with. He was a great leader, great player who did it at both of the end of the pitch. He was a social manager who would get the lads out for a few beers."

The United players paid their respects by having T-shirts made, which they wore for training, reading, 'I've had a Pally.'

"That was a disgrace!" he says. "They said that I was the

worst trainer, but they'd obviously not studied Paul Ince and Brian McClair training. I wasn't blessed with great stamina and with my height I found it hard to do the long distance runs, but I was quick."

The Middlesbrough he rejoined was unrecognisable from the club he'd left. "It was largely down to Steve Gibson, who is a very enlightened chairman. He stood on the Holgate End as a kid and he fulfilled a dream, not of playing for the club, but of owning it and fulfilling his passion that way. He built them a new stadium and Boro have spent years in the Premiership."

Paul Gascoigne was among his new teammates at Middlesbrough. "He has OCD, was generous, hyper, funny, insecure and had his demons. He was a genius as a player and a lovely fella, who was always up to mischief. I walked out of the toilet one morning to find him squirting shaving foam into my boots. Another time, he nicked the brand new team bus at Middlesbrough and crashed it.

"He was a complex character and I feared that when he quit football his insecurities would come to the fore and that's what happened. He became a lost soul and he's struggled to come to terms with it. I just hope that he gets the right help."

After three more years at Middlesbrough, Pallister quit playing in 2001, aged 36.

"I was going to take a year off, but Sky approached me to be a pundit. I'm now doing it with the BBC and MUTV and enjoy it. I do bits and bobs for the FA and the PFA and I'm trying to get my golf handicap down. I play off 14 at the moment. I'll try and guide my two girls, Lauren and Eve, in the right direction in life."

Pallister still keeps in touch with Sharpe and Bruce from his United days.

"I also see Robbo now and then and Parks though MUTV. It's difficult when you are all over the place with separate lives. It was great when we were at Old Trafford, but while you have that bond while you are there, it is soon broken when you leave to play elsewhere or retire. It's great when I meet up with the lads, but we don't do it often.

"Life becomes a little more mundane when you stop playing," he concludes. "You look back and crave a lot of the excitement you had as a player, the adrenalin rush which you used to get from playing in big matches or playing at Old Trafford. You do become used to it when you are going through it. And then it's gone."

11
MARTIN EDWARDS
The chairman

MARTIN EDWARDS
MANCHESTER UNITED

Saturday 19th August, 1989. It's an hour before kick-off and Manchester United are about to start the new season with a home game against champions Arsenal. United's long-time kitman, Gorse Hill born and bred former taxi driver Norman Davies, is tasked with finding a strip for United's new chairman-elect Michael Knighton. In the rare sunshine half an hour later, 47,000 watched as Knighton ran onto the pitch wearing boots and a United training top, before juggling a ball in front of an ecstatic Stretford End, who went home even happier after United won 4–1.

United's supporters were so thrilled because Knighton, a charismatic property speculator, had come in with an offer to buy out the unpopular then-chairman Martin Edwards with the promise of pumping enormous sums of money into rebuilding parts of the ground.

Knighton's performance did not generate the same response elsewhere. As he watched Knighton on a monitor from his office alongside Arsenal manager George Graham, Alex

Ferguson had a bad gut feeling about this publicity stunt from someone who had yet to conclude any deal. The mood was far worse in the directors' box.

"I was horrified," admits Martin Edwards. "Absolutely horrified. I was sat in the stand thinking, 'What the hell have I done?' I couldn't believe what I was seeing. I kept saying to myself, 'What the hell have I done?' I realised that I'd made a big mistake. The other directors felt the same. They cringed and began to turn on Knighton."

Many still find it hard to believe that Martin Edwards seriously contemplated the sale of one of football's prime assets. But Edwards maintains it made perfect sense. There were serious problems at Old Trafford. The 47,000 gate that day was almost 10,000 more than the average crowd from the previous season and a figure which would not be bettered all season.

United's average attendance had slipped below Liverpool's the previous season as the club finished 11th. The average was 38,000, but crowds as low as 23,368, 26,722 and 30,379 had watched United's three final league games of the season against Wimbledon, Everton and Newcastle. The club had taken just one coach of travelling fans to a league game at Queens Park Rangers, witnessed by a paltry 10,017.

Martin Edwards told his under-fire manager Alex Ferguson that he was going to sell the club, saying, "If you know anyone who would be prepared to buy my shares for £10 million, with a guarantee that he will spend a further £10 million on renewing the Stretford End, then he can have it."

Ferguson, who enjoyed a good relationship with his chairman, asked him why he wanted to sell and concluded that Edwards felt he could never win the fans over and had no other way out.

Michael Knighton appeared as a potential purchaser of United that summer.

"I wanted to sell the club to Michael Knighton for two

reasons," explains Martin Edwards, at his home in Wilmslow, Cheshire. "I had a huge debt to the bank, almost a million pounds. Since the rights issue in 1978, I'd put over £400,000 of my own money into the club. My house was the security against that debt. I couldn't go on feeding that debt for ever and I wasn't comfortable. This was pre-Sky television, when the economic climate was very different in football.

"The second reason was that the Stretford End needed rebuilding and the price would have been around £7 million. I didn't have the money. Something would have had to give. Michael Knighton arrived out of the blue and was prepared to give me £10 million, which was more than what my shares were worth. He also said that he was going to rebuild the Stretford End and would spend a further £10 million on that. It solved both my problems. And there's another thing – what if I had turned him down and it became public knowledge that I had turned down the money which would have rebuilt the Stretford End? In hindsight, it sounds ridiculous given the wealth of the club today, but at the time it wasn't a bad offer."

Edwards's first impression of Knighton was positive. "Michael Knighton is a very interesting guy when you first meet him," he says. "I thought he was serious, ambitious and I knew that he had backing from two very wealthy partners."

Although later portrayed as a maverick fantasist, Knighton correctly identified the huge potential in United. He said that the club had a major pulling power which had not been exploited. He predicted that it would become a £150 million business within 15 years. (Within 11 years United was valued at over £1 billion). He commissioned a study which identified several areas for development at Old Trafford such as television rights, merchandise, a magazine and a hotel – all of which were exploited in later years.

With the club sale set to go through, Edwards relaxed and a previously parsimonious United spent heavily on Neil Webb, Mike Phelan, Gary Pallister, Paul Ince and Danny Wallace.

There was much optimism among red ranks, and Knighton's juggling act on the pitch was taken to show that he had a genuine love for United, projecting an enthusiasm and a warmth that the reserved Edwards rarely evinced.

But now the directors began looking for loopholes to get out of the deal. Edwards is quick to point out that this wasn't purely motivated by their reaction to Knighton's tomfoolery. "Of course, there was an element of self-interest to them, as they wouldn't have gained from Knighton coming in."

Ultimately, Knighton didn't have the money to take over. Again, Edwards counters the widely held belief that Knighton had a made a fool of the United board.

"He'd proved that he had the financial backing, but then he fell out with the other two partners because they would have sidelined him eventually," says Edwards. "Knighton realised what was going on and he wanted to be number one. The backers pulled away. When the pressure came on, Knighton couldn't deliver the money."

Knighton exited; Edwards stayed. Over the next ten years or so, Edwards would get rid of his United shares bit by bit for a grand total of £85 million.

Knighton wasn't the first outsider with whom Edwards had negotiated about selling Manchester United. The controversial publisher and *Daily Mirror* owner Robert Maxwell had boasted about buying the club in 1984. A rampant egomaniac, Maxwell already owned Third Division Oxford United, but they were a long way from the perceived glamour of the top flight.

"I was never close to doing a deal with Robert Maxwell," Edwards puts the record straight. "He approached me. He was a really big noise at the time. I agreed to a meeting with him, only because Roland Smith was involved in the deal. He had been on the board with my father Louis Edwards and was his friend. He wanted me to meet Maxwell. I agreed, but as far as I was concerned, it was private. What did Maxwell do? He announced to the world that there would be talks about him buying Manchester United."

Edwards met Maxwell at his London office, Maxwell House. "We had little common ground," he recalls, "and I didn't particularly like him. I felt that he was trying to get United on the cheap and we were miles apart. When I was leaving, he said, 'We'll do a joint press release.' I got in the car back to Manchester, when I received a call from Maurice Watkins [the club solicitor and director] who was at the meeting. Maurice said, 'Maxwell has issued a press release.' It was very one-sided, covering himself and against me."

Edwards was strongly criticised by fans. "I look back now and I realise one thing," he says, "I never won the PR battles. I didn't win it with Maxwell and I didn't win it with Knighton, did I? I was never interested in public relations and I'm still not. I'm disappointed in today's world in the sense that with people like Tony Blair and Brown, it's all about image and PR. Where's the substance? Did Winston Churchill need a PR man? No. If I had to make a statement then I made it personally to the press."

Edwards acknowledges that communication wasn't his strong point.

"I wasn't good at dealing with supporters. I didn't want supporters running Manchester United, that was my concern. I knew what the supporters thought because I read all their correspondence. I would get hundreds of letters on big topics. I had a lot of friends who were supporters too so I knew what was going on, what the supporters wanted. I wasn't prepared to give a lot of what they wanted, nor did I feel that having a regular dialogue with supporters was going to help."

Even his biggest detractors would probably admit that long time United chairman and current club president Martin Edwards was the scapegoat for United's problems throughout his 20-year leadership. As chairman of the club and major shareholder, the buck stopped with him. If ticket prices increased – as they often did in the 90s, then Edwards, the son of former chairman and Sir Matt's confidant Louis Edwards, was blamed. In addition to the debacles with Maxwell and Knighton, Edwards took the flak for floating the club on the stock market in 1991, for the rebuilding of the Stretford End and for the ill-fated deal to sell the club to BSkyB. He was savagely criticised for being parsimonious in wage negotiations, for not communicating with fans and for being Martin Edwards, the former rugby-playing rich Cheshire kid into whose lap fell the greatest football club in the world.

By the late 1990s, the 'Blame Edwards' culture had even become ironic. One letter writer to the fanzine *United We Stand* made him culpable for everything from his wife's moods to the fact that the plants in his garden weren't flowering as expected.

Not everyone had it in for Edwards. The late, great, Anthony H Wilson, regularly defended the United chairman and said he was the most important factor in Manchester United's dominance of English football.

And Edwards was capable of communication, if he was so minded. If, as editor of *United We Stand*, I wrote a letter to him then Edwards answered immediately. If we wanted an interview then we got one, usually in his office overlooking the Old Trafford forecourt. If we saw him on pre-season trips he would always come over and say hello, no matter whom he was with.

I helped the writer Jim White, another United fan, on his excellent 2008 book *Manchester United – The Biography*. Jim told me that he had written to Sir Alex Ferguson, David Gill and Martin Edwards requesting interviews as a matter of course, but that he wasn't expecting a yes from any of them.

I had a hunch that of the three, Edwards would agree. And he did, prompting White to think that I had mystical powers.

Whatever fans say about Martin Edwards – and they've said a lot, most of it negative – he seldom fought his corner.

He presided over the biggest, most successful club in British football in the 1990s, a club which attracted admiration and envy, yet he remained loathed by many hardcore United fans. He made key appointments, from Sir Alex Ferguson to Edward Freedman, which would revolutionise United. He was responsible for signing Eric Cantona. And while many clubs botched up their stadiums with uneasily juxtaposed rebuilding after the Taylor report, Edwards oversaw the continued redevelopment of Old Trafford which stayed consistent to the plans laid down by his father in 1962.

I met up with Edwards at his Wilmslow home the morning after arriving back from United's World Club Championship success in Yokohama. He'd asked me to bring a match programme and upon seeing his office, it's clear to see why. Edwards owns virtually every printed book there is about United. A renowned United trivia fanatic, he used to get the club's former programme editor Cliff Butler to test him on questions. Many United fans chose to believe that he preferred rugby and had little passion for any other kind of football.

The request for this interview was accompanied with a copy of *We're the Famous Man United*, which he returned stating that he'd bought a copy when it came out. I couldn't see Malcolm Glazer telling me that. After making coffee and dealing with a phone call from his mum who wants to know what time United kick-off at Stoke, Edwards settles down.

"I was born in 1945," he says, "two months after the end of the war at Adlington Hall, a Cheshire manor house. During the war it was confiscated and used as a nursing home for officers' wives.

"When I was very young I used to wait for my father to come home from watching United and give me the match programme, which I collected. My first game was in 1952 against Wolves. I don't remember much about it."

Edwards was sent to boarding school when he was eight in nearby Holmes Chapel.

"There were around 100 male students and they were very keen on sport," he recalls. "I was in the rugby 15 and the youngest player to reach the school cricket team when I was ten. I loved sport, cricket and rugby."

Edwards then attended Cokethorpe, a public school in Oxfordshire, where Tony Martin, the Norfolk farmer who was imprisoned for fatally shooting a burglar, was also a pupil. Another classmate remembers Edwards as being a serious and quiet boy, which gave him an air of gravitas and maturity. Edwards was also considered popular with the opposite sex and there was talk of him having success with two maids, which won admiration from the other boys as they were older than the pupils.

"Again, it was a sporting school," says Edwards. "I was far keener on sport than the academic side. I played rugby at school and we had football kickabouts, but nothing more than that."

Edwards's father and uncle were equal partners in the meat trade. "My grandfather had started the business in the 1930s in Miles Platting," he explains. "Both my father and his brother were born in Salford – Salford lads. My father went on the United board the day after Munich disaster. The week before, he came up to be elected to the board. One director, Mr Whittaker, opposed him. Perhaps he was a little bit frightened of him.

"Harold Hardman, the chairman, told my father that he could have brought him on the board, but that he wanted the decision to be unanimous. He asked Mr Whittaker to think about things. That decision probably saved my father's life because he was due to travel to Munich. Fearing the embarrassment of the situation and being busy with business, he didn't travel. Instead, he cancelled his place on the flight. Mr Satinoff, a fan and friend of the directors, took his place on the plane and lost his life."

George Whittaker, who looked like a throwback to Edwardian times with a walrus moustache, was a United director who did not travel on the doomed flight, as he died in the team's London team hotel the night before the Babes' legendary 5–4 victory at Arsenal. It was the Babes' last performance on English soil and they wore black armbands as a mark of respect.

"Mr Whittaker's death meant that my father would have been selected at the next board meeting, but the day after the crash my father joined immediately."

Edwards was at boarding school at the time of Munich and didn't return to Cheshire until the next holidays, a month after the disaster.

"It was in those holidays that I became an avid United supporter," he says. "That's when I started going regularly to games."

Matt Busby's choice, Louis Edwards, became the most influential member of the United board. In 1962, he said "The welfare and continued progress of Manchester United are now my life ambition."

Son Martin left school in 1964 with an undistinguished academic record.

"I went into the family business, where I would work for 16 years," he says. "I moved back North and left most of my friends behind – though I keep in touch with many now. That's how it is at boarding school and I didn't have many friends in Cheshire after leaving school. I had to start making friends."

His first job was cutting up meat and boning out in the central butchery. "I was late on my first day for work by two minutes," he recalls. "I'd walked to the train station at Alderley Edge, then got a train to Manchester and a bus from Stephenson Square to Miles Platting. I was sent home. I was absolutely livid, bloody fuming. My mother wasn't impressed either, but Father explained that he wasn't treating me any different to any other person at work. It was my dad's way of saying that I was in the real world."

Edwards was sent to work in several butchers' shops, before being entrusted to run a single shop. "My dad wanted me to start at the bottom in the factory. The other lads teased me because I was the boss's son, but they were all right, decent lads who had a laugh. It was a good experience for me.

"I joined the works football team and played centre forward. I wasn't a bad goalscorer, but I lacked technique because I'd never played football at school. I was fit, though, and sporty. We won the league one year. Our captain Billy Myerscough had played for Aston Villa in the 1957 FA Cup final."

Edwards also played rugby for Wilmslow Rugby Club. "When the seasons overlapped I played rugby on a Saturday afternoon, football on Sunday morning and cricket on Sunday afternoon," he says.

The United chairman Harold Hardman died in 1965. "He had been poorly for a while and Father was really the leading light," says Edwards. "He was almost like an acting chairman and did most of the negotiation to bring players like Denis Law to the club.

"Matt Busby always said of all the players he had, the greatest was Law, and I'd have to agree with that. I was a teenager in those days, going along to watch matches with Father. To me, Denis from 1963 to 1967 was unbelievable. In the same way you could say Paul Scholes and Ruud van Nistelrooy did in 2001, or Cantona did in '96, he won the league for us in '65. He was just outstanding."

Louis Edwards had been buying up shares in United, but didn't have a controlling interest. He became the biggest shareholder and took over as chairman in 1965, with his son working at the meat company.

"The company was very successful. It had started off with a few small butchers, but the business grew and grew until there were around 70 shops in the Lancashire and Cheshire area. We also had the meat concession for around 120 Woolworths stores, so their meat departments were run by Louis Edwards – the name of the company. We also ran the in-house meat departments for around 60 cash-and-carry stores.

At the peak, we had around 200 retail outlets plus around 70 of our own shops. We had around 1,000 employees and the side of the business which I looked after had a £10 million turnover in the mid to late 1970s."

In 1970, Edwards, then just 25, was invited onto the United board by his father. "I was playing rugby for Wilmslow but had a couple of head injuries," he explains. "My father thought that I had stopped playing – and I think he wanted to discourage me from playing and invited me onto the board, but I didn't stop. I would attend board meetings during the week and watch midweek games, but I wanted to carry on playing. I loved playing rugby. It was only after I got concussed at the start of the 1971/72 season at Waterloo away that I stopped. The neuro-surgeon told me that I was in danger of becoming punch drunk like a boxer. He told me to stop playing. I was only 26, but I listened to him."

Edwards was by far the youngest of the United directors. "There was a huge age gap between me and the other direc- tors, who were all 30 years older," he recalls. "They were all very respectful, though. Les Olive was the secretary and he was very good with me. I was going through a learning curve and couldn't contribute much in those early days so I sat and listened. It was a tremendous advantage for me later on because I'd seen the board meetings, seen the dramas of players coming and going. I'd seen Matt Busby coming back, the Frank O'Farrell and Tommy Docherty sagas."

Louis Edwards died from a heart attack in 1980, a month after Granada TV's *World in Action* investigative series screened an edition called 'The Man Who Bought United.' It contained allegations of systematic bribery and corruption. Martin called it a "character assassination", saying, "Let's not kid ourselves. This is what brought about his premature death. What Granada did was complete character assassination. I have never seen anyone deteriorate so quickly."

The position of United chairman became vacant. Martin

saw his father's passing as his chance to fill the position, but the other directors didn't agree.

"Les Olive approached me on behalf of the other directors to say that they felt I was still a bit young to be chairman of Manchester United," he says.

"They wanted Matt Busby to be chairman, with me as vice chairman learning the ropes. I was 34. I'd been watching events for ten years. Matt was 71. He could have had another ten or twenty years and we didn't know what health issues he might have had. I felt that it was the right moment for me to be chairman. I told Les that I wasn't happy with his proposal and that I felt the time was right for me. I had experience and energy. I wasn't daunted by United. Indeed, when I joined United I moved to a much smaller company as United only had 100 employees and a turnover of around a million.

"While United was a much smaller operation, in terms of publicity it was very different. Only a few people were interested in the fortunes of the meat company, but at United it was a national interest on the way to becoming an international one. The exposure was huge, but the size of the business was not daunting."

Olive, the long-time club secretary and director, returned to the board and they discussed it. Edwards was in a strong position as his family had a controlling interest from Louis Edwards's shares.

"It was their decision and they decided to make me chairman and Matt club president," says Edwards. "My father had around 50 per cent of the club's shares when he died. He left 18 per cent to my mother, 16 per cent to my brother and 16 per cent to me."

Dave Sexton was United's manager when Edwards took over in March 1980 and the new club chairman soon flexed his muscles. "We finished second at the end of my first season after winning the last seven league games," he says. "The position flattered us and we finished eighth the following year. I felt that

Dave had had four years in charge and that United were not progressing. We were no nearer to winning the league. I also felt that the supporters were a little bit disgruntled with the style of football we were playing. We had some very poor attendances that season (attendances dropped from 54,394 on the opening day of the season to 40,165 on the final day). So I decided to dismiss Dave, my first major decision. I know that some players were not happy, but I felt it was right. The board saw me act decisively and I felt stronger in the position from then on."

Edwards's choice as Sexton's replacement was Lawrie McMenemy, the Southampton manager who had excelled at The Dell and led the Second Division side to surprise FA Cup success over Manchester United in 1976.

"I'd spoken to him and he indicated that he would come to United," says Edwards. "McMenemy then rang me and told me that his wife didn't want to move to Manchester and that he would not be coming. That left me in the lurch. My second choice was Bobby Robson. I spoke to him and he said that while he was very flattered, he had unfinished business at Ipswich. He explained that he had a young squad with players he had brought in and he didn't want to leave them."

Inconceivably, United were struggling to find a manager.

"So I was really in the lurch wasn't I? The next choice was Ron Saunders. He'd been successful and led Villa to the championship, but he wasn't interested and turned us down flat. United were different then," says Edwards, explaining Saunders's reluctance even to discuss the job. "While it was a big club, success was lacking. Between 1968 and '83, the club won just one trophy, the FA Cup in 1977. It was a bleak period. United didn't have enough money in the kitty either. Managers asked me how much money there would be. I was honest. They weighed up what I said and turned us down."

The solution was provided when journalist John Maddock approached Edwards and informed him that the West Bromwich Albion manager Ron Atkinson would take the United job.

"That was music to my ears," he says. "Ron was an up-and-coming buck doing well at West Bromwich Albion. He'd led his exciting side to a 5–3 victory over United at Old Trafford. He was under contract, though, so I approached Bert Millichip at West Bromwich. We met at a service station in the Midlands and did a deal where United would compensate West Brom. Bert wasn't happy, but he realised that Ron wanted to come to Old Trafford so there was little he could do."

There were no problems with Atkinson's personal terms, though Atkinson later claims that when he was discussing club cars, Edwards said, "Dave [Sexton] had a Rover" and the flamboyant Atkinson replied, "Well, I've got a dog called Charlie, Mr Chairman, but I thought we were talking cars." According to Atkinson, Edwards agreed to replace his existing car, a Mercedes coupé, for an up-to-date model.

Edwards shakes his head. "I can't remember that, I think it might be a Ronism."

What he describes as his lowest point as chairman was just around the corner.

"I'd not been in the job for long and we had just bought Frank Stapleton and John Gidman and spent a lot of money on them. Watford knocked us out of the FA Cup and I felt so disappointed. Tottenham had also knocked us out of the League Cup in the first round, beating us home and away."

Edwards was still closer in age to the players than his fellow directors.

"I'd knock about with the players a little bit on pre-season tours," he says. "I can remember hiring mopeds out in the Caribbean and that Gary Bailey was a reasonable tennis player. I never got involved in the hi-jinks, though, because I thought it was unprofessional.

"I never got to know players well, to talk to them about their personal lives. They were friendly on the surface, but perhaps a little guarded because of my position. These days I'm very keen on the United Former Players' Association and

I go to as many old boys functions as possible." Edwards asked that his fee for this interview be donated to the Former Players' Association.

There were no hi-jinks on United's trip to Hungary for a UEFA Cup match against Videoton in 1985. Edwards went for a walk close to the team hotel with fellow director Maurice Watkins when he saw two people struggling by a river. As they got closer, he realised that it was a policeman trying to stop a lady from jumping into the fast-flowing water.

"I did what anyone would do and went to help him," says Edwards. "I helped pull the lady back to stop her jumping in the water. She was really angry that we'd foiled her suicide attempt and bit my hand before running off."

Back at Old Trafford, the larger-than-life Ron Atkinson was a very different personality to the serious Dave Sexton.

"I had a good relationship with Ron," says Edwards. "Though he wasn't quite the character which he portrayed all the time. Ron liked exciting football and exciting players. His teams reflected that and he wasn't unsuccessful. He won two cups and we were never out of the top four, which at the time was quite good. It was the league that we were after, though, and we never looked like winning it. We had a great chance in the 1985/86 season when we won the first ten games on the trot, but then we started picking up injuries to key players and we didn't have the strength in depth to deal with that."

By 1986, Edwards had other concerns about Atkinson. "Ron took his eye off the ball a little bit towards the end," he says. "His marital circumstances probably didn't help as he'd separated from his first wife Margaret and had started a relationship with Maggie. The results were not coming towards the end – we were near the bottom of the league when he went."

Atkinson had previously offered his resignation. "Towards the end of the 1985/86 season, he came to me and said, 'I think I should call it a day this season. I think my time is up.' I wasn't sure and told him not to do it, suggesting that he should give it another season. What was disappointing, though, was that he went to the World Cup in Mexico that summer when I felt he should have been around buying players. He came back and wanted to buy one or two at the last minute, which wasn't ideal preparation."

Edwards was singled out as the instigator of the sale of United's star striker Mark Hughes to Barcelona in 1986 and a barrage of criticism ensued.

"The only way Hughes would sign another contract was with a get-out clause allowing him to leave," says Edwards. "If we hadn't given him a contract he would have gone for nothing. I put a clause in for £1.8 million and I did that to protect Manchester United. I didn't want Mark Hughes to go, United didn't want him to go, but Mark Hughes decided to go. That never came over in the media and I got all the stick. Maybe he had committed to Barcelona half-way through the 1985/86 season and maybe by the end he didn't want to go, but he'd signed a deal with them."

Off the field, United had issues with football hooliganism which Edwards had seen first hand in the 1970s and 1980s.

"The hooliganism was a little bit out of our control," he says. "Old Trafford was always very well policed. If there were ever any requests for something to be done to the ground, for better police facilities or surveillance, we always supported the police and local authority in whatever they wanted. The last thing we wanted was trouble.

"Away from Old Trafford, our influence was limited. We tried our best on the away travel and encouraged people to travel officially. I came in for a lot of stick by restricting people to official travel, but at least then we had control of our own fans, with good security.

"You always get fans who want to travel independently in Europe, though, because they find the official travel too expensive. Once they do that, they are out of the club's control. There were riots in Valencia in 1983 which were horrendous, absolutely horrendous. I was in the ground watching and I feared the ban coming for English clubs, but what could we do?"

English clubs were duly banned from European competition for the five years from 1985 to 1990. After the ban was lifted, United continued to encourage fans to travel with the club, while also selling tickets to independent travellers.

"Even after the ban, how could we control what happened in Turkey in 1993?" asks Edwards. "We cannot control the behaviour of our own fans if they book their own travel. It was completely out of our control. If we had a hooligan element attached to us, what could we do? We had numerous meetings with the police about hooliganism, but then some clubs in Europe ignore all the advice. British grounds are safe now, but you don't know what you are going to get in Europe."

Edwards also had several personal unsavoury encounters with United fans on European away trips. "I was sitting in Rome a few years ago having a meal with friends in one of the squares," he says. "A group of men, 20 or 30 of them, saw me and started singing, 'Martin Edwards, you're a wanker.' I get that, but a lot of people come up to me and are very pleasant. They say, 'We'd like to thank you for everything that you've done for Manchester United, it's unfair what has happened to you.' And if those in that group of men singing at me in Rome were alone and sober, their behaviour would be completely different."

If Edwards has been unfairly blamed for some of United's biggest mistakes, there is no doubt what is seen as his masterstroke as Chairman, though some people have even tried to take that away from him. Alex Ferguson was always United's first choice to replace Ron Atkinson.

"Without question," says Edwards. "I read somewhere that I was interested in Terry Venables and Bobby Charlton wanted Alex. That's nonsense. Mike Edelson [a United director] was the only one who mentioned Venables. Alex first came onto our radar when he took Aberdeen to win the Cup Winners'

Cup final against Real Madrid in 1983. He was clearly one for the future. I got to know him quite well when we did the Gordon Strachan deal, because Gordon had signed two contracts and we needed to unravel that. Alex wanted him to come to United."

Ferguson was a considered choice. "We felt that we needed a tough manager with a proven track record both domestically and in Europe, somebody who could handle big players. But it was still a big leap from Aberdeen to United."

In November 1986, Edwards flew north to see Dick Donald, the Aberdeen chairman, about signing his manager.

"The pair had an understanding that he would be able to go if Manchester United came in for him," says Edwards. "He agreed compensation, but then Dick said, 'You're not taking [assistant manager] Archie [Knox] as well, are you?' Alex wanted Archie to join United too."

The new Scottish management pair arrived and began a substantial rebuilding job. Another thing that Edwards is credited for is that way that he stuck by Ferguson throughout a lengthy rebuilding process which was slow to bring any reward.

"While the team didn't win trophies, we knew that Alex and Archie were working behind the scenes on the youth and recruitment," says Edwards. "We signed five new players in the summer of 1989 and they needed time to gel."

By the turn of 1990, United sat mid-table and the Knighton deal was off. Attendances were plummeting at Old Trafford, fan discontent high and speculation that Ferguson would be dismissed was rife in the media. A third-round FA Cup game away to Brian Clough's high-flying Nottingham Forest side was crucial. Lose, and many thought Ferguson would be sacked.

"The focus is always on that third-round cup game at Forest," recalls Edwards. "Despite the speculation, Alex wasn't going to be sacked if we lost that game. If we had been relegated or the crowds had started to drop, then we don't know what would have happened."

Edwards approached Ferguson before the Forest game. "I said, 'Irrespective of the result, your job is safe.' I never ever had a discussion with any other member of the board about whether Alex should stay or go. I could see what he was doing behind the scenes. It was definitely a concern that fans were protesting and gates were dropping. There would have been more pressure if we hadn't won at Forest and I don't know how long we would have withstood that pressure, so the FA Cup definitely came at the right time. Alex needed a lift and he got it through the cup run."

The 1990 FA Cup success was Ferguson's first trophy at Old Trafford. From then on, though United entered into its most successful period in its history, the criticism of Edwards shifted from matters on the pitch. The club was suffering acute growing pains for which Edwards received much of the blame. Everyone suddenly wanted to watch United, with demand often exceeding supply for tickets. Edwards was slammed for rising ticket prices and unfair ticket distribution, with fans annoyed that wealthier supporters had ticket priority.

"I thought I was fair on ticket prices," he says. "When it came to cup final tickets, it's a nightmare whichever system you put in. Unfortunately, sometimes we had to weight allocations to the higher payers. People are not going to pay £50,000 for a box if they can't get a cup final ticket with that."

Irritation over squeezing greater profits from ticket prices went back to 1987, when United introduced a membership scheme, with fans charged £5 a season for the chance to stand in certain sections of the ground like the Stretford End. Some saw it as a money-making exercise and a chance to oust David Smith, head of the supporters' club which had an office at Old Trafford. In 1987, Smith was advised that his organisation was 'surplus to requirements' and United endorsed a new commercially orientated club membership scheme to replace the supporters' club.

"Dave Smith was independent from the club and he was

making money for himself," says Edwards. "We felt that we should be controlling the supporters' club, not Dave Smith. If there were problems with fans then we wanted control of it." Smith wrote a book with Michael Crick entitled *Manchester United – The Betrayal of a Legend*. The book placed the responsibility for the perceived betrayal squarely in the "hands of the Edwards family . . . The fans . . . were being let down by a man who simply wanted to make money from his great club."

"I felt that he had betrayed me and therefore the club," comments Edwards simply.

In 1991, United became a public limited company. For many this was the first step in a process which led inevitably to the Glazer takeover. Again, Edwards argues it was necessary given the circumstances after Hillsborough, and makes the point that supporters could have changed the destiny of the club if they had not been so unwilling to participate.

"We needed money to rebuild the Stretford End," says Edwards. "We had to go to the City for that money. By then we had to comply with the Taylor Report to make Old Trafford an all-seater stadium. We did a rights issue. Every fan had a chance to buy shares in United. Most didn't. We wanted a third of the shares to be held by small individual shareholders, a third by institutional shareholders and the rest by supporters. That was what we were aiming for, maybe even more being held by supporters, but they never took up the shares. We raised the money to build the stand."

The construction was also paid for by far higher ticket prices. By 1992, United fans outraged at price hikes formed a group called HOSTAGE (Holders of Season Tickets Against Gross Exploitation). The fanzines were full of letters from fans who strongly objected to the 30 per cent price rises.

"Look what we spent the money on," counters Edwards. "We built the Stretford End. Look at Arsenal now, with a huge debt that they pay off each year. We always built stands out of the profits. The money that fans were paying was going back into the club. The share dividends were actually fairly small."

The new all-seated Stretford End stand didn't please everyone – United's continued success meant that it was too small.

"It fitted in with the rest of the ground," maintains Edwards. "There were sightline issues with having a bigger stand and being too far from the pitch."

United have since built bigger stands behind both ends. The Stretford End development also upset fans as an executive area of seating was placed in what was once the vocal heartland of United fans.

"I can understand why some supporters were not happy, but there would not have been a great payback on that stand if we had just put normal seats in," says Edwards. "I accept that the atmosphere was compromised, but we had to get a balance financially. And I know it's not the popular thing to say, but I was happy when Old Trafford became all-seater. I felt that after Hillsborough, it was the safest way forward for stadiums."

The loss of the terraced Stretford End was bemoaned as a further example of the movement away from football's working-class roots.

"There was a shift in the type of people attending games," acknowledges Edwards, "but a lot of the hardcore have stayed."

IMUSA (The Independent Manchester United Supporters' Association) was formed in 1995 and wanted a dialogue with Edwards – something he was not prepared to entertain.

"I felt that IMUSA would have always wanted more and more and more," says Edwards. "And I didn't want the independent supporters running the club. We had supporters on the board. Les Olive was a huge supporter, he always had the conscience of the supporters. Mike Edelson and Maurice Watkins were supporters in their own right.

"I would never have sold a player for a short-term gain.

My interest in the club always had to be long term because that's what my shares represented."

Another of IMUSA's concerns was the increasing commercialism of the club. In 1992, Edwards appointed Edward Freedman, who had led a merchandise revolution at Tottenham Hotspur, a club which had a bigger turnover than United in 1991.

"Edward Freedman was a good signing off the field," explains Edwards. "We'd just bought the club shop off Sandy Busby. While we didn't have the shop, there was a great opportunity being lost. We paid a fair price for the business and it brought the merchandise back in house.

"I got to know Edward through Irving Scholar at Tottenham. I could see that some of his ideas were ahead of their time, which had proved true since other clubs have copied them from United. Clubs were not printing names on the back of shirts, for example, which was Edward's idea. He introduced the video magazines which were huge for a time. He introduced a club magazine which sold 150,000 copies a month at one point. He brought in wholesaling, which meant that we were selling goods to stores around Britain and beyond. He anticipated events and trends. If Edward hadn't started that, Nike would never have paid us what they did for that huge contract to merchandise United for 15 years."

The appointment of Freedman was met with hostility by the existing United directors. "There was a lot of opposition to bringing Edward in, especially from Bobby Charlton and Mike Edleson," explains Edwards. "Roland Smith, the PLC chairman came to me and said, 'Do you really want him?' I did. And I never regretted that.

"Edward arrived at the right time, because it coincided with the advent of the Premier League and Sky television, who had a huge influence. The higher profile and increased coverage was almost immediate. I would sit in my office on a Saturday watching the huge crowds queueing to get into the club shops."

Whereas Liverpool had failed to capitalise on their popularity, United did not. From Burnley to Barcelona, clubs copied and opened up megastores. It was merchandise money which paid for United's signing of Roy Keane from Nottingham Forest in 1993.

"Other clubs copied us," says Edwards. "But their biggest problem was that they spent all the money on players. We spent money on players, but we were sensible. We improved the stadium – and United are now getting the benefits from that. At other clubs, the money just washed right through, with nobody retaining any of it."

Edwards suggests that this prudence was because he had put his own money into United.

"It's very easy for a chief executive or somebody who has no shares or equity in the company to go and buy players because somebody else will pick up the bill in five years' time," he says. "That's an easy way to become more popular with the supporters. I never had that luxury. I always had to balance the books and look after United because I had £1 million of debt in the club. I had to get a balance between buying players, improving the stadium and pleasing the supporters by not charging too much. When you judge my reign, don't judge it on one thing. Judge it by how successful we were financially, how successful the team was, whether the ticket prices were fair and whether the club was run successfully. I could never please everybody, but over the range I wasn't that bad. I could have charged £1 a ticket to please a lot of people, but we wouldn't have been around for very long."

The football journalists certainly prefer Edwards to United's new regime. "I had a good relationship with the football media," he says. "The news guys will have a go at you in any way they can including your personal life." Edwards was involved in some sexual peccadilloes which were splashed across the tabloids. "They would slaughter me, but when it came to football I had a good relationship with the football writers. David

Meek of the *Manchester Evening News* was a delight to work with. I trusted him on anything, Stuart Mathieson too and I never had a problem with him.

"Peter Fitton would ring from *The Sun*. I would make a deal with him to not write something in exchange for another story. If the journalists let me down once I would never trust them again."

The journalists had plenty to write about in November 1992. Edwards's involvement in what would possibly be seen as Ferguson's greatest ever signing is not widely known.

"I got a phone call from Bill Fotherby at Leeds enquiring about Denis Irwin," explains Edwards. "I told him that I would have a word with Alex, but I also told him it was unlikely that Alex would want to sell Denis.

"The agent Dennis Roach had told me that things weren't right with Cantona at Leeds so I said to Bill, 'What about Cantona? Would you sell him?' I'd not even spoken to Alex about Cantona.

"Fotherby replied, 'It's funny you mention that, because Cantona hasn't got the best relationship with Howard. I'll come back to you on it.'

"He came back and asked me about Irwin and I said, 'No way.' Bill went on, 'We'd be prepared to sell Cantona, but it would have to be done quickly, very quickly.'

"The Leeds fans liked Cantona and if it dragged on there would have been a lot of pressure not to sell him," says Edwards, "So I rang Alex at The Cliff.

"'Would you want Cantona?' I asked. 'Oh yes,' said Alex. 'Well I think I can get him.'

"'Great,' he said. 'What would you pay for him?' I asked. 'Whatever it takes,' he said.

"So I rang Bill back and said that we'd be interested in Eric. 'What would you want for him?' I asked. '£1.6 million,' replied Bill. 'We can't pay 1.6,' I said. '1.5,' Bill said. 'I've had a word with the manager and he won't pay more than a million,'

I replied. '1.4.' I said, 'He's a problem for you and we're taking a risk with him.'

"'1.3.' I said, 'Come on Bill, you're taking the piss. And you owe me one for Gordon Strachan, who has done very well for you.'

"'The best I can do is 1.1,' said Bill, 'but you've bloody robbed me.' We agreed to 1.1.

"Given that Eric turned us around, that's probably the most satisfying deal that I ever did. Peter Schmeichel comes close. Brondby wanted something daft for him, but he would have been out of contract in December 1991, which I told them. 'But you don't want him in December, you want him for the start of the season,' said the official at Brondby. We took hours and hours battering them down to £505,000. Denis Irwin was another good one - £650,000 plus £75,000 if he reached a certain number of caps for the Republic of Ireland."

Not that United always got their man. "I had some disappointments, including Paul Gascoigne," says Edwards. "We really thought that we had him, but he moved to Tottenham. Alan Shearer was another disappointment because we'd agreed personal terms with him. We'd agreed a fee of £12 million too, but then Newcastle suddenly came in with an offer of £15 million. Jack Walker never wanted to sell him to us, so that suited him."

Edwards was delighted with Cantona, but he wasn't his favourite. "While Eric was the most influential player in my time as chairman, my favourite player was Scholesy," he says. "When they were all young, Brian Kidd said to me, 'The jewel in the crown with this lot is Paul Scholes. He'll be the next Kenny Dalglish.' Scholesy has got a brilliant football brain. Everything goes through him, even now. He has passing range, skill factor and influence on the game. He has great vision, rarely gives the ball away and scored a lot of goals when he was younger – over 120. But I also have to say that Giggsy has been great."

Edwards's high point was, inevitably the treble of 1999. "Those ten days were magic from beginning to end," he recalls. "Winning the league at the end after Andy Cole came off the bench at half time against Tottenham. We were a goal down, then Beckham equalised and Cole put us ahead as soon as he came on. Then we won the FA Cup final against Newcastle, while resting a few players. And then Barcelona. I saw the board go up for four minutes of extra time. Then bang bang, and we were European champions. I was sitting next to the Sports Minister Tony Banks. I was stunned. I was so relieved when the first one went in that I hadn't recovered by the time the second one went in. I felt faint. I kept thinking, 'We've done it, we've done it.'"

Despite this, Edwards doesn't consider the treble-winning team his best. "I still think that the best team in my time was the 1994 side. Schmeichel, Parker, Irwin. Irwin was exceptional. Pallister and Bruce were solid as rock and complemented each other. Brucey wasn't the best centre half by any means, but he worked perfectly with Pally. Then you had Ince and Keane in midfield, with Robson if needed. Kanchelskis and Giggs would fly down the wings, with Cantona feeding Hughes. Fantastic. That team played together 12 times and won every one."

It's for his decisions as chairman rather than fan memories which people will remember Edwards. "People say that I don't get on with Alex Ferguson," he says. "If I go to Old Trafford, Alex always welcomes me. I get on fine with him. In any company there are times when relationships are tested – that's normal. I remember being disappointed at the end of the 1998 season. I felt that we were not improving and I said to Alex that I felt he was taking his eye off the ball with the horse racing and everything else. We had words. The following year he came back and won the treble.

"But look at the achievement in the 14 years that we worked directly together; look at the trophies. We worked well together."

It's interesting that Edwards mentions 1998, for in September of that year he received another offer for Manchester United. There was little chance of the potential buyer being unable to raise funds – it was Rupert Murdoch with a £623 million bid for the club. Against a backdrop of vocal, organised fan dissent, Edwards recommended the bid to United's shareholders.

"I thought Sky would have taken Manchester United to a level where nobody could have got near us," he says in his defence. "That's why I recommended their offer in 1998. When they approached us, we had gone 30 years without winning the European Cup. I felt that they could have pushed us onto the next level.

"I saw the way some supporters responded to the Sky bid and considered it over the top. And I saw that some fans were rejoicing when the bid didn't go through and maybe they thought that I was disappointed. I wasn't. That was the decision the Office of Fair Trading made and I could live with that. I just felt that we had to consider the offer on behalf of the shareholders of a public company. If we believed it was in the best interest of shareholders then we had to recommend it. We did that and it was turned down. I'd done my duty."

Edwards's legacy also extends to his responsibility for bringing in several employees at director level in the late 1990s. "David Gill came in as finance director," he says. "I was impressed with him in the interview and he had a fantastic CV. He was personable too – and I still think he is. I brought Peter Kenyon in because of his experience with Umbro and I wanted him on the merchandising side. I brought him in as my deputy, which disappointed David."

Edwards stepped down as Manchester United's Chief Executive in 2000, selling his final tranche of shares.

"I'd given my life to United and missed out on a lot of home life. My children had grown up and married. I hadn't devoted enough time to home life. My wife wanted me to retire at 50, but I asked her for another five years. I stuck to that.

"I didn't sell my shareholding when the price was highest. I sold some at the initial float, and a second chunk to put money in the children's trusts. My children should not have been reliant on Manchester United. I didn't want a large holding if I wasn't running the show."

Edwards was awarded the position of club president, with no executive powers.

"I go along to every game as a fan and sit in the directors' box," he says. "I go with friends and family. I enjoy it. I can go in the boardroom if I want, or the dressing room. There's a lot less pressure from when I used to worry about everything on and off the field. I still get butterflies if we are only winning 1–0 with five minutes to go and the other team are attacking, but I don't carry the burden like I once did."

And he was on the sidelines when Manchester United was finally sold to the Glazer family, in 2005.

"It was a *fait accompli*," he says. "If somebody had the money to buy the shares it was an inevitability. I thought that time would tell whether they would be good owners and I still think that. I don't think they have done anything drastically wrong so far. The crunch time will come when they exit. Will they saddle the club with the debt or just sell the club on for a profit because that's all they are interested in? How will they leave the club?"

Manchester United had debts of £700 million in 2009. "It concerns me that the club is in so much debt," says Edwards. "The club are not in control, that family are in control of the debt. I can understand where the fans are coming from with their concerns. I'm not going to make any accusations because up to now they have behaved fairly well, supporting the manager and they haven't disrupted the running of the club or the personnel within the club. Time will tell. But are the Glazers more of a threat than if the Irish (Magnier or

McManus) or other interested parties had bought the club? It's a free market."

Edwards remains convinced that the most important person at the club is the manager. "The manager is still very important," he says. "He's had one hell of a run. I think he'll think about moving on when he gets to 70. He will have done more years than Matt and his legacy will be there forever more. The next appointment is a huge decision and hopefully a manager will emerge to take over from Sir Alex."

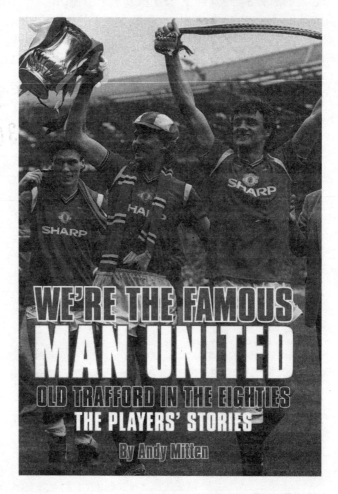